POCKET ROCKET

DON'T QUIT!

THE AUTOBIOGRAPHY OF WAYNE McCULLOUGH

POCKET ROCKET

Wayne McCullough

MAINSTREAM
PUBLISHING
EDINBURGH AND LONDON

First published in Great Britain in 2005 by
MAINSTREAM PUBLISHING COMPANY
(EDINBURGH) LTD
7 Albany Street
Edinburgh EH1 3UG

ISBN 1 84596 020 3

A catalogue record for this book is available
from the British Library

Typeset in Frutiger and Sabon

Printed in Great Britain by
William Clowes Ltd, Beccles, Suffolk

CONTENTS

I want to dedicate this book to the two women in my life whom I love more than anything. My beautiful wife, Cheryl, who is my soulmate and best friend, and my little daughter, Wynona Leigh Davis, who is a gift from God. Cheryl has been there for me through the ups and downs of my boxing career and has been the best manager I could ever have wished for. She has played tough in a man's business and come out on top.

Cheryl, I love you more than words or feelings can express. Thank you for being my co-pilot on my journey through life. Wynona, you are my precious little 'Pocket Rockette'. You captured my heart from the first moment I laid eyes on you. You were innocently born into the world of boxing and you have fitted in perfectly. I love you, Wynona. You will always be daddy's little girl.

FOREWORD
BY MICHAEL FLATLEY

My friend Wayne McCullough is a dedicated professional – he's one of life's super-triumphs. He always gives 100 per cent, especially for his fans – and then he packs in the extra work. He's got to the top in boxing and stayed there through hard work and discipline. I've been a fan since 1994 when I first saw him in Dublin. I instantly recognised that here was a man who knew no limits to what could be achieved by his own endeavours. Wayne has proved me right ever since, whether he has been winning fights or stepping away from some controversial decisions.

He's a virtuoso in the ring and is always brave. Whatever his opponents challenged him with – and he's consistently only fought the world's best – he's never backed down. If he takes one strike (or two, or three), he's always there to punch back. His attitude is: 'I'm going to hit you more than you hit me.' He's a rare breed; not a man to be intimidated by a rival's reputation or the size of an event.

He showed this in his 17th professional fight when he won the WBC world bantamweight title against Yasuei Yakushiji in Japan. This fantastic achievement early in his career said so much about this warrior, for Wayne found the strength to strip the champion of his title on his home turf. Wayne told me there were about 20 Irish fans in the crowd of more than 10,000 – and they made more noise than Yakushiji's supporters!

When he fought then WBO featherweight title holder Naseem Hamed in 1998, I walked into the ring with him. I was proud to be part of this athlete's entourage; he is the embodiment of the Irish spirit. Wayne's performance showed flaws in the supposedly invincible champ for the first time.

Over the years, we've become good friends. I've visited him and his wife, Cheryl, and their family in Las Vegas and have always been offered great kindness and hospitality.

He's now officially, legally, Wayne Pocket Rocket McCullough, but I always think of him as a fast-stepping little giant. He honours basic virtues like dignity and courage, and for that, and his achievements, he has my respect.

Salutations,
Michael Flatley

PREFACE

I realised by the tenth round of my WBC (World Boxing Council) World Championship challenge against Yasuei Yakushiji that I was going to be a world champion. Since the age of eight I had been working towards this moment. Sweating in cold gyms, punching my way through the amateur circuit and then making the transition into professional boxing, and now I had my chance in my 17th fight as a pro to take the title.

* * *

I had been waiting over a year for this moment. The bell sounded to begin the fight. The bantamweight world champion, Yasuei Yakushiji, came straight across the ring and hit me two cracking right-hands on the chin. I hadn't come to Japan to be beaten, so I acknowledged that he'd hit me, covered up and continued with my strategy. I knew he was a hard puncher and it was going to be a difficult night, but I was prepared and ready for anything he was going to throw at me. It was tough, but nothing he threw at me was going to take me off target. I'd started well, thinking it couldn't be this easy: but I knew Yakushiji was the best fighter in the weight division, so he was something special. If I wanted to beat him, I'd have to be better than the best.

The great Eddie Futch, my trainer, had told me in the dressing-room to jab my way in. I was practically beating the world champion with one hand. I knew I was well ahead on the scorecards. He was having a hard time getting away from my jab. It wasn't going to be easy, but I was going to try and keep away from any danger. I knew I was stronger than Yakushiji and it became obvious that my body shots were taking their toll on him. He was still trying to win, but there was no way I was going to let him. I wanted his Belt and I was going to make sure the judges saw I was doing enough to take the title from the champion.

He backed off. I aggressively stalked him. Eddie told me I was winning, but he said I should continue to use my jab and move around the ring in the last couple of rounds. I was taking the fight from him: coming to fight in his backyard, I knew I'd have to do that to get the decision.

Late in the fight Yakushiji had figured out my game plan. With two rounds to go Yakushiji came on strong: he stepped up the pace, so I fought him cautiously. I boxed him and stayed out of trouble, making sure I was still winning the fight and not allowing him to get back into it. I was positive I was not going to leave anything in the ring. I wasn't going to walk away without that Belt around my waist.

When the bell sounded to end the fight, I felt relieved. I dropped to the canvas and thanked God for getting me through the fight. It was over. Now the anxiety as I waited for the decision.

The ring announcer read the scorecards – albeit in Japanese – and I heard him say my name, then Yakushiji's. It was a split decision. I knew if I won, it should have been unanimous. He read the final name in his best English: 'Ma-Culla!'

I realised I had won. I was the champion of the world. I couldn't believe it. Although I knew I was well ahead at the end of the fight, it still came as a surprise to me that I was the winner. I had gone to Japan with the intention of winning the Belt, but when my name was announced, I was still amazed – delighted, but amazed.

I had done what most people said I couldn't do. I had conquered the world.

I went back to Vegas and looked to the future. I had already promised my fans in Belfast that I would fight my first defence there, so plans were put into place to defend my title in front of my home-town fans.

Who could have known then that I'd be where I am today? Through all the sadness and happiness, wins and defeats, there is nowhere else I'd rather be and no other way I'd have wanted to live my life.

1

IN THE BEGINNING

Wayne McCullough is one of the most talented and
dedicated fighters I have ever come across, and I think
his desire to succeed is amazing.
Paul Weir, former WBO mini-flyweight
and light-flyweight champion

We all have a special talent that God has given to us and I learned
at a young age that mine was boxing. Even though I began to
fight when I was seven or eight years old, it wasn't until I was
fifteen that I realised it was what I wanted to do for the rest of my
life. It might sound ridiculous since I was still only a kid, but I
really did know that someday I could be a world champion. I had
high hopes and big dreams. I knew I could reach the pinnacle of
the sport. And those high hopes and big dreams came true.

* * *

I was born in a terraced house on Percy Street on the Shankill Road
on 7 July 1970. My family moved out of the area when I was just
two years old, so I have no real memories of the house or the
neighbourhood, but I know that the street had taken a direct hit
during the Second World War and much of it had had to be rebuilt.
At one end of Percy Street is the Protestant Shankill Road and at

the other is the Catholic Falls Road. When the Troubles started in 1969, a wall was erected as a security barricade to separate the two communities, commonly known as the 'Peace Wall'.

My family has always lived in Belfast, except for a two-year spell when Mum and Dad moved out of the city. After this we settled back at the top of the Shankill Road in the Highfield Estate, where I lived until I moved to America in 1993. Highfield is part of Greater Shankill, the area in which the Troubles were at their peak while I was growing up during the 1970s and '80s. British soldiers would patrol the streets carrying rifles, and, to me, this was normal. Sometimes I'd bump into a soldier on the way home from my early morning run, and he would stop me and ask where I was going or where I was coming from. Friends in America talk about their cities' ghettos; I expect they would class the area where I lived as one too.

Growing up in the Shankill area was tough. Bombs were a regular occurence and I've witnessed a few shootings, but I've never had any interest in being involved with any paramilitary organisation. I think going to the gym kept me out of trouble. There were nights I came home to find that some of my friends had been arrested.

The local community centre in Highfield was the hangout for kids in the area. When I was younger, we used to play on the roof. I remember a bomb going off there in broad daylight. It was only about 200 metres from where we lived and most of the windows in the houses around the estate were blown out. My dad and his friend were the first people on the scene and, of course, all the kids followed them to see what had happened. The story went that there was a guy inside making a bomb and it went off prematurely and blew him to pieces. Half of the community centre was gone too. The guy's head was still stuck to the ceiling when I went in, and then my friends and I were told to get out.

The Ulster Defence Association (UDA) and the Ulster Volunteer Force (UVF) were the main paramilitary forces in the area. There were riots between the kids on both sides of the Protestant and Catholic divide every night at the Springmartin peace line. I think a lot of the time they just did it to pass the nights because there was little else to do. Even though I was still only a kid, a friend, 'Big J', used to tell me to stay out of the way in case I got injured because he knew how important my boxing career was to me. I thank God I didn't get involved in it all.

Although I have six brothers and sisters, I felt I was the only one who didn't actually have a sibling to fight with – maybe that's why I went to the boxing gym. There were my two older brothers, Noel and Alan; my two older sisters, Joan and April; and my two younger sisters, Christina and Anne. I was closest to Noel and Christina.

One of my most vivid impressions of that time at home is almost all of my family smoking. When I was younger, I'd be sitting at home and everyone would light up at the same time in our tiny house. It would fill with smoke almost immediately. Being an athlete, I knew it wasn't good to breathe in second-hand smoke, so I'd go out and stand at the front door. I wasn't looking at anything in particular; in fact, I would just do a lot of thinking. I had always loved Belfast, but I'd think to myself that there had to be something better out there for me.

I attended Spring Hill primary school on the Ballygomartin Road. From about primary four I wanted to be like Ray Clemence or Pat Jennings, and since I was good with my hands I was put in goal for the football team. The balls that were flying at me never scared me. I could jump like a monkey and I saved a lot of shots. I also played rugby. I loved having the ball in my arms and running towards the players on the other team, and vice versa, when they came in my direction with the ball. Most of the players were a lot bigger than me, but I would attack them head-on.

I enjoyed mathematics and English all through school, and both have certainly helped me during my career in boxing.

When I was about ten years old, I was a Teddy boy. I loved going to discos in the local community centre and dancing all night long. The in thing that year was Elvis-style blue suede shoes. I knew my mum and dad didn't have money to go out and buy me a pair, so I asked for them for Christmas. I already had the drainpipe trousers and the pink socks with the black stripes, so all I needed to complete the outfit were the shoes. Imagine my delight when I woke up on Christmas morning and the shoes were there waiting for me. I couldn't wait to get them on and go dancing.

I remember having to babysit my two younger sisters, Christina and Anne, on Saturday nights. My friends would be out enjoying

15

themselves and I wanted to go out too, but most weekends I couldn't. Looking back, I know I didn't enjoy the same sort of upbringing as other kids, but I didn't know anything different and saw no reason to complain.

At that stage my brother Noel, who was six years older than me, was living out of the family home, but we still hung around together. We would go out on our bikes on Sundays and ride into the mountains at the top of the Glencairn Estate. When McDonald's opened in Belfast, we'd cycle into the city centre at lunchtime and get a burger and then cycle back home. In the evening I'd often either run or cycle to the Chinese takeaway and pick up dinner for everyone. After that I'd go round to Noel's house and listen to the weekly Top 40 presented by Rick Dees. That was the highlight of my week.

I was always really close to my mum when I was growing up. She never came to watch me fight because she was afraid I was going to get hurt, and I understood that. My dad came to some of my fights, but I felt as if I had very little emotional or financial support in the early days. My mum and dad didn't encourage me; I wasn't praised when I won fights. But I kept going anyway. I did it for me, no one else. It wasn't until I won my Commonwealth Games gold medal that my parents became involved in my career.

Some of my fondest memories of this time are of going out shopping and visiting my grandparents with my mum. We would walk, or sometimes we'd take one of Belfast's familiar black taxis, from Highfield down the Shankill Road to where my grandparents lived. Mum would sit and talk to my granny while I talked to my granda about my boxing. I was close to my mum's parents but I always felt closer to my Granda McCullough, who passed away on my 13th birthday. He's the one person I think I take after. He was a gentleman and respected everybody who came into his house. Mum and I would then shop for groceries and walk or get a taxi back home.

When my brothers got married, I couldn't go to either of their weddings because I didn't have any decent clothes. My mum and dad would go out drinking every Saturday night. They always seemed to have enough money for that. I didn't have a birthday party until I met Cheryl when I was 19.

* * *

When I first started boxing, I only weighed about 3½ stone. I was a wee boy with a big heart and that has not changed. I remember walking across the West Circular Road in Belfast, heading to the Albert Foundry boxing gym with my two brothers, Noel and Alan. I had seen the trophies they had won and wanted one too. I have always been smaller than most people, but at Albert Foundry I didn't feel that way. Back then, the gym was full of both amateur and pro fighters. British champion Davy Larmour trained there. He won a bronze medal at the Commonwealth Games in 1970 at flyweight, and went back in 1974 and brought home the gold. He went on to represent Ireland at the Olympics, then in 1983 became a pro. He was someone I looked up to.

I would jump rope at the back of the gym and stay out of the way, observing the older boxers while trying to pick things up from them. I watched Davy hit the bag, hit the pads and spar. He may not have known it, but I learned a lot from him. When I was older I sparred with him a few times, and he was very hard to hit! He was always teaching me new moves, and I took it all in. I respected him for making the time for me.

Many a winter's night I would walk across to the gym from my house. Often it was below zero outside, and some nights I would have to climb over the rusty green iron railings because the gates were locked, then walk across the icy or waterlogged running track. There was no electricity or heating in the building and on most of these nights it felt colder inside than it did out. And it was not only the running track that was waterlogged; a lot of times the floorboards in the gym would be floating. Whatever it took to get to the gym, I did it. That was the enthusiasm I had for boxing.

After I had been at Albert Foundry for a few years, my amateur coach, Harry Robinson, bought a brand new generator to power the lights, but we still had no heating. Later he built a wooden sauna where I would jump rope in order to make weight for my fights. I would go to the gym all bundled up in three or four tracksuits during winter just to stay warm and sweat. But the cold just made me work harder. You could see your breath. And it wasn't pleasant when you sparred and got hit in the face with a cold glove.

It was the total opposite in the summer months: the asbestos roof would get really hot and sometimes we'd have to keep the doors open to let in some air. But no matter the weather, I knew I was destined for greatness and I continued to push towards my goal of becoming a champion someday.

I was about eight years old when I took part in my first amateur fight in Ballyclare, a town 13 miles from Belfast. I had been training at Albert Foundry for about a year before that and I knew I was ready. My opponent that night had been in a lot of fights and was far more experienced than me. I only weighed about 4 stone back then and was a little nervous because I didn't know what to expect. I needn't have worried; I stopped him in two rounds. I had picked up boxing pretty easily; it came naturally to me. I hadn't liked it to begin with because it was taking too long to make progress and I didn't see anything happening in terms of a fight; I wanted to get into the ring. But I had to put in the time in the gym first. Boxing had grown on me, though, and I was hooked.

When I first started out, amateurs boxed using 8-ounce gloves and had neither headgear nor mouthpieces. There were no regulations. I didn't have boxing boots until I was older, so I always fought in running shoes. Nor were there official weigh-ins: when we arrived at a fight venue, we would stand beside a boxer who looked like he was about the same size. The officials would say, 'That's a match,' and we fought each other. We didn't start doing weigh-ins until we fought in one of the championships. I could have picked up a fight every week, they were held that regularly. Before I was 12 years old I had probably participated in 100 fights.

For a long time there was only myself, my brother Alan (a professional boxer) and another two fighters, brothers Gary and Neil Burns, in the gym training. There were a few guys who came in just to keep fit. Big Bert was always there working hard, along with Big Eric, Ginger and Sammy. Davy, another guy, used to come and work out, and when he wasn't training, he'd come back to walk his dogs. They were all regulars, even when it was cold. The members paid about £1 a week, but I didn't start paying dues until I was about 16. There was an older man called Geordie Allen who helped around the gym when I was younger. I remember him telling me I'd be a champion one day. Harry's other friend, 'Wee' Geordie, helped out too. He would work the corner at my fights, putting the stool in the ring and giving me water.

When I trained with Harry, we would concentrate on the different moves I could use in the ring. I worked on a lot of things I'd picked up from Davy Larmour, and some things I added on my own by watching fights on television. I loved to watch Barry McGuigan. I followed his whole career. I loved how he fought, full of energy with non-stop punching, and, just like me, he excited everyone with his style. Barry later became my friend. He has just recently been inducted into the Canastota Boxing Hall of Fame for his tremendous accomplishments as a professional boxer. Someday I will be inducted there too, to join fighters like McGuigan, Muhammad Ali, Joe Frazier, Henry Armstrong and many others.

Harry would hold the pads for me in the gym. I threw combinations that I knew would work and he would catch them. We just clicked and it felt right. In the old days, after a full training session, we would go to the back of the gym and play football. I had so much energy when I was a kid, I felt like I could go on all night. Harry would bring in oranges and when we were done messing about, we'd sit and talk about fights or read the *Boxing News*. The big-time American fights weren't televised very often in Belfast, so I would catch up that way on old fighters or contests that we hadn't seen. I was dedicated and worked hard. I loved the one-on-one aspect of boxing. You're on your own in there; no one can help you.

Harry would take me to box on the Shankill Road or the Falls Road; in fact, we fought all around the country. Boxing has no political boundaries. When you are in the arena, it doesn't matter who is in the ring with you; if you are a spectator, it doesn't matter who is fighting, Catholic or Protestant. You are there for the sport. It's a different story for some outside of the arena, but inside I've always found there are no dividing lines.

There came a point when I went to fight venues and everyone knew me. There was always a buzz surrounding the successful fighters, and I became one of them. The only problem is that I went to over a hundred venues and I couldn't get a match-up. So the fights didn't happen. No one wanted to challenge me, probably because they knew I could beat them. I was fast becoming a star of the boxing world.

2

LEARNING MY TRADE

While I had never met or seen the young Wayne McCullough, the buzz was big. He had won a silver medal for Ireland and was considered one of boxing's elite prospects. My pre-fight interview with the young boxer was typical, but I knew immediately that he was indeed something special. He showed a glint in his eye that exuded a rare confidence and focus I see only in boxers who become world champions. He was indeed a man on a mission to fulfil a destiny to achieve greatness.

Jimmy Lennon, world-renowned ring announcer

I won my first amateur competition when I was 11: the Northern Ireland Boys' Clubs Championship. I remember celebrating my victory with Harry afterwards. He took me out for fish and chips at a sit-down restaurant. That was a special treat for me.

Overall I fought over 300 amateur fights and only lost about ten. When I was competing in the County Antrim Championships, the decisions went against me every year, so I'd say I probably only lost five or six. I used to beat up my opponents really badly, but I would still lose the decision. Maybe they went against me because I was one of the very few Protestants in a Catholic-dominated sport. For me, it didn't matter which religion you belonged to. I was a boxer. This just made me more determined to fulfil my dreams.

I remember when I was 12 years old or so, our community centre organised a cross-community trip to Holland, whereby two pupils, one Protestant, one Catholic, would stay with a family and try to bridge the religious divide. I really wanted to go – I'd never been out of the country before – and was delighted when I was chosen. But even though we had a good time in Holland, it didn't really help my partner and me to build any bridges and we didn't keep in touch after the trip.

Finally, at 14, my last year as a juvenile, I won the County Antrims. In the same year, I won the Ulster Championships and went on to take my first Irish title in Cork. I know if I had got the decision when I was younger, I'd have been the Irish champion long before then. While we were in Cork for the Irish Championships with the County Antrim team, we stayed in a flea-ridden guesthouse. The fleas were everywhere and some of the boys were covered in bites. But it didn't bother us. We still did our training. We put our mattresses up against the wall and punched them like heavy bags. The dust was flying everywhere, so we had that to deal with as well as the fleas.

By 1986 I was in the youth boxer class. As I was still just 15 years old, I could also enter the Gaelic Games, a competition in which any country with a Gaelic language can take part. Scotland, Wales, Canada and Ireland were all taking part. Boxers weighing 7 stone were the lightest competitors allowed to enter in the first-class youth category. Even though I was only about 6 st. 9 lb, I really wanted to go. The Gaelic Games were in Wales that year and we stayed in the Butlins holiday camp. The food was terrible and I doubt I weighed anywhere near 7 stone. In my first fight, I fought John Williams from Wales. He was much bigger than me. I took two standing counts before the referee stopped the fight. I wasn't hurt, but it gave me a wake-up call: I knew I was too small and shouldn't have gone to the Games.

Just before I went to Dublin for the All-Ireland Youth Championship in 1987, Fidel Bassa's camp asked me to spar with him. Bassa was the WBA flyweight champion and he was in Belfast to fight Dave 'Boy' McAuley. I went in against Bassa and threw about 1,000 punches. He took it easy on me, but he loved my work rate. It was an honour to be sparring with a world champion. He taught me a lot of moves and we worked well together. He asked me to come back to spar for the rest of the week. I was torn: I wanted to stay and spar, but I had planned to fight in the All-Irelands. Bassa went on to beat McAuley in one of the fights of the year.

I went to the Gaelic Games again in '87. I stopped my first opponent then beat Scot Neil Armstrong in the next to win the tournament. I had redeemed myself by taking the gold medal and I felt as if I was walking on the moon.

That same year I went to England with the Young Ireland team to challenge Young England. I was matched against Mark Reynolds, one of the top English fighters. I wasn't supposed to win, but I went out there and threw continuous punches and stopped him with body shots in the second round. When we went back into our dressing-rooms, Barry McGuigan came in to talk to some of the fighters. I was speechless and in awe of him. My hero was standing right in front of me. He talked to the other boxers and then turned to me and told me that I would need to slow down a little or I wouldn't last. But that's the way I fought and, like everyone else, Barry later found out that I *could* keep going, but at that moment I was just happy to be standing there next to him, listening to what he had to say. At the end of the night, former world flyweight champion Charlie Magri presented me with the Best Boxer of the Night award.

In the 1987–88 season, I won the Ulster and Irish Youth competitions, the Irish Under-18 title, and the Ulster and Irish Junior and Senior titles. I was only 17 when I won both the Ulster and Irish Seniors and I received the Best Boxer of the Tournament in both championships.

Boxing promoter Barney Eastwood was good enough to let me train in his Castle Street gym for free while Alan sparred there as a professional. It was very hot in the gym, but I loved the heat and I made weight easily while training there. I sparred with world champion boxers Dave McAuley and Paul Hodkinson.

I was maturing at this time and the type of sparring I was getting against world champion fighters really helped me. Back then amateur boxers weren't supposed to mix with the professionals, but I thought it would benefit me more to work with them than amateurs. The experience I was getting was amazing.

* * *

After I passed my 11-plus and had left Spring Hill, I could have gone on to grammar school but because the Cairnmartin secondary school was closer to my house, I decided to go there. I wasn't pushed by my parents; to me, you went to school, got a job and that was your life. I was never told how important it was to get a good education and leave school with qualifications.

By the time I started at secondary I hadn't grown enough to stay in goal, so I was put in midfield in the football team. I much preferred being a goalie because I sometimes felt players got greedy with the ball and never passed it to me. You'd be alone in goal, but that is what I liked about it. I was also involved in cross-country running at the time and played for the field hockey team. I even used to play short-mat bowling with my dad. We'd often play against the team at St Columbus church. Halfway through the matches we used to stop for a cup of tea and sandwiches. I was only a young teenager and everyone else was probably over 40, but I loved bowls because it helped me relax after training.

I was an all-round athlete who would try any sport once, yet it was boxing that always appealed to me the most. Because of this, and because everyone at school knew I was a boxer, I gained their respect. Although I never got into a fight, if somebody was getting bullied, I stood up for him and told the others to leave him alone. And they did.

There were a bunch of about 15 of us that ran around together until I was about 16. Sometimes we'd play cards in the middle of the street and we'd bet each other 2p. Sometimes we'd up the stakes and bet 5p! We also played 'throw the coin': using 5ps or 10ps, we'd try to get our coin closest to the wall. I was an expert and on a good night I'd make £1!

John, better known as 'Murdoch', and Ronnie also boxed at Albert Foundry and we hung out for many years until I started dating Cheryl. We would collect wood for the bonfires on the Eleventh Night (the celebrations before the Protestant marches on 12 July) and we used to camp out beside them in the weeks leading up to it so that nobody would steal our wood. We all had a great laugh when we were together. It's what young kids did in our area. It was normal for us. But I never smoked or did drugs. I had my first taste of alcohol when I was about nine or ten years old. There was plenty of it going around and it was the thing to do, but I would only drink occasionally because I was training and fighting regularly.

My dad was a foreman at the brick works on the Ballygomartin Road when I was growing up, but Dad has been unemployed since it closed down. I remember him working as a volunteer at Barnardos for years. We didn't have much when we were growing up. At Christmas we'd get some new, but mostly second-hand, toys and clothes. But we never complained; we always had food on the table. Some days I would go to school with only a biscuit or a dry piece of toast for breakfast. I couldn't buy anything at break time like my classmates because I didn't have any money. It was embarrassing not to be able to buy treats, but I never grumbled about it. I was entitled to free school dinners and I always looked forward to them.

I was in the top class at school and didn't mind going every morning, but since my birthday fell in the summer months I was able to leave after fourth year. And I couldn't wait. Now I was able to concentrate on my boxing career. Looking back, I probably should have stayed on and got some qualifications behind me before jumping into the ring, but fortunately for me it paid off.

I went straight into a Youth Training Programme (YTP) and was making £27.30 a week. I thought that was great. My mum took £13 from me every week for my keep and I still had to buy my own lunches. I worked on the YTP scheme for a year, training to be a carpenter. I enjoyed working with wood and making bits and pieces to take home. Before I set off for work in the mornings I would go running and every night when I came out of work at five o'clock I would run home in my steel toe-capped boots. It was about three miles. I got a snack and went straight to the gym.

My whole day was taken up with work and boxing, and that's what I wanted.

When I had completed the YTP scheme, I signed on for the dole for a year. I remember my mum sending me to the corner store at lunchtime to buy a quarter of Spam, a quarter of cheese and some soda bread. I'd bring it home and toast it. I never got sick of eating it.

I found a one-year position at St Columbus, the church where I'd played bowls, through a government scheme after that. My job was to polish the floors, carry out repairs and cut the grass. I was the caretaker. It was only 16 hours a week but I earned £45 – a lot better than I was earning on the YTP scheme. I had the church spotless. Because I had the keys, I would sometimes go up on Fridays at midnight to polish the floors. I worked flexible hours and was my own boss. The job allowed me the time to do my training as well. I loved it, but it only lasted a year.

* * *

From about 1986 I had been fighting at light flyweight (7 st. 7 lb 13 oz). I was a strong young kid, so I was stopping most of my opponents inside the distance. In the Ulster Seniors I'd taken the title from the reigning champion, P.J. O'Halloran, inside three rounds. He was about 26 years old at the time. I was a boy in a man's world, but I kept wanting more. After the Seniors, the IABA (Irish Amateur Boxing Association) wanted me to fight P.J. again in a box-off for what I thought was a place in the 1988 Olympic Games team. I was just 17. I stopped him again in the third. P.J. was a real comedian and we became friends after that and travelled to a few international boxing tournaments together in the USA. I enjoyed being in his company.

I fought my first international as a Senior against Scotland in April 1986 and stopped my opponent, Donald Glass, in two rounds. It was a busy year for me. I also fought in an international with Cuba at the National Stadium in Dublin in May. I was matched against Daniel La Rosa, a Cuban with a record of only five losses out of ninety-nine fights. Just before I went into the ring, one of my teammates told me that the Cuban was a star – he more or less warned me that I was going to get beaten. But I went out and stopped the Cuban in the second round. I thought I'd sealed my ticket to the Olympics in Seoul.

In June 1988 Ireland fought against Canada at the Guild Hall in Londonderry. I was to fight Arturo Gatti. He has gone on to become one of the most exciting fighters in the professional boxing world and has won several world titles in different weight classes, but this night his corner threw in the towel in the first round after I had given him two standing counts. He is a great boxer and I enjoy watching him fight. A couple of days later, Gatti fought against another member of the Irish team but knocked his opponent out this time.

I was confident I was going to Seoul now, but boy was I wrong. The European Junior Championships were coming up and the Irish Board wanted to send me there instead. I had the best record out of the Senior team that year, stopping 12 guys straight inside the distance, and I would rather have gone to Korea.

When the Irish Olympic Council chose the team, I wasn't on it. I was devastated. Harry was still hopeful because he knew I was talented enough to make the team and thought he could change their minds. One day in July while I was doing weights with Noel at a gym on the Shankill Road, Harry came in and by the expression on his face I knew he had good news. 'You're going to the Olympics,' he said. I couldn't believe it. I was so happy I was literally jumping for joy.

Harry took my measurements for my suit – I'd never had one – and the rest of the team clothing. There were tracksuits, shoes, everything I needed. I'd never had a new tracksuit before and the only pair of new running shoes I'd owned were ones Harry had bought for me.

In Belfast, I did most of my running on the Glencairn and Ballysillan Roads. The old Glencairn Road up to an old well covered over with cement was a mile and a half of steep hill. You were fit if you could run up that hill, and it definitely built up your stamina. When I got to the top, I used to stand on the well and do a couple of rounds of shadow boxing. You could see all over Belfast.

One day I was running up there and I could see cows ahead. As I ran towards them to try to get around them, they started running up the hill too. I didn't actually get past them – they made it to the well before I did. They must have been fit! On the way back down I was jogging when a farmer jumped out from behind a bush with a pitchfork in his hand. He scared the life out of me. He yelled at me for chasing the cows up the road, but I told him I was just trying to get around them. I ran straight home and told Noel what had happened. He got on his mountain bike and went up the mountain to the farmer's house to confront him and ask why he had shouted at me. The farmer still had the pitchfork in his hand. Noel told him if he ever screamed at me again, he would take the pitchfork from him and stick it where the sun don't shine!

I hadn't intended to cause hassle and it didn't stop me from running past his farm. In fact, after that he couldn't have been nicer. Every time he saw me he'd shout, 'Hello, Wayne,' and ask how the boxing was coming along.

Making weight was getting tougher. I was growing. Sometimes after a big meal I knew I was not going to make weight. On occasion I'd make myself sick to get rid of the food I'd just eaten. I thought I had to do it to keep my weight down. It wasn't the smartest thing to do, but, at the time, I felt it was the only way. I didn't have an eating disorder as such, but, looking back, I'm sure it could have led to that. I only did it to make weight in my boxing career, but I can sympathise with others who have experienced a similar thing. It's not a disorder that only affects women, as I know first hand. I was young and it was the only way I knew to lose weight. I kept this a secret for years. I didn't tell Cheryl until 1994 and up to now she was the only person I had told. I didn't have a nutritionist or anyone helping me with my diet. Now I know differently, that eating the correct food and training hard is the only way to lose weight and stay healthy. I have become a certified personal trainer and sports nutritionist, so with my experience I can now advise others in the same situation as I found myself.

* * *

The Irish Olympic team trained in a small town just outside Sneem in County Kerry. It was in the mountains and it was freezing cold, even though it was summer. We stayed there for five weeks. We ran along the beach every morning and trained in the hotel function room in the afternoon. It was the first time I'd ever met the Irish team coach, the Cuban Nicolas Cruz Hernandez. He worked the fighters hard and not many people liked that, but I loved it. The only thing I wasn't keen on was the touch sparring, but he understood that and instead I worked on the pads with Mickey Hawkins, one of the coaches for the Northern Ireland and Ireland teams.

I was the lightest, shortest and youngest boxer on the 1988 Olympic team. My teammates were experienced world travellers and a lot older than me. Most had already competed in the World Championships or at the Olympics – this was my first boxing trip out of the country and here I was on my way to the Olympic Games. Joe Lawlor, John Lowey, Paul Fitzgerald, Michael Carruth, Billy Walsh and Kieron Joyce, who were all on the team, treated me well, and showed me the ropes and their tricks – which I didn't fall for. It was Kieron who gave me my ring nickname – he said I was small enough to fit into his pocket and that I threw punches like a rocket – the 'Pocket Rocket' was born. It has stuck with me ever since – so much so that I legally became Wayne Pocket Rocket McCullough in 2004.

Coaches Mickey Hawkins and Albie Murphy joined us in Korea – I don't know why, but Nicolas didn't come – and Pat McCrory, president of the Ulster Boxing Council, came as the team manager. We all met at Dublin airport dressed in our Olympic apparel and really looked like a team. Our luggage was branded with the official logo as well. Finally, it was beginning to sink in that I was going to the Olympics.

When we got to Korea, I couldn't believe how hot and humid it was. We first had to go through security and get our credentials to give us access to the Olympic Village and the boxing arena. There were over 10,000 of the world's top athletes in the Village. Security was extremely tight because of the conflict between the north and south of the country.

The team stayed in a luxury high-rise apartment complex, and

I shared a room with John Lowey. It was really hard to take everything in since I was so young. I had never experienced anything like it before. I was star-struck seeing all the athletes I had watched on TV. I got pictures with Carl Lewis and Sergei Bubka. There was a bowling alley and a 24-hour restaurant in the Village. Everything was free. I was like a kid in a candy store. At night we would trade Olympic pins or our tracksuits with athletes from other countries. I thought it was great. Albie Murphy was like a father to me out there. We went shopping and ate meals together, and sometimes just sat down for a cup of tea. He was a great guy.

Before the opening ceremony, Pat McCrory came to my apartment and asked me if I would carry the Irish flag at the opening ceremony because I was the youngest member on the team. I thought about it for a while, but what choice did I have? I don't think I should have ever been asked: if I had said no, then I would have been dubbed a hypocrite for fighting for Ireland; if I had said yes, I knew I would have been criticised as a Protestant from the Shankill Road for carrying the Irish flag. After some consideration, I told him I would carry the flag for sport. I wouldn't do it for politics because I am a sportsman, not a politician.

The press had a field day beaming pictures around the world of Wayne McCullough from Highfield Estate carrying the Irish flag at the opening ceremony, but when I walked into the stadium I immediately forgot about everything that had been whizzing around in my head. There were probably a billion people watching the ceremony on TV from countries all around the world. I was a part of it and that was totally amazing. The experience is indescribable. Walking into the Olympic stadium, knowing I was just a wee boy from the Shankill Road, was exhilarating. Then the games began.

It was open competition in boxing back then. There were about 60 fighters in my weight class. I got a bye in the first round, so I was straight into the last 32. My first fight was against the Ugandan Fred Muteweta. He was a good, tall, rangy boxer, but I stayed close and worked his body on the inside. In the second round I dropped him with a left-hook right-hand combination.

29

He bravely got up and finished the round, and actually fought back in the final three minutes. But the fight was sealed for me and I won a unanimous decision.

I was through to the last 16. My next fight was against Scotty 'The Bulldog' Olson, who was the Commonwealth champion. He was a short, stocky guy and he could punch with both hands. He said he was going to knock me out. His prediction almost came true in the first round. He gave me two standing counts after hurting me to the body. I didn't know how to block those shots at the time. I came back and won the last round. That was typical of me in the amateurs: I always started too slow and finished strong at the end. Scotty won the decision.

That was the end of my Olympic dream, for then. That fight taught me a lot. Scotty was experienced, I wasn't. I was only a boy. But I had gained a lot of knowledge to take with me if I was to continue to compete at this level. After the fight Scotty told me that he couldn't believe how I'd come back at him in the last round.

I met him again when I moved to America in 1993, five years after we'd met at the Olympics. By then he was a successful professional boxer, and when I approached him, he didn't recognise me. He was still really short, but I had grown about 3 inches. I was a couple of weight classes above him, so I'd never have to take another of those crushing body shots.

I went back to a hero's welcome at the Highfield Estate. Davy Larmour had organised a bus to drive me to the Rangers Supporters Club on the Shankill Road for a party in my honour. The Shankill Road Defenders flute band walked in front of the bus. No one said anything to me about carrying the Irish flag. They were there to support me and acknowledge my achievements.

I wanted to turn professional right away because I thought I'd reached the peak of my amateur career by going to the Olympic Games, but Harry discouraged me. 'You're young,' he told me, 'you haven't fully developed yet. Wait until you're a grown man.'

I took his word for it and it turned out that he was right.

* * *

The last Irishman to beat me was my friend Paul 'Butsy' Buttimer in the Senior Championships in Dublin in 1989. All I was thinking about was turning pro, and this fight woke me up. I wasn't mentally prepared going in there. My mind was elsewhere. I shouldn't have been thinking about anything else except the fight. But I was, and Butsy beat me.

3

BRINGING HOME THE GOLD

Watching Wayne on the podium, flowers in hand and an exciting smile, receive his gold medal, with 3,000 voices singing 'Danny Boy', was, and still is, for me a very moving, emotional experience.
Bob Gibson, official who sang 'Danny Boy' at the
1990 Commonwealth Games

I won the Ulster Senior Championships in 1989, the build-up year to the Commonwealth Games in Auckland, New Zealand, in January 1990. Each reigning champion fought in a multi-nation tournament that took place in the spring of '89. If you, as an Ulster champion, were good enough to go to the Games, the Ulster Boxing Council picked you to represent Northern Ireland there.

After the Olympic Games in 1988, I had moved up to flyweight (8 st.). I was making weight easily and I felt strong and comfortable. The multi-nation tournament I fought in took place in the Ballysillan leisure centre in Belfast. I had all the support since I only lived a couple of miles away.

England, Scotland, Wales and Northern Ireland all competed in the tournament. If I won this competition, I'd be more or less guaranteed a place on the Commonwealth Games team. I got a bye in the first round, so I was automatically in the final, where I fought

Englishman Johnny Armour, who had won his first fight with no trouble. I got a good look at his style and I knew what I was up against. This fight could have been a tough one for me. Armour was a southpaw, so he led with his right hand, but he was a come-forward fighter and I couldn't miss him with any shot I threw. His plan was to stand and trade toe-to-toe, but instead of doing what I normally do and getting into a battle with him, I backed up and used my boxing skills: threw my jab, picked my shots, turned and moved around the ring, making him miss. I broke his nose and there was blood everywhere. I made the fight so much easier for myself and I won a clear points decision on all three cards. Armour went on to become a good professional boxer.

My summer was pretty quiet and even though I didn't fight, I kept on training. I have always trained twice a day, every day, no matter what. I do that to try to perfect my talent. In November, two months before the Commonwealth Games, I went with a team to Prague to fight in an international against the Czechoslovakian team. Harry came along as the team coach. It felt good knowing my own trainer was there with me.

I beat the Czech fighter easily and was expecting to have my hand raised. I couldn't believe it when the judges gave the decision 2–1 to my opponent. The judges were from England, Czechoslovakia and Ireland, so I automatically thought the Czech and English judges had given against me. Little did I know it was the Irish one. We all knew that the Czech judges were not giving us the decisions unless we knocked out our opponents, but I couldn't understand how the Irish judge could have given him the victory. Straight after the fight he told me that I'd fought well. He also told me he thought I had won – obviously not enough to give me the fight on the scorecards. When I found out a few hours later, I confronted him. 'How could you tell me that I won when you were one of the judges who gave against me and cost me the fight?' I asked. The guy was speechless and in a panic. I just walked away in disgust.

My right arm was hurting after the fight and so I was taken to a hospital where it turned out no one could speak English. When we arrived at the hospital door, we had to put covers over our shoes. The doctor looked at my arm, but I couldn't understand what they were saying to me. I was fitted with a cast and assumed my arm was broken, even though it didn't feel like it was. When I got back to Belfast, I went to my own doctor. First he had to figure out what the doctor's report said because it had been written in Latin! The Commonwealth Games were only two months away and I thought I was out of the competition with a broken arm. Lo and behold, when the doctor translated the report it said I had a torn ligament and the doctor in Prague had put the cast on because I was travelling home and he didn't want my arm to move too much. My doctor just cut off the cast, which brought a smile to my face. Two weeks later I was punching again and was ready to go to training camp for the Commonwealth Games.

I didn't have to lose too much weight because I'd left Prague lighter than when I had arrived. Even though the city was beautiful, I thought the food was terrible; I lived on bread and yoghurt for a week. It was the first time I'd had trouble finding food I could eat, but it wouldn't be the last.

The Commonwealth Games team met at the Greenan Lodge (now the Balmoral Hotel) on Blacks Road in Belfast for training camp right after Christmas. Blacks Road was on a side of Belfast I didn't know very well, so I wasn't really sure where I was. It could have been Timbuktu for all I knew. I thought the Shankill Road was the whole world. My teammates for the Games were Paul Ireland, John Erskine, Eddie Fisher, Joe Lowe, Jim Webb and Paul Douglas ('Big Paul') – who, by the way, lived right next door to me in Highfield when I was growing up. As usual, I was the lightest boxer on the team. We all knew each other from fighting in the Ulster Championships together, so the atmosphere was light and friendly. Paul Ireland and I shared a room. During the first week the team ran on the surrounding roads. In the afternoon we went to Andersonstown leisure centre for weight training and to work on our technical boxing moves, and in the evening we trained in the Holy Trinity gym.

I was always the fastest when we were out running – John Erskine was pretty close behind me. We usually ran in a big circle around the streets because we'd worked out the route was about three miles long. One morning I took off like a rocket. I didn't know where I was running and I took a wrong turn. I was in the lead and just kept on running, but soon I realised I was lost. It was about 6.30 a.m. I saw a number 73 bus parked at a depot (I knew the number 73 went to Springmartin, just above Highfield) and if I'd had money in my pocket I would have got on the bus and gone home. But I hadn't, and so I had to try to find my way back to the hotel. That wasn't easy. I hadn't a clue where I was. No one had followed me, so I was on my own. I just kept running. I looked at my watch and saw that what was supposed to have been a 20-minute run had turned into 40 minutes at this stage. I knew I had to get back, but I didn't know how. Even though I lived in Belfast, I didn't know this part of it.

After about an hour, Mickey Hawkins and Nicolas Cruz, the team trainers, drove up alongside me in Mickey's white Mercedes-Benz. They asked what had happened to me and I told them I'd got lost. They thought it was funny that I couldn't find my way around my home town, but I wasn't laughing. My excuse was that it was a dark, winter's morning and I couldn't see the street signs.

After this incident, we decided to use the nearby running track. It is named after Northern Ireland's athletic hero Mary Peters. She won gold at the 1972 Olympic Games while competing in the pentathlon. She also won gold at the Commonwealth Games two years later representing Northern Ireland. Mary came to Auckland in 1990 to cheer us on. She is someone I have always looked up to and I consider her a friend.

We'd drive to the Mary Peters track about 6 a.m. every day. Most mornings it was freezing – it was January after all – and the track was covered in ice. We did the majority of our running around the outside of the track because there was gravel to grip on to. We did our sprints on the track on the mornings when there was no ice. We had a good training camp. It was fun and with seven guys staying in a hotel there was a lot of joking around. The *craic* was great. It was the best training camp I had ever been in as an amateur.

We left for New Zealand about a week before the competition started. The journey was really, really long. It took us about 30 hours to get there from London. We had a few stop-offs to refuel and we were allowed to leave the aircraft for a little while to stretch our legs. I was young then and I don't remember thinking about being tired. I was just excited about getting to New Zealand and fighting.

When we got to Auckland, it was summer. It was about 80 degrees and quite humid, but I thought the weather was lovely. Thankfully, we had about a week to acclimatise, having just come from freezing Belfast in January. The first thing we did when we arrived was pick up our credentials. We then went to the running track and did a light training session to loosen our bodies.

We stayed in what I'd call mobile homes in the Commonwealth Games Village – the best way to describe them would be wooden chalets. There were four bedrooms and two bathrooms in each one. The boxers were in one house and, just like at the training camp in Belfast, we all had a lot of fun together. We trained every day at the front of our homes, outside in the sunshine. We shadow boxed, jumped rope and hit the pads. It was warm outside and I was able to get a good sweat going. We also did our running on a grass track that had been set up in the Village.

All the Commonwealth countries were there with their teams. It was like the Olympics, but on a smaller scale. There were about 2,000 athletes competing in different sports compared to about 10,000 at the Olympic Games. The Village was pretty much like the one in Korea two years earlier as well. There were good training facilities and everything was free.

A few days before competition started, while I was hitting the pads with Mickey, I connected wrongly with my right hand and it immediately began to hurt. I thought I'd broken it. We went straight to the on-site doctor. He X-rayed it and told me I had bruised it but that the bone wasn't broken. I got physiotherapy treatment on it three times a day and my hand was back to normal in no time.

On the day of the first weigh-in, we got up and did our usual run. None of us were fighting that day. Big Paul and I were the only ones who could eat breakfast: I was making weight easily and he was able to eat because he was a heavyweight. After training my weight had dropped to about 4 lb below the flyweight limit and the trainers discussed whether or not to move me down to light flyweight. I knew I'd had problems making that weight and I was against it. I was happy where I was, so they allowed me to stay at flyweight.

The draw was held after the weigh-in. In my weight class there were 15 fighters. That meant that there would be seven fights and one contestant would get a bye. Big Paul and I waited behind with the trainers while our teammates went back to the Village for their breakfast. I thought for sure I'd be fighting in the first round, but as the names came out of the hat mine still hadn't been called. When the last name was read out, it was mine. That meant I got the bye and went straight into the quarter-finals, the last 8, right away. I was delighted.

Everyone except Big Paul and me fought in the first round. The competition for my teammates didn't start well at all, as each of them lost their first fight. John Erskine was totally robbed, but that's boxing. This was the strongest team I'd ever been on, but it wasn't meant to be for them to win. Big Paul got to the semi-finals and picked up a bronze medal.

When I entered the ring against Benjamin Mwangata from Tanzania, there was a lot of pressure on me to win the fight. Mwangata had already won his first fight easily enough and he was loose and ready to go. He was tall but that wasn't a problem for me. My punch output was just too much for him and I won on a wide unanimous decision, securing a bronze for the Northern Ireland team.

My second fight was against a very strong fighter named Maurice Maina from Kenya. He had fought in the Olympics in 1988 as a flyweight, but our paths hadn't crossed back then. He pushed me backwards and I had to box on the back foot. A lot of people didn't think I could fight going back, but I proved I could. I jabbed and moved, turning him as he came in, and made him miss with a lot of shots. I was landing at a rate of four punches to one. He was definitely a stronger puncher than me, but I was landing a higher volume of shots and won the fight by a unanimous decision. That win guaranteed me at least a silver medal. Harry Carpenter, who was commentating at ringside, said I was a 'model to all British boxers who fight in these championships'. He advised, 'You must train hard and have stamina.' He was so right.

I met Nokuthula Tshabangu from Zimbabwe in the final. I was the only boxer from my team left in the competition at this point, and Northern Ireland hadn't won a gold medal in boxing at the Commonwealth Games since 1978 when Barry McGuigan and Gerry Hamill had won theirs. So I was determined that I was going to win. Nothing was going to stop me.

About ten minutes before my fight we were preparing in the warm-up area made up of cubicles separated by curtains. I was getting ready and Mickey started to slap his pads together; it sounded as if I was punching like a heavyweight. I was hoping my opponent was standing outside listening!

Mickey and I were confident of the victory. We were ready to go in and win this gold medal. The first round was pretty even. Tshabangu was a very hard puncher. But I was just getting warmed up. In the second round I took over and he started to fade. Harry Carpenter, who was also commentating on this fight, said I was 'doing absolute wonders for Ulster boxing and Ulster morale'. I had 'swept the opposition aside with non-stop attacking'. In the final round, I landed a barrage of shots, forcing the referee to give him a standing count. With less than 30 seconds to go, I hit Tshabangu with a left hook that sent him straight to the canvas. I knew I had secured the win and a gold medal, for myself and Northern Ireland.

When I left the ring, I met up with all my teammates. They were delighted for me. There were no hard feelings. They had supported me 100 per cent throughout the competition, even though their dreams had ended early. I remember standing on the rostrum after having the gold medal put around my neck. There were three Africans sharing it with me. I looked like a little boy beside these full-grown men. I was expecting the Northern Ireland anthem to be played, but there was silence. Unbeknownst to me, the player had jammed and instead of me hearing a recording of 'Danny Boy', Bob Gibson, one of the Games officials, took over the microphone and started to sing. It was a very emotional moment, especially when fans in the arena started singing along. Bob had saved the day. I later found out that he was originally from Belfast but lived in New Zealand. We have stayed in touch to this day.

During the closing ceremony I carried the Northern Ireland flag into the stadium as I was the only gold medallist in our team. No one ever said anything to my face about me carrying this flag either.

There was a big party in the Village afterwards and all the athletes mixed together. New Zealand is a great country. Shortly after the Games I received an offer to go back and live there with the prospect of representing New Zealand at the 1992 Olympic Games. But I was a home bird and wanted to stay in Belfast. It would have been a great opportunity for me, but I hoped there would be bigger and better ones lying ahead where I was.

I arrived home to a hero's welcome in Belfast. There were parties everywhere for me. I became a superstar in Northern Ireland overnight. Everyone knew who I was. The local Shankill leisure centre presented me with a lifetime membership to use their facilities for free – and I have on plenty of occasions.

I was also invited to 10 Downing Street to meet the prime minister at that time, Margaret Thatcher. Harry accompanied me on the flight, but I was escorted in to meet her alone. It was an honour to meet her and shake her hand.

I got letters from people all around the country. The only politician who sent me a congratulatory letter was Gerry Adams, MP for West Belfast and leader of Sinn Fein. A lot of young girls sent me letters, but I only replied to one and I don't know the reason for that; God has a way of bringing people together. It was from a wee girl from East Belfast called Cheryl Rennie – who later became my wife.

4

OLYMPIC DREAMS

Wayne is one of the true upstanding gentlemen of the sport and as an ambassador sets an excellent example to all young fighters. In the boxing ring, Wayne fights with endless energy and fierce determination. This comes from living the passion of the sport you love.

Kevin Barry, boxing manager and trainer

After winning the Commonwealth gold medal I was on the dole, making no money, and the offers to turn pro were flooding in. As I was still only 19 years old, with no money in the bank and a gold medal behind me, the offers were very attractive.

When I became successful, more and more people started to recognise me. One night I was heading home from Cheryl's house – since I didn't have a car, I had to take two buses across town – and there was a group of guys hanging out by the City Hall. They shouted, 'Hey, boy, come 'ere.' I knew they were out looking for trouble and walked over to them, ready to defend myself, and then they recognised me. Their tone of voice changed and they said, 'Wayne McCullough, give us your autograph.' They wouldn't try to beat me up then!

I got a walkover in the Ulster Championships about a month after the Commonwealth Games and in the March I went on to win the Irish title. The Irish Amateur Boxing Association (IABA) wanted me to stay amateur until after the Olympic Games in Barcelona in 1992. The IABA met with the Irish Olympic Council and presented me with a financial offer that was tempting, to say the least. Each month, until after the Olympics, they would pay me £250 in my hand and deposit the same amount in an account for me. If I kept my promise and stayed amateur until after the Games, I would get the money they had put away for me in a lump sum. I agreed because it was just too good to refuse and I believed I had time on my side to learn more as an amateur.

The IABA knew I could win a medal at the next Olympic Games and that's why they took the chance on me. So I became Ireland's first-ever paid amateur boxer, which meant I could train full time. I knew the Cuban and American teams trained full time and that's why they were so successful. I had always hoped for the same type of opportunity and here it was.

In April I joined the Irish team on a trip to America. I fought twice while I was there, the first time just outside New York and the other in Indiana, where I fought Tim Austin and beat him. Austin was a world-ranked amateur then and went on to become a world champion as a professional.

* * *

In June, Michael Carruth and I were chosen to box on the European select elite team against a North America team in Salt Lake City, Utah. Mickey Hawkins was the coach for that trip. When we fought the Americans, I remember Oscar de la Hoya (who was only 17 at the time) being there; even back then he was their superstar. De la Hoya went on to become a multiple-weight professional world champion and is now an extremely successful boxing promoter.

The North America team was made up of select elite athletes from Canada, Cuba and America, and in the end they won the tournament 11–2. Fortunately, I won my fight, beating Tim Austin yet again. Maybe the American team was trying to get revenge on me. But that didn't work. I beat him twice on American soil but, boy, could he hit hard! The Austin fight was my last at flyweight.

41

In November 1990 I moved up to bantamweight (8 st. 7 lb) to fight in the World Cup championships in Bombay, India.

Before we left, the team doctor notified me that I would have to get some immunisations. I thought nothing of it, since I'd been immunised before going to Korea in 1988; however, this time was different. I had to get protection against tetanus and hepatitis, and a booster. The day I got the booster I had planned to meet Cheryl in Belfast city centre to see Santa Claus arriving at a shopping centre. I got a bus there from Highfield and by the time I got to the top of Royal Avenue, a quarter of a mile from where we were meeting, I could hardly move my leg – I had to drag it behind me – and I was starting to feel sick. When I finally made it to our meeting point, I had to prop myself up against a shop wall. When Cheryl arrived with her mum and sister, she asked me what was wrong. I told her that I felt sick and I couldn't move. They practically carried me to their house and put me into bed.

Only four weight divisions went to each qualifying tournament. Out of four eligible fighters, Ireland only sent Billy Walsh and me to the World Cup, with my trainer, Harry, as the coach.

The World Cup was one of the toughest competitions in which to win a medal because, unlike the Olympic Games and the World Championships, where there are one gold and silver and two bronze medals, there is only one bronze in the World Cup. The fights were held outdoors in a cricket stadium and it was about 90 degrees with 100 per cent humidity.

My first impression of Bombay was that people there were either rich or poor; there was no in-between. Billy and I would go running in the mornings along the Bombay promenade and after leaving our luxury hotel would literally be jumping over homeless people who were sleeping on the streets. I have never seen so much poverty. It was everywhere. When we were travelling to the fight venue in taxis, parents would knock on the doors with their kids in their arms. Some of them had no arms or legs and they would be being used to beg for money. I felt sorry for them the first few days and gave them money, but it got to a point where I didn't go out of the hotel unless I needed to because it made me feel so sad.

For my first fight I was drawn against M. Pingle from India, whom I beat. Then I defeated D.K. Park from Korea. I lost my next fight in the semi-finals to the world champion Serafim Todorov of Bulgaria. We fought over five two-minute rounds. He won the first three and I came back and won the last two, but it was too late. I was happy with the outcome of the fight, though, because I had just moved up a weight class and I had fought the world amateur champion and pushed him to his limits.

My left eye was swollen after the bout but I knew I had to fight the next day against the other semi-final loser to determine who would win the bronze. It turned out to be my friend Fred Muteweta. I knew from past experiences that when I had beaten someone, he would come back in the next bout and fight me harder, so I was well prepared. During our fight it started to rain and since the fights were taking place outdoors the ring was getting wet – it became really slippery and was more like an ice rink than a boxing ring. We were both sliding all over the place. In spite of this, I beat Muteweta on points. It turned out that each time we fought, it was easier to beat him than the time before.

The world's top fighters all compete in the World Cup as there is prize money at stake for medal winners. I received $1,500 (about £1,000) with my bronze and as an amateur that was a fortune. It felt good to be paid for fighting, and to get a medal too. The World Cup operates a points system, so I was ranked after the competition. The losing semi-finalists fight so the amateur boxing governing body can determine who is number three and who is number four in the world. So, after only four fights as a bantamweight, I was ranked number three in the world.

For me, the Ulster Seniors in 1991 was, at the time, the most prominent fight I had taken part in. I was scheduled to fight the reigning champion, Johnson Todd. He had knocked out almost everyone he'd fought. I had people walk up to me on the streets of Belfast before the fight and tell me to my face that I was going to get knocked out. I just laughed at them and told them to come to the fight and see. Since Todd was a southpaw, I wanted to move away from his big left-hand. My brother Alan turned southpaw for me and I used him for sparring. We worked on different moves in the ring, with Harry working on my strategy. The goal was to box and move. The Ulster Hall was packed to capacity on the night; I'd never seen it like that before. People were turned away at the door. I had a lot of support, but I know a lot of people came to see me possibly get knocked out as well.

Todd came out in the first round with his big winging shots, but I kept the fight under control by sticking my left jab in his face. I used my footwork to stay out of range and I stayed cool and relaxed. In the second round I threw a three-punch combination of a left-right-left that staggered Todd. The referee, Jack Poucher, stepped in to give him a standing eight count. Todd was very durable and came back with big shots that landed on my chin, but they didn't move me. The talk beforehand was about Todd's 'big punch' but right at the end of the round I put him to the floor with a big punch of my own. My left hook knocked him down in his own corner, but he was saved by the bell.

In the final round I played with him. I boxed and moved, giving him angles. I won a unanimous decision on really wide scores. Commentating for the BBC at ringside that night, Jim Neilly said that I had shown I was the best at light flyweight and flyweight, and I had proved I was 'beyond all reasonable doubt, the best fighter at bantamweight'. He went on to say that I was continuing with 'what had been a remarkable amateur career'. In my opinion, this was by far my best amateur fight.

When I went to the All Irelands, the National Senior Championships, four weeks later, I drew Johnson Todd again in the first round. The rumours were that Todd was sick when he fought me the first time and he said he was definitely going to knock me out this time. But I did exactly what I had done in the first fight: I gave him a standing count in the second round and won again on wide scores.

A week later I was scheduled to fight Joe Lawlor in the final. My sister, April, had recently recovered from chickenpox and when I woke up on the Sunday prior to the fight, I was covered in spots. I must have picked up the virus from her. So, one thing was for sure, my fight with Lawlor was off.

The European Championships were coming up around May and I wanted a box-off against Lawlor to see who would go.

Because of the dissolution of the USSR in 1991, the Olympic Council had changed its rules so instead of boxing being an open competition, only 32 fighters from around the world in each weight class were allowed to compete. Now we would all have to fight it out at qualifying tournaments. If Lawlor won a medal at the Europeans (which was one of the qualifying tournaments), he would be guaranteed a place on the Olympic team and I would miss out. I did a fitness test about four weeks after I'd had chickenpox in Dublin. Of course, I passed the test with flying colours. Lawlor was sent to the Europeans anyway, and I had no say in the matter. It made me very angry. Thankfully, for me, he didn't win a medal, and so he didn't qualify. We would meet each other again in the Irish Senior final in 1992.

In November 1991 the Irish team went to Sydney for another Olympic qualifying tournament. There were only four boxers picked to go: Paul Griffin, Billy Walsh, Dennis Galvin and me. If Paul Griffin and I were ever on the same team, we hung out together. He's a good guy and we always looked out for each other. Kieron Joyce and Nicolas Cruz Hernandez were the team coaches. It took us about twenty-four hours to get to Australia and we arrived only two or three days before the competition.

I stopped Felipe Costa from Portugal in the second round of my first fight. Then I beat Joseph Zabakly from Australia in my second. It was a tough fight. He had good support but I had great support from a group of Irish guys that had turned up to cheer us on.

My third fight was against the Cuban world champion, Enrique Carrion. This was for a medal and a place on the Olympic team. I went out there and took my time in the first round. In the last two rounds I practically ran him out of the ring. We were confident I had won. Nicolas was jumping for joy in the corner, but, of course, the decision went to the Cuban. I didn't just lose out on a medal, I also lost out on a place in the Olympic team. I was disgusted. When I fought one of the favourite boxers, it seemed as if they would get points up before they started. To this day, I think there are too many politics in amateur boxing.

We had a couple of days left in Australia before we returned home, so we went out and did the touristy thing. We visited the

Sydney Opera House and Bondi Beach, and we partied a little too.

As soon as I got back from Australia I realised my nose was cracked. The Ulster Senior Championships were being held in December 1991 and the Irish Seniors in January 1992 because the Olympics were coming up. I won the Ulster Seniors by stopping my opponent in the second round. I wasn't 100 per cent fit and I was still fighting, even though my nose hadn't healed yet, but I was determined not to let anything, not even a cracked nose, stand in my way.

When the Irish Seniors came around, I was up against Joe Lawlor again, the reigning champion. The winner would go on to the Olympic qualifying tournament in Germany. Joe and I had been friends since 1988, when we had trained together for my first Olympics. We travelled to Dublin for our brain scans and I spent the night in his house before returning to training camp in Kerry the next day. Even though we were friends, once that bell rang I knew I had to win. Joe was a good puncher and a tough guy, but I just threw too many punches and overwhelmed him. I won the fight on points.

I went to the qualifying tournament in March in a town called Halle in what was then East Germany. I had to win at least two fights to be guaranteed a place on the team going to Barcelona. I won the two fights I needed to qualify for the Olympics and some on the team suggested that I pull out of the competition at that point. But I would never have done that and I went on to win the entire tournament.

In the final I fought Dieter Berg, a German who was also going to the Olympics. He was a former European champion and was a tall, rangy southpaw. I beat him around the ring like I had never beaten anybody before. We could see the computer scoring from the ring. But after the first round I came back to the corner and saw I was losing on points. I couldn't believe it. Nicolas told me not to worry about the computer scoring, but it was in my head. I totally dominated Berg in the second round and came back to the corner to see that I was 8–3 down. What did I expect? The fight was in Germany and he was a German.

At the beginning of the third round the home fans started cheering for me. There were some Cubans from another boxing tournament who were also watching and as Nicolas was in my corner they were going crazy for me too. I continued to beat Berg around the ring and, with five seconds to go, as the referee broke us out of a clinch, I took a quick look at the scores – we had eight points each. 'No way!' I thought. They were going to rob me. I ran straight at him with a few seconds to spare and threw about ten punches. When the bell rang, signalling the end of the fight, and with the crowd going wild, I looked at the scores: from that ten-punch combination I had managed to score one point and secure a win of 9–8. I was overjoyed. Even though the scores should have been about 20–3, justice was served. I didn't get a trophy or a medal, I got something bigger and better: a place on the Olympic team. That would do, for now. When the team arrived back home in Belfast, I was thankful I didn't have any injuries, even though I'd fought four great fights. I knew I was getting better with every bout.

In April I travelled to Spain with an Irish team to compete against the country's Olympic fighters. We stayed in a resort in Tenerife, which was a real party spot for holidaymakers back then, with nightclubs and bars everywhere. There was a lot of temptation outside the apartment, but I knew there was plenty of time for fun when the competition was over. It was quite warm and I had no trouble making weight. Paul Ireland and I roomed together in an apartment. One morning as we set out for a run about 6.30 a.m. we met some of our teammates just coming in after a night out. A few of them were due to fight the next day and I didn't think they were taking boxing seriously. When we fought Spain, we were beaten something like 8–2. I didn't fight that day, but Paul did, and he was one of the winners. It was probably the best I've ever seen him fight. He boxed beautifully and deserved to win. When I went to a competition, I trained hard and fought, and afterwards could relax and party if I wanted to.

About four days later we fought the Spanish team again and this time it was my turn to fight. The guys who were out partying had done a complete 180, and waited until after the competition to go partying, as I had advised them. We beat Spain the second time around. I stopped my opponent, who was also going to the Olympics, in two rounds. It was the type of fight where I was busting him up so badly I wanted to ask the referee to stop it. I had him over in the first round and I gave him four standing counts. The referee was Spanish, so I think he allowed it to go on longer than it should have.

This would be my last fight until I got to the Olympic Games in Barcelona. I continued to train twice a day and I kept my weight under control. When it was time to go to training camp, I was more than ready. My goal was to get a medal. Everyone thought I could at least come home with a bronze, but in the Olympics anything can happen.

5

SILVER IN SPAIN

Wayne, without a shadow of a doubt, is the best Irish boxer of all time. His dedication, discipline, courage and willpower cannot be compared because they are his trademark. Nobody works as hard as he does. He's the best. The one and only.

Nicolas Cruz Hernandez, Olympic boxing coach

Only six Irish boxers qualified for the 1992 Olympic Games in Barcelona out of a possible twelve. This time I wasn't the smallest fighter on the team, Paul Buttimer was. Paul Griffin, Paul Douglas, Kevin McBride, Michael Carruth and me had all gone to qualifying tournaments to secure our places on the Irish team.

I never stopped working out. I did most of my training with Harry in Belfast and used Alan for sparring. I was really looking forward to these Olympic Games. I was bringing with me the experience of Seoul and using what I had learned over the past four years, so I believed I could win a medal.

With 78 days to go before the start of the competition, I wrote in my training diary: 'I will start preparation for the Olympics ten weeks before it starts.' By writing down that statement, my second Olympic dream felt real. Michael Carruth and I were the only two boxers on the team who had fought with the 1988 team;

we were the more knowledgeable fighters this time around and we sort of knew what to expect.

The IABA organised for the team to go to training camp in Cottbus, a town in Germany. We flew in on 23 June with the intention of staying for four weeks and heading straight to Barcelona. We didn't know what to expect when we arrived because no one had gone to check it out beforehand. The whole team, fighters and officials, stayed in hostel-type lodgings. There were three of us to a tiny room and there was only one shower and one toilet for everyone to share. It was over 100 degrees in Cottbus and there were no laundry facilities. Since we were training twice a day, we had a lot of dirty, sweaty clothes. As soon as I did a workout I washed my clothes in a sink and hung them out of a window to try and dry them, but because it was so humid when I put them back on they still felt damp. After about two days our rooms were stinking and there were fleas everywhere.

We were taken to a running track in the mornings to do our roadwork and in the afternoon we trained in a top-class gymnasium. Training took my mind off the awful conditions we were living in, but that only lasted a couple of hours because I always knew I had to go back.

The Thai Olympic team was in Germany at the time as well, but they had come well prepared. They'd brought their own food and drinks. We had to eat what we were given and half the time I didn't even know what that was – it was probably better that way. And all we were offered in terms of liquid were fizzy drinks. There was no clean water and after training I needed some. No one was able to supply us with it and I was definitely not going to drink it from the tap.

We sparred with the team from Thailand and training went well. Michael Carruth's dad, Austin, and Nicolas Cruz Hernandez had been picked as the Olympic coaches. Nicolas could see I wasn't giving my training 100 per cent. It was suffering because I wasn't comfortable and I kept thinking, 'If I spend four weeks in this place, I will be mentally drained and unable to fight.' Some of the fighters started complaining; I certainly wasn't the first. We all knew how appalling it was and decided as a team that we should go to Sean Horkan, the team manager, and tell him how we felt. We decided to give it another couple of days before we took any drastic action; however, on 30 June the state of the living conditions got to me. Mentally, I was shattered. I couldn't take it any more. I am a clean freak and the conditions were disgusting. I remember walking into one of the bedrooms where most of the fighters were relaxing – I can still see them lying on the beds – and asking if we were going to go and ask for our tickets. 'I'm ready to go now,' I said, but I got no reply. I looked at them all and knew I was on my own. As I walked out of the room I kicked the door and it almost fell off the hinges. I was so mad.

I walked straight into Sean's room and told him I wanted my ticket to go home. He said the flights could not be changed and I wouldn't be able to use my ticket to go home. So I got on the phone to Harry. I had been updating him daily on the horrendous conditions, so he wasn't surprised to hear that the situation had worsened. He sent me a ticket so I could fly back to Belfast. I got a taxi and left camp. As I was leaving, I felt a weight being lifted from my shoulders. The taxi to the airport cost over £100, but I was leaving at any price.

Harry had been informed that I was off the team before I arrived back into Belfast. I didn't care at that point because if I'd stayed in Germany I wouldn't have been fully prepared to fight anyway. If I was off the Olympic team, I was going to turn pro and the Irish Board knew it.

The next day I went out running. Not only did I want to continue my training, I wanted to clear my head. I was jogging along the Ballysillan Road and one of the officials from the Boxing Association pulled up alongside me in his car. I stopped to talk to him. He said if anybody asked me why I was home, I should say my rib was sore. I knew there and then that I was still on the team. He could also see that even though I had just returned home the night before, I was out pounding the roads, preparing on my own in familiar surroundings.

Later that night my diary read: 'HOME AND HAPPY TRAINING.' That said it all.

The IABA's plan was for me to go to Dublin on 6 July to the Blackrock Clinic for X-rays on my 'sore rib'. I knew what they were doing, so I played along because I still wanted to go to the Olympics. Some Irish officials flew out to Germany to visit the training camp and brought the team home a couple of weeks later – on the tickets that I was told were not changeable. So I did everyone a favour and cost myself close to £1,000.

I was supposed to meet up with the team on Friday, 10 July in Drogheda, a town near the coast about 80 miles away, but there were bomb scares on the bus and railway lines between Dublin and Belfast. I got a phone call at home on the Friday afternoon. Someone yelled down the phone at me: 'Get yourself down to this effin training camp, or you're off the team,' then hung up. To this day, I still don't know who it was. How was I supposed to get from Belfast to Drogheda if I had no transportation? On the Monday morning, I took a bus to Drogheda and began what was to be the final stage of training camp for the Barcelona Olympic Games. We used the local boxing club, which I'd been in a few times. I had always had fun there.

I knew one thing for sure: I was mentally and physically ready because I'd trained hard on my own in Belfast and my mind was clear. The Irish team went out to Spain a week or so before the competition started. We went through the usual procedures of picking up our credentials and so on. By now I was used to it. It was warm in Barcelona, but still very comfortable. The fights were to be held in an indoor stadium, so the heat wasn't really an issue.

In the mornings we went running along the front of the Olympic Village at about seven o'clock. It was three miles or so from our apartment to the running track and back. We then shadow boxed in front of our accommodation. All the athletes were staying in the same complex and some of them complained to the president of the Olympic Council about the noise we were making. Us boxers were up bright and early, training hard to try to win a medal for our country. After that we were forced to shadow box around the back of our apartments so we didn't disturb anyone's beauty sleep! We still did our workout at the front of our building in the afternoons, as the noise wasn't a factor then. After training every day I was about 2 lb under the weight limit, but I was feeling very strong.

There wasn't much to do during the day, so we made our own fun. One day all the boxers went up on to the roof of the complex and, because it was nice and warm, started throwing water at some of the other athletes on the Irish team. One of them allegedly slipped on a wet patch and went to the team president and complained about us again. We were called in to a meeting and told that if we didn't stop the horseplay, we were all going to be sent home. I sat there and thought I was back in school. We were only passing the time and having some good, clean fun. The boxers were the life and soul of the party and plenty of the other athletes were happy to hang out with us. I think some people looked down on us, but we produced the goods.

Competition started on 26 July, the day after the opening ceremony. A few of us didn't attend because we were fighting the next day. I had a hard draw. My first fight was against Fred Muteweta. This was the third time we'd meet centre ring. I bumped into him in the Village after the draw. We had been keeping in touch and had become friends since our meeting in 1988. Now we'd have to fight again. We hugged each other and said that's the way it goes. If Fred had been on the other side of the draw, I believe he would have gone home with a medal. Our fight went much the same as the other two had gone: I dominated the fight and gave him a standing count on the final bell. The computer score from our bout was 28–7. One fight down, still four to go.

Next up, I fought Ahmed Abbood from Iraq. About 30 seconds into the first round I hit him with an overhand right. I thought I was going to stop him because, for a moment, he was out on his feet and the referee had to give him a standing count. Before the end of round one I hit him with a left hook but at the same time his elbow smashed into my left bicep muscle. The pain was excruciating, but I wasn't going to stop. I beat him 10–2 in the end. After the fight I was straight on the phone to Cheryl. I was in tears. I didn't think I'd be able to fight on. I went to get treatment on the muscle and saw the physio as much as possible over the next three days before I was due to fight again. It was beginning to feel better, so I was good to go.

In the quarter-finals and fighting for a medal I boxed

Mohammed Sabo from Nigeria. He had also been at the Commonwealth Games in Auckland in 1990. He won a gold medal at bantamweight. So now, here we were, two Commonwealth gold medallists fighting each other. Sabo was a southpaw who tried his best to keep up with my punch rate in the first and at the end of the round the score was 6–6. But I was just getting warmed up. I started getting into a rhythm in the second and I began to get through with the straight right-hands to which southpaws are susceptible. Sabo was slowly fading and I was getting faster. After the second round I was 16–10 up. I went out in the third and simply kept hitting him. I ran through him and my right-hand was working wonders. When the final bell rang, I knew I'd done enough. I ran to my corner and jumped into Nicolas's arms. That fight was the highest-scored bout in the 1992 Olympics. The final score was 31–13. I had picked up an amazing 15 points in the final round.

The Irish fans were definitely the biggest contingent at the Olympics. My teammates sat among the fans while I was fighting, and shouted and sang and cheered me on.

My next fight was against Gwang-Sik Li, a North Korean. He had beaten Todorov, the world champion, in the quarter-finals just before I had beaten Sabo. I remember hearing Todorov squealing in the dressing-room beside me after he'd lost. Li was strong. He kept coming forward and was the hardest puncher I ever fought in my amateur career. It was 6–5 after the first round; I was leading by only one point.

After the second round my left cheek was hurting. I didn't know what was wrong with it, so I didn't say anything. I was still only one point up after round two, so even though I started the third round leading 11–10, I knew I had to win convincingly in the final round. The last round was always my strongest. I knew I was going to step up the pace in the final three minutes. For the first time in the fight I pushed Li backwards and it was obvious he didn't know how to fight on the back foot. At this point I was landing two punches to every one of his, and in the last thirty seconds I totally took control. I beat him 10–6 in the final round and the score was 21–16. I proved once again that I always come back in the last round. To this day a lot of people tell me this fight was the best they'd ever seen in an Olympic Games.

My cheek was slightly swollen after the fight and it was really painful. I knew if I said anything to the coaches or the team doctor that they would pull me out of the competition, so I phoned Cheryl again in Belfast and told her that my face was really painful; it was numb. I knew she couldn't help me, but it was just good to tell someone.

Since Michael Carruth and I were the only boxers left in the competition and none of the other fighters needed to train, we did most of our final preparation together. It was history in the making: Ireland had never won a gold medal and it had been 40 years since we'd even won silver at bantamweight. It was up to us and there was a lot of pressure to perform. We were guaranteed medals at this point, but neither of us were quitters: we knew what we were there for.

Six weight classes fought each day during the two-day Olympic finals. They alternated the weight divisions, so the day I fought, the light flyweight final took place first. Right after my match Oscar de la Hoya won gold for the USA. He fought at lightweight.

I was in the dressing-room, warmed up and ready to walk to the ring, when we were stopped by an official and told that they were going to hold the light flyweight medal ceremony before I got into the ring. I had to sit down again. Just then something came over me and I began to get worried. All of a sudden I realised that if I won, I'd have to stand for the Irish national anthem while the Irish flag was being hoisted above me. I don't know why I started thinking about this. I was part of the Irish team and would have been honoured to win a gold medal for Ireland, so I was unsure as to why I was thinking about flags and anthems. But God has a reason for everything.

Cheryl had decided at a day's notice that she couldn't miss seeing me fight in the Olympic final. It cost her a fortune to get to Barcelona – after all, there were no low-cost airlines back then – but she didn't care. My dad and my sister Anne were there on an all-expenses-paid trip, courtesy of Calor Gas in Belfast. As I walked out into the arena, I could see Cheryl. I was still confident

I could win the gold and the support I had from the fans was unbelievable. I had been in arenas before where I had great support, but this was the Olympic Games – I was in the final and fighting for a gold medal. I was on cloud nine and couldn't wait to start.

I was up against Joel Casamayor from Cuba. He'd had an easy semi-final fight, since his opponent had dislocated his shoulder in the first round and had pulled out. Casamayor was a southpaw puncher and he moved around the ring while I ran after him. I forced him to fight in the first round and in my opinion the round was pretty even. When I got back to the corner in between rounds, I took a glance at the scoreboard; I had to look back twice because they had me 6–1 down. I couldn't believe it! Nicolas told me it had been a close round and said to forget about the scores.

I went out in the second round and Casamayor hit me with a right jab, followed by a straight left. They weren't big shots, but I certainly felt them. They sent me backwards. It was as though there was electricity shooting through my face. I stepped back and covered up on the ropes, but he couldn't do anything to hurt me. The referee looked at me and I couldn't even open my left eye. Casamayor stepped in; we got tied up. Coming out of the clinch, he hit me a right hook on my left eye. I had to take a standing count. I didn't know what was going on. The pain was unbearable. I had never been hurt like this in the ring in my life; I was wondering why it had to happen in the Olympic final. After I took the count, I fought Casamayor for the remainder of the round with my eye half-closed. He still couldn't stop me; in fact, he wouldn't even come near me. As the end of round two drew near, he hit me with a light straight jab on my left cheek. The sensation that shot up my face was so severe I had to shake my head because of the pain. I still couldn't believe what was going on. Every time he hit me on the left side of my face it felt like I was being electrocuted with a live wire. At the end of the second round, I went back to the corner telling myself to forget about the pain and go out and do it in the final round. I was 10–2 down. In between the second and third rounds, Nicolas asked me what was wrong. I told him my whole face was numb. I honestly couldn't feel anything. The corner were going to pull me out, but I protested. I would never quit.

Going out into the centre of the ring for the final three minutes of the Olympic final, I told myself it was do or die. I went out and forced Casamayor to fight me. I had blood coming out of the corner of my left eye, but I wasn't cut. The blood was coming out of my eye socket as a result of the damage that had been done to my cheek. During the last minute of the final round, I hit Casamayor with big shots and had him going, but it was just too late. I won the last round 6–4, but it wasn't enough to win the fight. The final score was 14–8.

Casamayor went on to become a world champion professional boxer after he defected from Cuba in 1996. I met him in Vegas a few years ago and he asked if I had a copy of our fight. I sent him the final and also his semi-final. We have become good friends. How often do you hear of two fighters who compete in the Olympic final meeting up again, never mind becoming friends? That is what is great about this sport. Once the fight is over, we boxers are ordinary, decent human beings.

The fans celebrated after my fight because I hadn't lost the gold, I'd won the silver. And I was delighted. I knew God had a reason for everything and this just wasn't my time. I became a bigger hero for my gutsy performance than if I'd won the gold with ease. People all over Ireland and in the USA still talk about me fighting such a brave fight.

Immediately after our fight, Casamayor and I had to take a drugs test. We sat in the room together and chatted as much as we could – I can't speak Spanish and he knew very little English. We exchanged Olympic vests. The officials wouldn't let us leave the room until we had taken our drugs tests, so I had to sit there in the dressing-room area watching and cheering for Michael instead of being in the stands with the fans while he won his gold medal. I was so proud of him. I picked up Ireland's first silver medal at bantamweight in boxing since John McNally in 1952. That same day Michael won Ireland's first-ever gold medal.

The whole Irish team went out and celebrated our medal wins. I brought Cheryl along, and my sister and dad. We had a lot of fun. Those Games will go down in history as one of the best for Irish boxing.

I went to the hospital after the fight in Spain, but the doctors couldn't find anything wrong with my face. I think it was because it was so swollen. A few weeks after I returned to Belfast I went to see a specialist at the Ulster Hospital. He told me that my cheekbone was cracked in three places and the nerve that runs from the eye down the left-hand side of the face to the top lip had been ripped apart. That is what had given me the most pain. Thankfully, my cheekbone hadn't moved. The doctor told me if it had, I would have needed surgery to repair it and my career could have been over. He said to rest and that I shouldn't get punched on my face for six months in order to give my bone time to heal.

* * *

There were thousands of fans at Dublin airport when we arrived home from Barcelona, even though it was the middle of the night. The support we received was incredible and we thanked the fans for coming out. Michael and I became very good friends, as did Cheryl and Paula, Michael's wife. We all stayed in a hotel that night and the next day we were taken in an open-top bus along Dublin's O'Connell Street with what looked like 50,000 people on the streets waving and cheering for us. They were out with Michael and me celebrating. At the invitation of Dublin's Lord Mayor we went to Mansion House, where we were presented with awards. From that day forth, our lives would be changed for ever. I spent most of my time over the next six months in Dublin, Wexford and Drogheda, making appearances. We were invited to the Ireland v. Latvia football match that year and at half-time the Football Association of Ireland (FAI) brought Michael and me onto the pitch and presented us with Dublin Crystal footballs. Mine still sits in my home in Las Vegas.

My face was slowly getting better, but I was almost driven insane with the itch I had over a few months. There was nothing to scratch, it was one of those itches under your skin: a sign my cheekbone was healing.

When I returned to Belfast, the people of Highfield had a big street party. There was free food and drink for everybody in the estate. A few days later another open-top bus took me down the Shankill Road to the Plaza Hotel in Belfast city centre where a function had been organised in my honour. Joseph Rea, the Jewellers, presented me with an engraved Rotary dress watch – and it is still keeping good time.

A reception was also held for me at the City Hall. While I was waiting to go into the function room, I was told that the council had been hesitant about celebrating my victory. Michael Carruth hadn't been invited, even though I had attended several functions in the Republic of Ireland. Their alleged reason was that I had fought for Ireland. I was happy to fight for Ireland, but I'd had no choice since boxing is an all-Ireland sport. I walked up to the Lord Mayor and told him I wasn't impressed; in fact, I was disgusted. I fought for sport not politics. I was ready to walk out. The guests were seated, and so Pat McCrory advised me to 'do it for the boxers'. I thought about it for a few minutes and then agreed to go in for the dinner, but I made sure the Lord Mayor knew I wasn't happy about it. Like everything else in Northern Ireland, politics supersedes sport and my boxing achievement was no different. Sadly, no matter what individuals achieve in my home country, politics finds a way in. I didn't make many PR appearances in Belfast. I don't know why, I just did most of my work outside the city.

A short while later I received an invitation to a garden party at Buckingham Palace. Cheryl and I already had plans to go on holiday to Greece, and we were young and naive. We didn't realise the significance of such an invitation. We'd drop everything to go if the same thing happened today.

People told me that if I won an Olympic medal, I'd be set for life. But I was still on the dole and making very little money for appearances. I got the remainder of the money from my Olympic sponsorship at the end of 1992. It took me a while to get it because the IABA was trying to entice me to stay amateur for another four years until the 1996 Games. They offered to double what I was already receiving, but I thought I'd kept my promise long enough and it was time to move on. I was sick of the amateur game. I'd wanted to be a professional boxer since I was 15. My mind was made up: I was turning pro.

6

LIVING THE AMERICAN DREAM

There's only one Wayne McCullough! I first met Wayne as he was about to turn professional, and across those years, with the incredible ups and downs of his life, he has always remained the same. Warm, natural and intensely committed to family and profession. There's not a phoney bone in his body. A true champ. It's an honour to be counted among his friends.

Dermot Lavery, documentary film-maker

With the Olympic Games behind me, my goal now was to get a good contract to turn professional. Harry and I continued to train, although I couldn't spar because of my cheek injury. PR work was non-stop. Every other day I was travelling from Belfast to Dublin, making appearances, and there was food and drink everywhere we went. No matter what was happening, I always trained beforehand. I never stopped. Cheryl and I went all-expenses-paid to Miami in late 1992 courtesy of local department stores Penneys and Primark. We stayed in the Sheraton Bal Harbor Hotel – a real hot spot for celebrities. We had the time of our lives.

I had professional offers from Britain and Ireland and I was considering them all. But I had imagined that, being as I was Northern Ireland's first Olympic silver medallist in 40 years, the offers would have been more attractive. I wanted to be a full-time pro but with some of the offers I would have also had to hold down a regular job just to make ends meet. Harry and I took our time considering the offers: my face was still sore and I didn't need to rush into anything.

Around October 1992, I got a phone call from Barry McGuigan. He talked to me about Mat Tinley, an American TV executive with Prime International, who was interested in signing me. Mat is from Denver, Colorado, and he and Barry were friends; in fact, Barry worked for Mat as a commentator at Prime International. Meeting up with Mat sounded like a good idea, so from this point on Harry took over negotiations. Harry was a father figure to me in the gym when I was growing up. He knew everything there was to know about me. He was probably my best friend at the time, but things change and we've now lost touch.

* * *

I was scheduled to attend a dinner at the Burlington Hotel in Dublin on 3 December, so we set up a meeting with Barry earlier that day to sit down with Mat and see what he had to offer. The first thing that struck me was that Mat had taken the time to come over from the States to meet me. I thought that he must really be interested in me.

We chatted for a while and then Mat made the offer. He talked about seeing me at the Olympics – and how U2's Bono had suggested Mat attempt to become my manager! Mat had only heard good things about me and wanted to see if we could work out a deal. When he told me what the offer was I thought, 'Is he joking?' I had only ever *heard* about that amount of money before and now he was offering to give it to me, for doing something I loved to do.

Mat was offering me a high five-figure sum to enter into an initial two-year contract with him, just to sign my name. I thought that was amazing. He also offered me an extra bonus if I accepted before the end of the year. I would be contracted to a minimum of seven contests in the first year and a minimum of eight in the second. The purse amounts were incredible for someone who was on the dole. The contract also stated that Mat would pay for my accommodation and transportation in the States, so I knew I'd be taken care of. Since the Olympics, almost six months previously, I had made some money through appearances, but nothing I could live off long-term.

We left the hotel and I shook hands with Mat but we didn't sign the contract. Between December and February, Harry was negotiating long distance with Mat and he would write everything they discussed on bits of paper. He would then show these to me at the gym. Since neither Harry nor I had experience in this field we decided to hire a legal team to examine the contract. Mark Orr, an American law expert, and Maureen Hill did a tremendous job, and Mat and I both got what we wanted.

* * *

At the beginning of 1993, a new nightclub opened up in Belfast. A couple of my friends and I went there for the evening. We were minding our own business, talking about boxing, when one of the bouncers came over and said the manager wanted me to leave. When I asked him why, he told me the manager didn't like me. One of my friends stood up for me, and the bouncers got upset and made him leave. I stayed for a while and then left of my own accord, but the next day a Belfast newspaper published a story on the front page that I'd been thrown out of the club and beaten up by the bouncers. I didn't have a bruise or cut on me. Some people will do anything for money and publicity.

* * *

On 9 February 1993, Harry and I met Mat in his room at the five-star Culloden Hotel, close to Holywood on the outskirts of Belfast. He had flown back over from the States and with my lawyers present, behind closed doors, I signed the contract and turned professional. That night in my diary I wrote: 'Aim: World Championship.' We made the formal announcement at the Europa Hotel in Belfast the next day and then went to Dublin for another press conference in front of the Irish media.

We went out that night to celebrate. Barry was there and was the life and soul of the party. His jokes never stopped. Just as we were leaving, Mat told me I was going to be based in Baltimore, Maryland, and training with Janks Morton, Sugar Ray Leonard's former trainer. I was to leave within two weeks, so I had to get my visa sorted quickly. Mat had scheduled my first fight in Los Angeles for 23 February 1993. He said he'd see me when I got there. At that point it hit me, and I thought, 'Am I going on my own?' So, timidly, I asked, 'Can my fiancée come with me?'

'I didn't realise you guys were serious,' he replied. 'Of course she can come.'

That made me feel more comfortable about leaving home and going to the States. Cheryl gave her notice at the Belfast City Hospital where she worked. Her colleagues were very supportive and understood her situation. Cheryl knew how much boxing meant to me, so she gave up everything to join me in my quest to conquer the world.

I did all my training for my first pro fight in Belfast. About a week before I was due to leave Northern Ireland, Mat told me I wouldn't be training with Janks Morton after all. Instead, Eddie Futch was going to train me. He was 82 years old at the time and working with Mike 'The Body Snatcher' McCallum and Riddick Bowe, both former world champions. He hadn't been sure if he'd have the time to focus on my career but had taken one look at my Olympic performance, thought I could be a world champion and agreed to take me on. I was amazed that the legendary Eddie Futch was going to be my trainer. Everyone in boxing knew him. He had worked with Joe Frazier and Ken Norton in the past and now I was going to be working with him and living in Las Vegas. We were going to be residing among glitz and glamour in a city where people go to hit the jackpot. We had seen it on TV and thought it was just a street of casinos. We were shocked when we got there.

Our visas still hadn't arrived by 19 February and we were scheduled to leave for Los Angeles the next day. Mat had been in touch with immigration and finally, on the Friday evening, we got a call to say the visas were coming through the next morning. A staff member at the US Consulate opened the office early on the Saturday morning so we could go in and get our visas stamped into our passports before we left – so early, in fact, he did it with his slippers on! Without him, I probably wouldn't have made it for my professional debut.

We rushed to the airport and our families came to see us off. They were heartbroken, but they knew it was the best thing for my career. It was a ten-hour flight from London to Los Angeles, where my first fight was scheduled three days later, at the Country Club in Reseda, California. Sitting on the plane on the way there, we talked about what lay ahead and wondered if we were crazy leaving everything behind. We had both been living with our parents, so really we had nothing to lose. We left Belfast with two suitcases each and about £500 in our pockets. Cheryl was 19, I was 22, and we thought, 'We'll give it a go.'

We arrived at the Tom Bradley International terminal at Los Angeles airport at about 6 p.m. local time. Tom Brown, who was working for the promoter, had been sent to collect us. To this day we have stayed friends with him and often talk about Tom being the first person we met when we arrived in the States – he jokes that he missed the fight between Gabriel Ruelas and Azumah Nelson that night because he was at the airport picking us up! He took us to the Carriage Inn on Sepulveda Boulevard, in Sherman Oaks, Los Angeles.

The next day Tom took us to Ten Goose Boxing Gym where, with no time to think about jet lag, I did a light workout. I shadow boxed and hit the bag to get a sweat going and checked to make sure my weight was under control. I wanted to begin my career as a super bantamweight, but I started off as a bantamweight. This meant I had to weigh a pound less than I did when I was an amateur. In amateur boxing you weigh in kilos, so bantamweight, 54 kg, works out at 8 st. 7 lb.

Eddie Futch was unable to attend my first professional fight, but his assistant, Thell Torrence, came to my room right before the weigh-in with his cornerman, George Holt. It was the first time he had seen me. He knew I was capable of training on my own. I weighed in at 8 st. 6 lb. As part of my contract, I was guaranteed my fights would be televised in America and Europe. I was to get exposure fighting on the undercard of major World Championship matches.

My first opponent was Alfonso Zamora from Mexico. His record was one win and one loss. He was a typically tough Mexican fighter and the nephew of his namesake, 1970s bantamweight world champion Alfonso Zamora. The main event featured Rafael Ruelas and Robert Rivera. Ruelas defended his NABF Belt that night and went on to become the IBF lightweight champion. The promoter of the card was Dan Goossen. Even though he didn't promote all my fights, we have reunited and he is my promoter again today.

Mat organised my ring outfit. He arrived at my hotel room with a pair of green shorts emblazoned with a white four-leaf clover. I thought I'd left behind the politics I was so sick of in Irish amateur boxing. We agreed I would pick my own colours to fight in from then on. Mat had also chosen the music for my ring walk – at least he got that right: I walked in while U2's 'In the Name of Love' was playing. I assumed Mat had chosen U2 because they were Irish and Bono had suggested that he sign me up. It was my first taste of their music, though I had heard of them, and it stuck.

When I stepped into the ring, the crowd was going crazy for me. The arena was filled with Irish fans from Ireland's 32, a Los Angeles bar, and Scottish fans from another pub nearby. Dan gave me a $1,000 bonus because he knew I had helped sell out the arena.

I was hyperventilating and a little nervous before the fight began; I was thinking if I lost the fight, my career would be over. But as soon as the bell rang, I went straight out and threw a barrage of punches. The nerves were gone. It felt good to be back in the ring. I felt like I belonged. It was my first fight since the Olympics and I had missed being in the ring. My opponent was tough, but after the first round I took over. I was landing punch after punch, and in the third round I hit him with so many shots I thought the referee was going to step in and stop him. But the good thing for me was, unlike in an amateur three-round fight, I had another round to go. At the beginning of the fourth I hit

Zamora with a right-hand and dropped him. He got up, but I swarmed him with punches and the referee, Rudy Jordan, stepped in and stopped it 39 seconds into the final round.

I enjoyed watching my fight on television afterwards. Even though I'd only been in the country a few days the commentators talked highly of me. Sean O'Grady, the former lightweight world champion, said I was 'very impressive in [my] pro debut' and described me as 'an excellent young prospect'. His co-host Al Albert noted I was 'a very exciting young fighter . . . the type of guy you want to see again'. I did my first American radio interview with Jim Sullivan, who has now become a good friend.

I was paid $5,000 for my pro debut and during my first ten fights, Mat, as my manager, didn't take his cut from that. He made his money selling the TV rights to my fights, which was fine by me. He also paid my trainers their percentage in the beginning, so all I had to pay were my own expenses.

After the fight I was invited to a reception/celebration dinner put on for me at Ireland's 32. When we left the reception, Mat, Cheryl and me went to McDonald's. I had my first win under my belt. I was now a professional boxer and I felt as if I was on top of the world.

The next day Cheryl and I got up bright and early and took a short flight to Las Vegas. We were really excited. Mat and his associate, Jonathan Spinks, flew up from Los Angeles with us. When we got to Vegas for the very first time, the temperature was about 16 degrees, but it felt warm to us since we had just come from Belfast. It was winter in Vegas but it felt like a lovely summer's day to us. We could see the hotels on Las Vegas Boulevard, affectionately known as 'the Strip', from the plane and we couldn't wait to go and see them for real.

We stopped off at Carrows, a restaurant near the airport, and met up with Eddie and Thell. Eddie talked about my fight and how good I'd looked. He said he was going to mould me into a champion and I hung on his every word. I liked Eddie from the very beginning. He made me feel at ease in his company. He was a true gentleman.

We still had nowhere to live so Mat took us to view a few

apartment complexes. They were like holiday resorts. They had saunas, tennis courts, gyms and swimming pools – everything you could ever have wanted. At one complex there was a real cowboy on the staff! Well, he had the Stetson, the boots, the belt buckle; he was just what I'd always imagined a cowboy to look like and here he was standing right in front of me. We eventually went to view the luxurious Meridian Apartments on Flamingo Road. I turned to Cheryl to say, 'We can't afford to live here.' Even though Mat was paying for all our expenses, we still worried about the day-to-day costs of a lifestyle like this. But Mat told us that he wanted us to live there; he said he was more comfortable knowing it had a guard gate and that we were safe and protected. He was happy, and so were we. It cost $1,150 per month to rent a one-bedroom furnished apartment and Mat paid the three-months' deposit.

We stayed at the St Tropez for the first week while the apartment was being prepared. On our first venture into Vegas, Cheryl and I mistakenly took the scenic route to the Strip. It should normally take 20 minutes or so. We were dressed like typical Vegas tourists in shorts and T-shirts since it was sunny and warm. We went around the backstreets, past the MGM Grand, which was under construction at the time, and finally arrived at the Strip about an hour and a half later. There is a lot more to Vegas than the Strip: at the time it was a biggish city with a population of about a half-million; today, the population is about 1.7 million. The sun had gone down by the time we got back and we were shivering. We didn't realise the desert got so cold at night. We'd assumed it stayed warm all the time!

* * *

I was going to be training at the Top Rank gym, right behind the casinos. Eddie wanted me to be there around 11 a.m., when the gym opened, so he could give me his undivided attention. I was going to be doing my roadwork about seven o'clock in the evening when the sun had gone down. I didn't like this routine – I'd rather have run in the morning – but to get time with Eddie Futch I would have trained in the middle of the night.

Thell picked me up from the St Tropez in his truck the next day. I knew I was taking him out of his way, so I said I would walk to the gym from then on. We'd stopped by the gym the day Mat was in town, so I knew where it was. When I walked in, I got the 'stare down' from almost all of the fighters who were working out there. Eddie introduced me to Mike McCallum. He talked about the Olympics and he knew who I was and made me feel at home. Mike was a two-time world champion and went on to win his third Belt in 1994.

I was new bait, as I'd only just arrived at the gym, and everyone wanted to spar me, but most of my sparring was done with Eddie Cook, the bantamweight world champion at the time. He didn't go easy on me; in fact, he tried to take my head off, but I held my own. I'd sparred with world champions in Belfast and I knew what to expect.

After the first couple of days of walking the 45 minutes to and from the gym, I decided to buy a mountain bike. It now took me about 20 minutes to get there, but the heat was rising. It was now almost 30 degrees. The first day I took my bike to the gym I wheeled it in the front door. The gym was a big, open warehouse with plenty of room, but Mitch, the gym manager, came and asked me what I was doing. I told him I was putting my bike against the wall, and he replied that I couldn't leave it inside the gym and asked me to keep it outside. I told him I didn't have a lock for it and I couldn't leave it there, but he insisted. 'OK. Fine. I'm leaving then,' I said. As I walked out of the door, he came running after me and told me it was fine to leave it in the storeroom. I never wanted to cause any problems; it was only a bike after all. From that day on, Mitch and I became good friends.

After the St Tropez we moved to the Mirage, a hotel in the heart of the Strip. It was easy to tell the time in the evenings: after the sun went down, the volcano (a tourist attraction at the front of the hotel) would erupt every 15 minutes. Our room looked straight onto it, so we heard it erupting every time. The first night it was fun but after it had happened five or six times it started to get on our nerves.

Cheryl and I didn't have a car when we first moved to Vegas, so we'd either walk or take a taxi to go anywhere, including to get groceries. The nearest store was about two miles away. If we walked to get a taxi to the store, it was about three-quarters of a mile in the opposite direction, so most of the time we just walked the whole way. When we got our groceries, we would phone a taxi to take us back to our apartment but 99 per cent of the time it wouldn't show up, so we'd end up walking home weighed down with groceries. We tried to go to the store at night, so it wouldn't be as hot, but that didn't matter in the summer months because it was hot 24 hours a day. One night I had just come back from a run and must have been dehydrated when Cheryl and I went out to get groceries. When I went outside, the heat got to me even more and I almost passed out. Cheryl had to run to a corner store and buy me some water. Most people in Belfast thought that I went to America, and I was lifted and laid, but I wasn't.

I paid my membership dues at Top Rank on time, the first day of every month. Mitch didn't have to chase me like he did other fighters. I was there to do a job and I got to the gym by whatever means possible. I had to battle my way through four lanes of traffic across the Strip every day on my bike. I strapped two bags to the handlebars stuffed full of my boxing gear. On several occasions I almost got knocked over by articulated lorries. Nothing would stop me from going to the gym. I never complained.

Eddie and Thell worked on my technique. They had me repeat combinations over and over again in front of a mirror. Thell would hold the pads for me while Eddie told him which combinations I needed to work on. All in all, we were a great team. Hedgemon Lewis, a former welterweight world champion, was also part of the training team, as was Freddie Roach, who was a great fighter in his day. He moved away to open up his own gym in Los Angeles a while later. Thell, Hedgemon and Freddie all came from the Eddie Futch school of boxing. Eddie had guided their boxing careers.

Eddie wasn't worried about hard sparring. He taught me new things every day. I dropped Cook with a right-hand one day in sparring and that was the last time he sparred me. I could see that I had improved so much in a few months.

My buddy, Brian Clements, whom I had met at Top Rank in

1993, only recently told me that after I'd walked into the gym he and Jerome Coffee (whom I fought in my tenth fight) watched me train and both thought, 'I could take him.' He also told me his nose had never bled before, but during our spar it did and it didn't stop for four rounds. They realised they had been wrong about me. It was different watching me to sparring with me. I was deceiving. I looked easier to hit than I was. I don't remember sparring Brian back then; I was a scared young kid in that gym and I was just there to survive.

7

STAYING BUSY

If you're looking for a formula on how to become a genuine world champion, just borrow Wayne McCullough's ingredients.
Conn McMullen, former opponent and friend

Mat wanted me to have a busy fight schedule. And he got what he wanted. Within sixteen weeks, I was 7–0 as a pro with six knockouts (KOs). The timetable was perfect. I was fighting on a regular basis. Eddie and Thell were working with me in the gym and, slowly but surely, fight to fight, they could see my development. I was turning into a real professional fighter. I'd fought mostly between 8 st. 6 lb and 8 st. 10 lb, and I was still deciding whether to campaign at the bantam or super bantam weight limit.

My second fight was on 18 March at the Paramount Theater in New York. This is a smaller arena that is connected to Madison Square Garden. Cheryl and I were really scared walking around in New York City. We expected it to be frightening, like how it's portrayed in *Hill Street Blues* and the movies. The city was covered in snow at the time.

I fought Sergio Ramirez, himself from New York. He was a Golden Gloves champ and was making his pro debut against me. As we were walking to the ring, I heard his trainer say, 'We're gonna knock this white kid out.' I just laughed. Ramirez didn't know what he was in for.

He came out trying to catch me off guard in the first, but I took my time and picked my shots. I battered him around the ring until, in the third, I knocked him down with a left hook to the body. He got up, but after a flurry of punches I forced the referee to give him a standing count. I was right back on him and he went down again. I threw 15 punches and he went down once more. He stayed down this time. I got the KO win in the third round in front of a full house packed with Irish fans.

We went back to Vegas and then on to Los Angeles for my next fight, eight days later on 26 March. I had hurt my left hand in the fight in New York, but I thought it would be OK going into this one. Barry McGuigan had come with me to the weigh-in the day before, as he was there to commentate on the fight for Prime International. I weighed in at 8 st. 6 lb.

The boxer I was supposed to fight pulled out right after the weigh-in, so the promoter had to find someone else. Oscar Zamora, from Guadalajara in Mexico, was also at the weigh-in and he didn't have an opponent either, but he had weighed in at 9 st. 1 lb. They asked if I would fight him, even though I was 9 lb lighter. Zamora was told to go away, drop some weight, come back and weigh-in again. He did, and came back at 8 st. 13 lb. My trainer was fine with his weight, so the fight was made. They weighed me again just before the fight, after I'd eaten all day, and I was still only 8 st. 10 lb.

Zamora was much bigger than me but that didn't matter at all. I went out there and pummelled him over four rounds. I beat him up bad. He was also a Golden Gloves champion making his pro debut. My left-hand went in the first round and when I went back to the corner at the end of the round, I told Thell again and again, 'I hurt my hand, I hurt my hand.' But because of my Belfast accent Thell didn't have a clue what I was saying.

'Keep throwing your left jab,' he'd reply and I'd think to myself, 'I just told you my hand was sore. Why are you telling me to use it?' I finished the next three rounds throwing mostly right-hands and I won the fight easily on points. As Thell took my glove off in the dressing-room, he saw that my left hand was really badly swollen and bruised. It was only then that it dawned on him what I'd been telling him between rounds. 'That's what you were trying to tell me after the first round,' he said. We laughed about it, even though my hand was in a bucket of ice and I was in pain. I had practically fought and won the fight with one hand.

I saw a specialist in Los Angeles right after that fight because I'd been having a lot of trouble with my hands. I was fighting in the smaller 8-ounce gloves and it was tougher on my hands than it had been in the amateurs. The first thing the doctor said was they would to have to operate in order to help me. I looked at him, shocked, and asked him about the success rate. He said it was 50–50. I didn't want to take that chance. I'd only started my career. He gave me a cortisone injection, which helped to ease the pain, but I wondered if my hands would hold out.

Three weeks later, on 16 April, I fought Oscar Lopez in Boston, Massachusetts. Barry trained me for a few days because Eddie and Thell were in training camp with Riddick Bowe. George Holt, who had prepared with me in Vegas, travelled with us to Boston and, along with Thell, worked my corner. Lopez was another durable Mexican fighter, but I hit him three punches to one. He got a cut in the fourth round and retired on his stool before the fifth, handing me a TKO win.

Barry commentated again for this fight and before the bout we made a few promotional appearances at local bars. At each one we met Sean Mannion, a tough ex-fighter from Boston. Mannion had lost a 15-round decision to Mike McCallum in 1984 for the light middleweight championship. Sean was drunk, but somehow always made it to the next bar before we did. He had plenty of interesting stories to tell from his days in the ring. We were taken care of in Boston and Cheryl and I really liked it there. Its architecture and greenery reminded me of home. The city will always have a special place in Cheryl's heart because while I was training, she was out shopping – for her wedding dress.

After each fight I would usually go straight back home to Vegas and into the gym to work with Eddie, but not this time. We flew to Roanoke, Virginia, where Riddick Bowe and Mike McCallum were in training camp with Eddie and Thell. I knew that was where I needed to be if I wanted to continue learning. Training camp was in the middle of nowhere. There were two shops, one with very sparse shelves; a café, where we got gorgeous sandwiches, and the best coconut cream pie I've ever tasted; and a restaurant. There was nothing to do between training sessions but sleep. Everyone else stayed in a hotel but Cheryl and I stayed in a B&B close by. It was a really old-fashioned town, like something from *Little House on the Prairie*. The owners of the B&B took really good care of us. Training was good but we only stayed there for about a week before going back home to train with Hedgemon Lewis. One morning Riddick, Thell, Mike and I went out for a run. After a few minutes I realised I could walk faster than they were running, so I took off.

My next fight was in Denver on 4 May. I arrived there just three days before the contest. I didn't realise it was known as the mile-high city and that the altitude would affect me. I could hardly breathe. Of course, I fought another Mexican, who was used to the altitude, living at 10,000 feet. His name was Manuel Ramirez. I weighed in at 8 st. 7½ lb. I remember during the fight the altitude made me feel like I was fighting in slow motion. I felt as if I couldn't get going. But I got through it. I knocked Ramirez down in the fifth round with a left hook. He got back up, but I went marching forward again and threw a barrage of punches. The referee stepped in and stopped the fight, giving me the TKO win later that same round. If I ever had to fight in Denver again, I told myself, I'd stay there for two weeks before the fight.

Cheryl and I had planned to get married on 7 May in Las Vegas. Since I had a fight a few days before, I told her to make all the arrangements to prevent me from focusing on anything else. She was happy to do that. In the fourth round, of course, I found myself thinking about the suit I was getting married in – just as Ramirez hit me two right-hands on the chin. I told Cheryl we would never plan anything for right after a fight ever again. I had also been worried that I might get a black eye, but thankfully I didn't. Cheryl would probably have made me cover it with make-up for the pictures!

My next fight was scheduled for 1 June and although I'd been on my honeymoon in Hawaii, I had been training twice a day. When we got back home, Cheryl flew on to Belfast to renew her visa and I flew on to training camp in Washington to meet up with Riddick Bowe. I stayed at a hotel on my own, while Eddie and Thell stayed in another with Bowe.

Bowe had an open workout arranged and about 500 people were there to watch. Eddie put me in to spar with a light welterweight and he tried to take my head off. I stepped up the pace and in the end Eddie had to stop the sparring session because I was in control and nearly knocked him out. Bowe had Dr Su, from Korea, there with him and we arranged for him to work on my hands over the next couple of months, trying to stretch my ligaments, as they were giving me the most trouble.

After about a week, I headed back home to finish preparing for my next fight. I sparred with a Japanese world super bantamweight champion at Top Rank and I got the better of him. He didn't know who I was, but I knew him. It was good for my confidence levels.

A couple of days before my fight in Philadelphia I arrived in the city. My opponent, Luis Rosario, had fought the week before and entered the ring with a black eye. This was the only fight in my professional career that Cheryl missed and the first one Eddie worked because, up to then, he had been busy with Bowe. The fight was made at super bantamweight and I felt comfortable there. The weigh-in was held on the day of the fight, not the day before, which is the norm. This happened a few times early in my career.

I started the first round quickly and punished Rosario round after round. In the fourth I threw an amazing 245 punches. Rosario's face was a total mess and the referee finally stepped in to save him in the fifth.

* * *

I'd moved to 6–0 with five KOs and left Philadelphia to travel to Belfast for my big homecoming fight. I'd become an overnight success in the USA, with fans in every state, and since this was my first fight in Belfast for almost a year, I thought the arena would be bursting at the seams. In the lead-up to the fight I did a few television interviews and Cheryl and I were invited to chat on UTV's *The Kelly Show*. While I was home, my friend, Roderick McKee, organised a brand new car for me to drive from Toyota GB.

Eddie and Thell both came to Belfast for the fight. I was excited to have them there because I was honoured that they trained me. It was certainly a sight to see Eddie in my old boxing gym. The kids from the surrounding areas came by each night, not to watch me train but to see Eddie and Thell. Back then many people in Belfast had only ever seen black people on the television. They loved Eddie and Thell. They were very well received and everyone respected them.

Thell brought his wife, Eunice, over from the States with him and she was really scared to see British soldiers everywhere, walking around patrolling the streets, something she had never seen before. I heard that when she got back to her hotel room, she put the wardrobe in front of her door so no one could get in.

Preparation had gone well and there was a good vibe in the city about my fight. I was happy to be back fighting in Belfast. On 18 June 1993 I fought the reigning Irish champion, Conn McMullen, from Carnlough, Northern Ireland, at the Maysfield Leisure Centre. I stepped up to fight him in my first ten-rounder. Conn was a good little fighter. He was strong, but, as in most of my fights, I was throwing more punches than him. I was giving him angles, hitting him with shots to the head and body, and I knew Eddie's training had really helped me. I stayed on top of him and, in the third round, could see my body shots were hurting. But he was durable and he took them. A left-hook right-hand combination staggered him back onto the ropes. I went straight back on top of him and kept punching. Near the end of the third I hit him with two body shots and he stumbled back to the ropes. I threw about 25 shots without reply and the referee, Barney Wilson, stepped in and stopped the fight. My homecoming was complete. Conn and I have become good friends since then. He lives on the East Coast of America now and has been to support me at a few of my fights.

I was really disappointed that the arena hadn't sold out. It holds about 2,000 people, but there was only a crowd of about

1,000 there. Most of the supporters were my family and friends. I told Mat after the fight that I didn't want to come back to Belfast for a while because I didn't feel that my home town was coming out to support me. I'd had bigger crowds in America. We decided to return when the fans wanted me.

Cheryl and I stayed in Belfast over the summer and took a trip to the Greek island of Crete in July. This holiday was another all-expenses-paid trip, this time from Aisling Travel, who had presented it to me after I won the Olympic silver medal. We had a wonderful time. We flew back to the States in August and went straight to training camp with Bowe in Big Bear, California. A fight that Mat had scheduled for me in August was cancelled, so my next contest was to take place on 24 September in Dublin.

* * *

Cheryl had looked into buying a car, but before we did anything I had to take a driver's test. I did mine in August. I thought I'd just have to go to the office and tell them I had driven in Belfast, but I had to sit a written exam and take a full driving test. Thankfully, I passed both with flying colours. Now all we had to do was get a car.

* * *

I'd fought most of my amateur career in Dublin, so I was a very popular sporting figure there and I knew the fans would come out to support me. We arrived in the city about a week before the fight and stayed in a guesthouse in Dunshaughlin, just outside Dublin. Brian Peters, a local boxing promoter, looked after us while we were there. He has since become a very good friend. A couple of days before the fight I remember developing shin splints from running on hard surfaces. After that I was driven to Phoenix Park, one of the largest parks in Europe. The grass was a lot softer to run on, but I was still in a lot of pain.

The fight against the Algerian Boualem Belkif took place on 24 September in the Tallaght National Basketball Arena, which holds about 3,000 people. It was sold out and a couple of thousand people couldn't get in on the night. The atmosphere was electric. It was a hot September day and the heat inside was intense. There was no air conditioning and temperatures in the ring got up to well over 30 degrees. It didn't bother me, though, because I was used to the Las Vegas heat.

Montell Griffin was also on the card. We were in the same stable and Eddie trained us both. Montell went on to be the first boxer to beat Roy Jones Jr and become the light heavyweight champion of the world.

Belkif was a short, stocky guy, and his record didn't do him justice. He'd had ten wins (six KOs) and ten losses, and while it showed he'd lost as many as he had won, he was still really tough. Beforehand, Barry had said that this was a definite step up in class for me and Belkif was going to be a hard guy to beat. He imagined Belkif was going to go into the later rounds and perhaps take me the distance but still hoped I would win. Belkif kept both hands up well. He had a peekaboo defence, so I used my left hand and pitter-pattered his hands to try to open up his guard. I banged hard left and right hooks to his body to try to wear him down. Round after round I chipped away at him. I took my time and picked my shots.

In the fourth round Belkif was cut over his left eye. I feinted a punch and then threw a left-hook right-hand combination straight onto Belkif's chin. He went down onto the canvas. He got up again, but I jumped on him, throwing punch after punch. I hit him with a lot of shots and I thought Fred Tiedt, the referee, would have stepped in, but he let it go on and Belkif was able to finish the round. I started the fifth where I left off in the fourth: right on top of him. As Belkif hit me with a shot, I slammed my gloves together as if to say, 'Right, let's go.' I worked his head and his body as I backed him into his own corner, then I threw a right uppercut that dropped him to his knees. Tiedt still allowed him to continue. After a 17-punch combination with no reply from Belkif, the referee finally stepped in and stopped the fight.

I was so amazed by the Dublin fans. The atmosphere in the arena was fantastic; I was on a high. I felt wanted and appreciated. I told Mat that I wanted to come back to Dublin as soon as possible. Win number eight was under my belt and I had my seventh KO win.

＊ ＊ ＊

I had always wanted to watch a big fight live at the outdoor arena at Caesars Palace on the Strip and my dream came true on 6 November when we went to see the rematch of Bowe and Evander Holyfield. Mat got us tickets in the stands, but it was a cold winter's night in Vegas and the metal seats sent shivers right through my body. What a difference to June or July, when it is nearly 40 degrees in the evenings. This was the same night that the 'Fan Man', James Miller, parachuted into the arena and got tangled up in the ropes during the bout. What a fight to see! Only in Las Vegas!

＊ ＊ ＊

My next fight was in Fargo, North Dakota, on 9 November. The main event was world champion Virgil Hill's defence of his WBA light heavyweight title against Saul Montana. It was freezing cold that night and the snow was almost above our heads. Virgil was the local fighter and the support he got was fantastic. I fought Andres Gonzalez from Tucson, Arizona. It was probably my easiest pro fight. I hit him with a few shots in the first round that hurt him and it looked like he didn't want to know. In the second round I caught him with a right uppercut that lifted him off his feet and he fell flat on his face. He didn't even attempt to get up. It was good to get a quick win because it meant I didn't hurt my hands.

Jerome Coffee from Nashville, Tennessee, was next on 30 November. He had gone 15 rounds with former world champion Jeff Fenech. Jerome also trained at Top Rank in Vegas and he always watched me. I went to the gym to train before the fight and Jerome showed up too. I was 9–0 with eight KOs and he was 35–10–1 with nineteen KOs. His record showed that he had been in with world champions and he was very experienced. He was a featherweight and I was a bantamweight, but we fought

79

between those weights at 8 st. 10 lb. That didn't bother me, though.

Before the fight Jerome commented on national television: 'There are clear things I want to do to him and that is to dictate pace, take it up and down. Certainly, I want to attempt to show him things and do things to keep him off balance, keep him confused. I want to draw him into traps. Pull him into stuff. Make him think he's about to do something and then get hit with something. Keeping him wondering what I'm doing next.' Jerome also said I couldn't punch, but he was in for a surprise.

When we got to the fight venue in Pensacola, Florida, I found out I was on the undercard of Roy Jones Jr. This was a major fight card, since Roy Jones Jr was one of the best fighters in the world. I have always looked up to Jones and remembered him from the 1992 Olympics. It was an honour for me to be on his undercard.

Near the end of the first, I threw a right-hand and Jerome collapsed onto the ropes, but they held him up. He took a standing eight count, but finished the round. He knew then that I could punch. I stayed on top of him, keeping the pressure on in every round. In the fourth and fifth rounds I was throwing well over a hundred punches. Jerome decided to stay on his stool and not come out for the sixth. I'd been cut on the back of my head during the bout and went to hospital for four stitches.

Jerome told me afterwards that he couldn't believe how many punches I'd thrown and how strong I was. He said if he hadn't known me, or hadn't seen me in training, he'd have had me tested for steroids. We have remained friends ever since and I've played golf with him on occasion in Vegas. But that's the only sport I'll ever let him beat me at!

The USA network commentators again had only nice things to say about me. Sean O'Grady remarked, 'This relentless attack is reminiscent of [Rocky] Marciano. Look at this aggression. Look at the inside punches, combination hooks. He's a bell-to-bell bomber.' Al Albert just couldn't resist finishing with 'from Belfast'.

8

TRUE LOVE

Wayne McCullough is the epitome of a fighter. He has fought his whole life to get to where he is today. He deserves everything he has achieved along the way. I am proud to be his manager and even prouder to be his wife.

Cheryl McCullough

The area beside the pool at our apartment complex was lush and tropical. As soon as we moved in there, Cheryl and I knew that it was where we wanted to get married. We had always planned to go away to wed and this was the perfect location. Cheryl hired a wedding planner who helped her through every detail of the day, from the flowers and music to the catering. We intended to keep it intimate and chose to have a 'reception' in Belfast for friends and family at a later date. The wedding was scheduled for 6 p.m. on 7 May 1993.

I was in the gym working out as usual in the morning. The wedding planner arrived with silk flowers (the real ones would have wilted in the heat) and equipment to set up for the service just as Cheryl came downstairs. She assumed the real flowers for her bouquet and the tables had been forgotten and when I arrived home about five minutes later I found her sitting in the living room crying. 'The flowers are fake,' she sobbed. I told her I had seen the real flowers and reassured her that they just weren't out yet. Disaster averted!

That afternoon I met Harry Mullan from *Boxing News* for an interview. He was in town for the Lennox Lewis v. Tony Tucker heavyweight title fight the following day at the Thomas and Mack Center. Afterwards, I asked him if he was busy later that day. He asked why, and I told him I was getting married and invited him along. He told me he'd love to come. About 30 minutes before the wedding was due to begin, Harry arrived and saw me jog past the pool area on my way home from my afternoon run. There was just no stopping me.

Brian Peters was in town for the big fight and he also attended the wedding. Mat flew in from Denver to give Cheryl away. His wife, Kim, came with their son, Charles. Jonathan Spinks, Mat's business associate, acted as my best man.

Of course, the wedding didn't start on time. The flight from Denver had been delayed and by the time Mat and his family arrived and got dressed it was almost 7 p.m. My nerves were wrecked as I stood under the archway waiting for Cheryl to walk down the aisle. I had to lock my knees or I'd have fallen over. I was more nervous at that moment than I had ever been stepping into the ring. As Cheryl and Mat started to walk towards me, I started to think back on how we first met.

* * *

After the Commonwealth Games, Cheryl and hundreds of other people sent me letters to congratulate me on my success. Since she didn't know exactly where I lived, she addressed the envelope to me with Wayne McCullough, Commonwealth Games Gold Medallist, Highfield Estate, Belfast, Northern Ireland written on the envelope. And it got to me.

Her letter to me read:

Hi Wayne,
Congratulations on your great achievement on winning a gold medal for Ulster. I watched your fight on TV and you

were a real knockout! I would like to be your No. 1 fan! Well done!
> Love,
> Cheryl

She had enclosed a padded boxing glove key ring.

My reply read:

> Hi Cheryl,
> Thanks for the lovely card and glove. I'll put you at number one. I would like to get to know you better, so keep in touch and I will send you a photograph as soon as I get some printed.
> Well, goodbye for now.
> Love,
> Wayne

I got a walkover at the Ulster Senior Championships in 1990 and I was going to the Ulster Hall on 27 February to pick up my trophy. It had been widely reported in the press that I would be there that night. As I was sitting with my dad watching the fights, Billy McClean, the former fighter now turned boxing trainer, told me that a wee girl was out in the hall wanting to get a picture with me. I'd had photos taken with everyone that night, so I walked out to see her. Just as I was walking away, her mum, Georgina, said, 'This is the wee girl who wrote to you.' I realised then it was Cheryl. I wasn't dating anyone at the time, and neither was she, so we exchanged phone numbers.

I called Cheryl the next day to chat and arranged to meet her on the Saturday night. But I couldn't wait, so I called her back the next day and asked if she could meet me that night instead. Thankfully, she said yes, and we agreed to meet outside the City Hall in Belfast.

I got the bus from Highfield into the city centre with Noel, who was going in to do some late-night shopping. I arrived outside the City Hall a little before seven o'clock and she hadn't arrived. Little did I know she was waiting – and watching – across the street; she didn't want to stand at the City Hall in case I didn't show up. But I was always going to be there. I would never have stood her up.

A couple of minutes later she walked up to me and we said our hellos. Cheryl later told me that she thought I was just going to meet her and be her friend. She never expected to be my girlfriend. That first night Cheryl dragged me around *all* the shops in the city centre. I should have seen the warning signs!

Cheryl understood my training commitments and never complained about the time, or lack of it, that we spent together. I'd had other girlfriends but those relationships had never lasted longer than a month. The girls would pressure me into spending more time with them, even though I couldn't. They felt as if I put boxing before them and they didn't like that. I know that's one of the reasons Cheryl and I have stayed together: she knows that boxing is very important to me and accepts that.

* * *

Before I realised it, Cheryl was standing beside me at the altar in her wedding gown. She was stunning. I looked into her eyes and I knew I had been in love with her from the moment I'd met her. It was meant to be and we were confirming it that day. A Baptist minister married us in front of God and our friends. The ceremony was so romantic.

In 1997, Cheryl and I decided we were ready to start a family and it wasn't long before God sent us a precious bundle of joy. The baby was due in March 1998. Our beautiful baby daughter, Wynona Leigh Davis, was born on the 30th and our lives were changed for the better for ever.

I drove Cheryl to the hospital on the 29th and she was soon settled into her private suite. She went into labour in the middle of the night. Typical! I didn't leave Cheryl's side and by the time the doctor arrived to deliver our baby, Cheryl had been in labour for 18 hours. Her mum and sister had flown over from Belfast for the birth, so we all stayed in the suite together, celebrating Wynona's first night in this world.

The hospital put wristbands on Cheryl and me, and a band

around Wynona's leg. They were fitted with electronic devices that would alert hospital staff if, for example, someone was trying to leave the hospital with a baby that wasn't theirs. No one told me I couldn't take mine off, so I slipped it off my wrist and went to the gym to train for my upcoming fight scheduled for three weeks' time. After training, I went straight back to the hospital and bumped into one of Cheryl's nurses. She looked at me with a shocked expression and wanted to know how I could have left the hospital without my wristband beeping. I told her I'd taken it off – but I wasn't supposed to!

When Wynona was two days old, she made her entrance at the boxing gym and was introduced to the boxing world. She slept through the noise of the punch bags and bells. She's been in the gym ever since and is somewhat of a celebrity on the Vegas boxing scene. Everyone knows her. She has met some of the world's top fighters, such as Robert Duran, Christy Martin, Audley Harrison and Kevin Kelley. We even have a picture of her sitting on Mike Tyson's knee.

* * *

In boxing, many fighters are religious. Maybe it's because we risk our lives every time we step into the ring and we have to believe in something. I've always believed in God. I used to go to Sunday School when I was a child but that was more to get the sweets at the end than anything else. From 1990 onwards, my faith has been stronger. When our daughter was born, I wondered how anyone could think there is no God. We started attending Liberty Baptist Church in Las Vegas just after Wynona's birth and became members at the beginning of 2005.

In a lot of my fights, I have prayed to God to give me the strength to get through when I've had nothing left to give. I know He has helped me. I started going to church with Cheryl when we began dating and that was the first time I'd been introduced to church as an adult. The Bible is the most interesting book I've ever read. Sometimes it's hard to understand, but I believe it's the most powerful book ever written.

When I mention God, some people curl up into a shell and try to avoid it. They seem scared of the word God. I have worn different Bible verses on my shorts while fighting as a professional; that's my testament of faith. Hopefully, if someone sees the verse on my shorts, they will pick up a Bible and read it. Maybe my chosen verse will have an impact on their life.

One of the verses I use is found in the King James Version of the Bible in II Timothy 4:7. It reads: 'I have fought a good fight. I have finished my course. I have kept the faith.'

Another verse I use can be found in Luke 10:19: 'Behold, I give unto you power to tread on serpents and scorpions, and over all the power of the enemy; and nothing shall by any means hurt you.'

A lot of journalists have asked me what the verses say and I tell them to go look it up in the Bible. I'm not a so-called Bible basher, by any means, but I believe in God and I know I'm going to Heaven when I die. Hallelujah.

9

MY FIRST BELT

As a combat Marine, I was taught that the way to take an objective was by going straight at it. Wayne would have made a hell of a Marine. I can think of no higher compliment for a fighter. Or a man.

Pat Putnam, boxing writer

Following the Jerome Coffee fight, Cheryl and I had planned to go to Disneyworld for a few days. Orlando is only about an hour's flight from Pensacola by plane. We packed our belongings the night of the fight and Cheryl told me the flight was leaving at 1 p.m. the following afternoon.

We got up around 9 a.m. the next morning and had breakfast. We were taking our time getting ready and I asked Cheryl to check the exact departure time on the ticket to figure out when we needed to leave the hotel. The hotel was about a 30-minute drive from the airport and we would have to be there about an hour before the flight departed.

When she checked, she realised the flight was actually at 11 a.m. not 1 p.m. and we had missed it. She frantically called the airline and fortunately they were able to get us on another flight out later that day. I was really stiff from the fight, so all I could do was stomp around the room in a panicked frenzy.

From that day on, I have always checked the tickets so we get there on time!

* * *

Cheryl and I were miserable without a car. Las Vegas is a large city and nowhere is accessible on foot. We were hiring cars now and then but that was becoming really expensive so after I passed my test we decided to buy a car instead. In America, everyone has to have a credit score before they can get a loan. We came from Belfast, rented an apartment and had no credit cards in our name. We had a bank account but we'd only had it for a few months. Since we hadn't filed taxes, we didn't have a credit score. So Mat flew in from Denver and came with us to a car dealership. We picked out a car, Mat put down a deposit and co-signed the loan for us. We were now the proud owners of a white Honda Civic.

* * *

After 11 months as a professional boxer, I was going to be fighting for my first Belt – the North American Boxing Federation (NABF) title. Winning that would have guaranteed me a world top-five ranking and put me in line to fight for the World Championship.

The fight was scheduled to take place on 18 January 1994 against Javier Medina from Puerto Rico, in Omaha, Nebraska. It was right in the middle of winter and the day of the fight was one of the coldest on record for the area.

Harry Robinson, my old amateur coach, had visited us at our home in Vegas over Christmas. We'd worked out on the pads over the holidays. I had trained hard because I wanted to be completely prepared for my first title fight. With 11 fights in the same number of months, the schedule was tough, but I was enjoying every minute of it.

Medina was 9–0–1 and I was 10–0, so we were quite evenly matched. We weighed in the day before and I made weight easily. The main-event fighter that night was James 'Bonecrusher' Smith, the former heavyweight world champion. He was to be on the scales just before me and as I was preparing to weigh in he stepped up. Now, think of it this way – he can weigh whatever he wants because he's a heavyweight, but he got on the scale wearing white socks up to his knees and *nothing else*. Cheryl, who was sitting right in the front row, had to look the other way.

Before the fight, Medina had printed up leaflets that read: 'When Wayne McCullough fights me, it's going to be like he's fighting three of me. I'm going to be so fast he won't be able to hit me.' I saw some in the lobby and I thought he had a nerve. Cheryl lifted them all and took them to our room so no one else could read them.

The 'Tale of the Tape' is shown at the beginning of every televised fight. It shows a fighter's age, his height and weight, and his reach (measured from fingertip to fingertip across your back). I was surprised to find out when I watched the recording of the fight that our Tales of the Tape were identical:

McCULLOUGH		MEDINA
23	AGE	23
117 lb	WEIGHT	117 lb
5' 7"	HEIGHT	5' 7"
66"	REACH	66"

Prior to the fight, the commentators told the viewing audience that I was one of the sport's top prospects in the bantamweight division, as I was already ranked number nine in the world after only ten fights. 'He's on a mission. He wants to be a champion of the world,' was Sean O'Grady's comment. 'He's a fighter that most fighters look at and say, "Hey, he can't punch," but he continues to knock people out. All with the pressure style of the Pocket Rocket.'

Medina said he was going to give me lateral movement; he planned to move to the left and right. He said if he found out I was strong, he was going to change his game plan to box and counterpunch me. My plan was to get inside his jab because he was a tall, stand-up boxer. I wanted to work his body and his head, but I didn't want to take any chances in this fight. This was my first 12-rounder. The referee for the fight was former heavyweight contender Ron Stander. He'd challenged Joe Frazier for the world heavyweight championship 22 years earlier in that same arena.

Medina tried to move in the first couple of rounds. He was boxing and using his footwork, but my plan was working. I was able to get underneath his jab and nullify his punches. He was hard to pin down because he kept moving, but I was landing three punches to every one of his. In the sixth round I totally took over and I was starting to beat him up. He was taking a lot of shots. At the end of the round I continued to pound Medina and even the commentators were saying that the referee should stay close.

I knew I had Medina gone, so I started the seventh where I left off in the sixth. I pinned Medina on the ropes and a straight right-hand to the chin sent him to the canvas. Medina was in trouble, but he got back up. I jumped straight on him again. A left-right left-hook combination to the body sent Medina to the canvas for a second time. Sean O'Grady said the referee should have stopped it right there, but he didn't. I stayed on him and I knew I was going to get him out of there. A big right-hand sent him back to the ropes. He was out on his feet. I threw about 28 punches without reply and the referee finally had to step in and stop it.

Medina walked unsteadily back to his corner. I was overjoyed and jumped into Thell's arms – just as well he caught me! I had won the NABF title and I felt fantastic. The fans were going crazy and gave me a standing ovation. Medina never fought again. Eddie later said that, had I not fought him, Medina could have gone on to become a world champion. That's how good he was.

I was standing in the middle of the ring right after they had announced me as the winner. The NABF official strapped the Belt around my waist. They put it on upside down, but I didn't care – I could see it better that way when I looked down.

Dr Su came to Vegas in February to work with me in between fights. I was still having a lot of trouble with my hands and there was a lump on the back of my right hand. He treated me every day for about a week. He stretched my hands and gave me hot- and cold-water treatments. I couldn't punch for about five weeks after the Medina fight and I was a little worried because I had another fight coming up in March. I was finally able to punch on 22 February and my hands felt fine.

* * *

I was scheduled to fight on 19 March, outdoors at Millwall football stadium in London. I was on the undercard of the WBO (World Boxing Organisation) Heavyweight Championship of the World bout between Herbie Hide and Michael Bentt. The fight was televised on Prime International and ESPN in the States as well as on television in the UK. I was due to fight a boxer from Columbia. He hung about the hotel for five days before the fight, eating everything in sight at meal times. He was a big guy and I was thinking to myself that he wasn't going to be able to make weight. The weigh-in was to be held the day before the fight, and when I arrived I was informed that it had been switched. We would weigh in on the day of the fight instead. I was really angry. Psychologically, I wanted to get it over with, even though I only weighed 8 st. 6 lb and the fight was made at 8 st. 8 lb. I was then told my opponent couldn't compete and that the promoter was looking for someone else to fight me. I started eating as if I had weighed in because I didn't know at that point if I would fight or not. Later that evening I was informed they had found me an English opponent, Mark Hargreaves from Burnley.

The next day I went to weigh in, even though I'd already eaten my breakfast. I didn't know whether I was coming or going. I still only weighed 8 st. 10 lb. We hung around waiting for Hargreaves to appear, but by lunchtime I had decided to leave so I could eat and rest before the fight. Eddie and Thell waited for Hargreaves. A little while later an official came to take the scales away, so Eddie asked him where my opponent was. He was told he had already weighed in, to which Eddie said he must be invisible; Eddie and Thell had been there the whole time and they hadn't seen him. He was told that Hargreaves had weighed in elsewhere. Eddie said he needed to take a look at him to see what he thought. When Eddie saw him he knew he was well over 9 st., but was probably just overweight because he had been called in at the last minute. He was really a super featherweight, according to the record book, but Eddie allowed the fight to go ahead since he knew I could handle Hargreaves.

After what I had gone through, I was mentally burnt out. I had been dragged around during the week of the fight to do medical tests and then there were the problems with my opponent and the weigh-in. On fight night I had to wear a full sweat suit to walk to the ring because it was well below zero outside. When I took my tracksuit top off, I really felt the cold.

Hargreaves had a lopsided record. He was 7–8 with four KOs. He came out swinging in the first round throwing big right-hands, which everyone knows I am susceptible to. It was as if he had prepared for me. I hurt my left hand again in round one and the pain was almost unbearable. Dr Su was in my corner, but there was nothing he could do to help me until the fight was over.

I didn't get my rhythm going until the end of the third round, and at that point I started hitting him to the head and body. I knew I was hurting him with every shot. For every one I was taking, I was landing four or five of my own. With 30 seconds to go, he was truly in trouble. A right uppercut shook him all the way down to his boots. I threw 28 punches without reply and the referee stopped the fight right as the bell sounded to end round three.

I was glad to get this fight over with and I promised myself I would never be treated like that again. After the fight my diary read: 'I wanted to see him fall. I was frustrated because I was messed about all week. Other opponent wasn't allowed to fight. I think they were trying to get me beat. *Never*.'

* * *

Everyone may think my life with Cheryl is a fairy tale but our lives haven't been all plain sailing. After I won the Olympic medal, Cheryl and her family started receiving death threats, which only stopped after my fight against Hargreaves. The first letter read:

> We are watching you
> GOLD-DIGGERS

Cheryl is far from a gold-digger. She had a job when I met her and would buy me bus tickets or pay for petrol for my car (when I bought one). She would even pay for us to go out and have dinner when I had nothing to offer her but love. We were in this relationship together.

Another letter arrived a short time later that read:

> I love Wayne McCullough
> It's not his money I want
> I want his child and by hook or by crook
> I will get him. No one will stop me.

Several other letters were sent to Cheryl and I believe these people were maliciously trying to break us up, but they were never going to do that. I was in love with Cheryl and they knew that. When I mentioned the letters to people I suspected of writing them, the threats mysteriously stopped.

* * *

On 18 May I got a cortisone injection to ease the pain in my hand and I just hoped they would both hold up until I fought in June. When I started punching again, I wrote in my diary: 'Hand good, no pain.'

My 13th fight was to be the biggest test of my career to date. And it proved to be my hardest fight ever. The bout was set for 17 June 1994 at the Taj Mahal in Atlantic City. I was the main event and I was fighting former WBC bantamweight champion, and number one contender for the Belt, Victor Rabanales from Mexico.

I trained in Big Bear, California, for three weeks before this fight and brought Alan over from Belfast to help with sparring. Training went really well and my weight came down easily enough. We travelled to New York a few days before the contest, where we held a press conference at Dorran's Bar, then we drove to Atlantic City in a limo. I was number three in the world at this point and with that came perks – when we arrived at the hotel, we were shown to our suite, and it was gorgeous.

The weigh-in was the day before the bout. We both weighed 8 st. 5 lb. This was the fight the fans wanted to see. Everyone wanted to know if I could make it to the big-time. There had been a lot of hype surrounding my career up to this point and I felt I had to prove something. Coming into this fight, I hadn't lost a round as a pro. I was defending my NABF Belt and it was also a final eliminator for the WBC title. The winner would go on to fight the Japanese WBC champion Yasuei Yakushiji.

Rabanales thought he was going to knock me out in six or seven rounds. He expected me to come to him and he was planning to counterpunch me. On tape he looked easy to hit but when I got into the ring with him it was almost impossible. He was so awkward. I was disadvantaged in terms of experience going into this fight – it was only my 13th bout; it was his 49th. He had 19 KOs on his record, more knockouts than I'd had fights.

Cheryl and Kim, Mat's wife, were making their way into the arena through a back corridor and on the way stopped off at a storage room where a broadcast of the famous O.J. Simpson Bronco chase through the streets of Los Angeles was showing. Little did they know the fight they were about to watch would be even more exciting.

* * *

Brian Peters carried my NABF Belt into the ring while U2's 'I Still Haven't Found What I'm Looking For' blasted through the arena. There was good support from the Irish contingent, as a lot of football fans watching the World Cup in New York had made the trip to Atlantic City to see me fight. I tried to push Rabanales back in round one, but I found it hard to stay close to him because he was so awkward. I could never tell where his punches were coming from. In the second round, Rabanales hit me a right uppercut that looked like it came from the back of the arena. It caught me flush on the chin. I automatically raised my hands to cover up and took a few steps backwards to gain my composure. I moved around the ring for a few seconds and then nodded at Rabanales as if to say, 'You got me, but I'm still here.' I came straight back with a jab right-hand left-hook combination that caught him clean.

In the first six rounds of the fight I had taken the lead, but Rabanales was always there, strong and dangerous. This is the fight that showed that, even though I got hurt, I could come back and win. It also proved that I don't just have a *good* chin, I have a *great* chin. Rabanales' punches would have knocked most fighters out cold.

I can always hear Cheryl's voice when I'm in the ring and she was shouting 'Come on, Wayne,' rooting me on. I knew the crowd was cheering for me but I couldn't really make out what they were saying; I never can. But I could definitely hear Cheryl yelling at me because she does it all the time!

Before the Rabanales fight I had been working on the crossguard style. I hadn't perfected it and in this fight it wasn't really working for me. My defence was going through a transition period. I started to use my footwork and boxing skills in the ninth round because I knew he was too strong for me. We all knew it was going to be a tough fight. About a minute into the round Rabanales threw what looked like a body shot, but instead he brought it up over the top and hit me, full force, with a solid right-hand that landed directly on the centre of my face. The punch knocked my head right back. On television it looked as if my head might be ripped off my shoulders. That punch would have knocked anybody else out. But not me.

For what seemed like five seconds – it was probably more like a thousandth of a second – I thought I was sitting on the sofa watching TV in my hotel room with Cheryl. I imagine it's what being out on your feet must feel like. But my legs stayed strong. To this day, no other fighter has ever hurt me like that.

When I was coming around again, everything was black with white flashing lights. My vision was fuzzy and I couldn't see straight. I saw three Rabanaleses and didn't know what to do, so I hit the one in the middle.

On instinct, I continued to throw punches and move around the ring. I stepped back again and nodded to him, acknowledging he had hit me. Then I hit him with a left hook on the chin, just to let him know I was still in the fight. I had him cut over the left eye in the ninth round and I came back really well and finished strong.

In the gym I had already shown Eddie and Thell that I could step back and box, so in the last two rounds Eddie told me to back off Rabanales and box him because I was ahead on the scorecards. A lot of people were surprised to see my movement but maybe if I'd done that from the first round, Rabanales wouldn't have laid a glove on me.

Barry McGuigan, who was commentating for Prime International, said I had jumped up by huge degrees in the level of competition when I fought Rabanales and I had handled the fight admirably.

In the last round I just jabbed and moved. The movement was giving Rabanales trouble and he didn't know what to do. He hardly landed a punch. Commentator Rich Marotta, also working for Prime, said I'd turned boxer in the last round and done a great job. He said I'd surprised Rabanales with my final-round strategy.

The Irish fans were going nuts for me as usual. I won the fight unanimously on scores of 116–110, 117–110 and 115–113. This fight was a big learning curve for me. It was the type of fight that taught me what a tough sport boxing is. This was the first time I'd gone 12 rounds and I got through them in my trademark fast pace. I felt good, but I believe it was the hardest defence of an NABF Belt in history.

Rabanales' manager, Rafael Mendoza, complained about the judges' scores at the post-fight press conference. He thought I had won, but said the scores should have been closer. One judge had me winning seven rounds to five, which was close enough for me. Eddie and I both thought I won about eight rounds to four. I was happy with the decision and ready to move on. U2's Larry Mullen was at the fight supporting me. He came into my dressing-room after the fight and has remained a friend ever since.

When I went to bed that night, Cheryl was so worried that she kept waking me every half-hour in case I died in my sleep. She had never seen me like that after a fight. I don't think I had either.

A few days later I wrote in my training diary: 'I got busted up. My eye is black and my face has been swollen for days. Hands hurt. He hurt me to the body. Should have used crossguard to block punches. Learned a lot. Don't fight a fighter, just box. That's easier. Put me off a bit. But I'm number one now. Then champion. Sore.'

Kevin McBride, my buddy from the Olympics, was also on the card. He won his fight too and I'm happy to say that in June 2005 he beat Mike Tyson and is now on top of the world.

The next day Cheryl, Barry, Mat and I all travelled by limo to New York to watch the Irish football team beat Italy in the World Cup. I could hardly move and my face was bruised, but we had a good time at the match.

My training diary on 20 June read: 'Should be resting but can't. I did three miles on the treadmill and twelve minutes on the bike. Weights.' I couldn't relax.

On the Wednesday after the fight, Cheryl and I flew to Dallas where ITV had based themselves to report on the World Cup. The channel was showing my fight and had asked me to come into the studio to chat about it. On my way there a few guys stopped me and said something in Spanish. I thought they were talking about my fight against Rabanales, but when I spoke to them in English they began to understand what I was saying. Somehow they had mistaken me for the Mexican goalkeeper!

I thought I'd have to go on air wearing sunglasses as my eye was so swollen and black, but their talented make-up artist spent almost two hours trying to cover the bruising. She made me look like a million dollars. When I went on TV, you couldn't even tell I'd been in a fight. I was tempted to keep the make-up on for the rest of the day! The former footballer Ray Wilkins, who I'd looked up to when I was younger, was in the studio that day too. After we watched the fight, he said to the audience, 'I was speaking to Wayne during the fight and I'm actually delighted that I'm a footballer. That was really tough going and obviously Wayne spoke us through it. That was absolutely marvellous to watch. Great stuff.'

I took a long rest from fighting after the Rabanales fight but went straight back into the gym to work with Eddie. Even though I was number one in the world, I knew I had a lot to learn. After each fight I would go home and watch it and try to work on the mistakes I'd made.

Two-time world champion Steve Collins came to Vegas in late June and we got together during his stay. He had his world-title Belt with him and I thought it was amazing.

In August, Cheryl and I moved out of our apartment and into our first home. We bought a town house on the west side of Vegas. We'd been paying rent for almost a year and a half and thought this would be a good investment. I'd made a little bit of money, and buying a house was better than wasting it on cars. Although I have to admit that after almost every fight I traded in my car for a bigger and better one. Cars were always my downfall.

My next fight was in September in my adopted home town of Las Vegas against Andres Cazares, from Mexico. This was one of the longest breaks I'd had between fights. The fight with Cazares was made at super bantamweight. Cazares was only five foot tall, so I looked much bigger than he did. I just played with him. I landed a right uppercut in the first round and immediately blood started pouring from his nose. I could have knocked this guy out any time I felt like it, but I took my time. After the Rabanales fight, I was raring to go.

In the third round I threw a triple left hook to the body and down he went. Referee Richard Steele counted him out. Cazares complained when he got up, but the referee could have counted to 20 before he would have been ready to continue. I got another KO win and I was marching confidently towards the championship.

As usual, I went straight back into the gym to work with Eddie. One day a trainer came up to me in the gym and told me there was a man there who talked just like me. His name was Romolo Fusco, originally from Belfast but living in Las Vegas. Before he'd moved to Vegas, he'd lived only a few miles from my family home in Belfast. We became very good friends. He and his sons, Frank and Tony, would often come to visit with goodies to celebrate a win with me, or just to chat about the good old days. Tony is a walking encyclopedia. Closer to fights, I'd tell him not to bring any more cake or chocolate since I was on a diet. Romolo had owned a chip shop in Belfast and at weekends we'd go to their house for traditional fish and chips – it was like our own Belfast appreciation society!

For my 15th fight we went back to Dublin. Since we'd had such a good crowd in Tallaght, we decided to go to a bigger venue, the Point Depot. I was scheduled to fight Spaniard Fabrice Benichou, former IBF super bantamweight champion, on 12 November. Eddie had trained Benichou for a while in Las Vegas, so he was confident about me fighting him.

Even though I was the number one contender for the World Championship, I still took this dangerous fight. Benichou, from Madrid, was campaigning at featherweight, so we fought at a catch weight of 8 st. 10 lb. He was a short stocky guy covered in tattoos.

Brian Peters and a good friend of ours, Jim Aiken, of Aiken Promotions, were the local promoters of the card. In the hotel room just before we left for the fight, Mat told me I was only getting paid $20,000 instead of $100,000. I was absolutely devastated by the news. The arena was sold out, and US and UK television were both broadcasting the fight, so a lot of money was made on that show. But suddenly my earnings get cut by $80,000 right before the fight. It's not good psychological preparation for stepping into the ring.

I told Mat I would fight on. I was young and foolish then. If I'd thought about it, I should have told Mat I wasn't fighting and made him go into the arena and tell the fans why. But I didn't want to let the fans down.

Benichou's record was 36–14 with 19 KOs. The Irish fans showed their appreciation for him by applauding as he entered the ring. The 7,000-strong crowd at the Point was electrifying throughout the ten-round fight.

Benichou was tricky and hard to hit. When I threw a punch, he swayed his body back and forth to try to slip them. You could see he was a veteran pro. Then he'd try to come back with a right uppercut. I stayed on the outside for most of the first round but right at the end I hit Benichou with a double left-jab right-hand combination and he fell back into the ropes and almost went down. I smiled at him as the bell rang to save him.

Round after round I used my jab and moved using my footwork. It was as if I was reliving my old amateur days. I was getting in, hitting him and getting out without taking any punishment. I was enjoying this fight. Freddie Tiedt, the referee, stayed out of the way. He didn't have much work to do anyway, as we did our fighting and didn't get into any clinches.

Benichou hit me on the kidneys a few times, but I never complained. Later on I had him gone on a couple of occasions as the rounds were drawing to a close. He looked like he was ready to quit, but he showed his experience and why he was a former world champion by always fighting back.

This was a tough fight for me but I knew I was winning every round. The general talk in the press beforehand was that this fight was too much too soon for me, but I proved that I was ready for this step-up in class.

At the end of the ninth round Benichou looked as if he was out on his feet, but he stayed in there with me. I kept trying to knock him out, but he just wouldn't go. In the last round the crowd were going mad. I kept my jab in his face. I threw more than one punch every second before the end of the round. The commentators were hailing it as one of the fights of the year. We got a standing ovation from the crowd.

My face was clean. I probably threw over 1,000 punches that fight. The referee scored the bout 100–91, giving me every round and him a share of one. Afterwards Benichou came into my dressing-room and told me I'd be a champion someday. I really respected him for that and I learned a lot from our fight.

After the fight my urine was almost black, but that had become normal for me. It would happen the first time I used the bathroom after a fight if I'd been hit on the kidneys. In December 1994, my urine was red with blood after every run. I began to get worried, so I saw a doctor. I was injected with a dye and underwent an MRI on my kidneys. The doctor told me to take six weeks off and do absolutely nothing. Well, that lasted about two weeks. I started doing weights and I was sitting on the exercise bike soon after. I *couldn't* take time off. Doing weights pumped me up in no time and I started to look like Hercules.

I thought my next fight was the title bout in March, but

Yakushiji wanted one more contest before he fought me. His people paid me $50,000 to step aside while he fought another voluntary defence of his title: Mat took his 25 per cent managerial cut out and I got the rest.

I took a fight just to keep busy and so I stepped into the ring with Geronimo Cardoz, from Mexico, on 14 March 1995. The fight was in New Orleans, Louisiana. I brought Dan Milam along with me, a Vegas doctor who had been doing a great job of taking care of my hands. We all stayed in a tacky motel right under the flight path of the local airport. Every few minutes a plane would fly overhead, coming in to land. If we looked up, we could almost see the faces of the passengers. Mat stayed in a luxury hotel downtown. Oh, the life of a boxing manager . . .

I couldn't get my weight down because I'd been doing so many weights, so the fight had to be made at featherweight. Cardoz was 22–6–2 with 16 KOs when we fought. I hit him with everything: hooks, body shots, head shots, round after round. This was a good fight to keep me busy and he was tough and durable.

In the sixth round I stepped up the pace and started hitting him with punch after punch. I hit him with a great left-right-left combination to the chin. Finally, after the seventh round, he was completely exhausted and couldn't take any more. He stayed on his stool and didn't come out for the eighth. I got the rounds I needed to stay sharp. Afterwards, I wrote in my training dairy: 'Tough guy. Good chin. Need to block uppercuts and lefts to body.' Another win, another stoppage. Next up, the World Championship.

10

ON TOP OF THE WORLD

I found Wayne to be a dedicated, loyal and hard-working fighter. He followed instructions well and will go down in history as one of the best bantamweights to have ever entered the ring. The sweet science produces many a great fighter but, in this case, it also produced a fine young man.
Eddie Futch (1911–2001), legendary boxing trainer

My World Championship challenge was set for the summer of 1995. The WBC bantamweight champion, Yasuei Yakushiji, wouldn't leave Japan, but I had informed Mat I wanted the fight brought to Belfast. Since neither party could agree on a venue, the WBC ordered a purse bid. This meant any promoter could bid for the right to promote the fight and stage it wherever they wanted. The champion was to receive three-quarters of the purse bid and I was to receive one-quarter. Mat placed a bid of just over $1 million, but the Japanese won the rights to promote the fight with a bid of over $2 million and chose to promote the fight in the champion's home town of Nagoya. The date was set for 30 July 1995.

It was now impossible to bring the fight to Belfast and I was very disappointed. To make matters worse, a Belfast newspaper ran the headline 'WAYNE SNUBS BELFAST' in bold capitals across the back page. It angered me because the decision as to where the fight was to take place was out of my control. I love Belfast and I am proud of where I come from. This is sadly the biggest headline I ever got! I made a promise that, when I won the fight, I would stage my first defence in Belfast.

This was only my 17th fight as a professional boxer and I was going to be paid over half a million dollars to challenge the world champion for his title, unheard of in the bantamweight division.

I was a little bit concerned about going to Japan. I'd competed all around the world as an amateur and had fought in opponents' home towns before, so this shouldn't have been any different, but it was always in the back of my mind that I might be robbed of a decision.

In April, Cheryl and I went on a cruise to the Mexican Riviera with Dr Milam and his wife, Janet. It was a great trip. I trained twice a day on board. I ran on the treadmill and shadow boxed in the gym. The other passengers probably thought I was nuts. I was supposed to be on holiday, but I saw no harm in working out.

Afterwards, Dan and Janet invited us to join Janet's family on a camping trip in Utah. It took a long time to drive from Vegas and when we arrived at the campsite, it was really late – and dark. Dan drove across a field and we followed him, but he got stuck in mud. We had to spend the night in the middle of a field, in the middle of nowhere, stuck in mud.

There always seemed to be some drama or injury to upset me in the run-up to a fight and Cheryl and I were half expecting something to happen here, but it was only a camping trip after all and my World Championship fight wasn't until July.

But then Dan and I went out riding on quad bikes. Dan was in front of me and I was trying my best to keep up with him. It was my first time on a quad – I didn't realise they were so difficult to manoeuvre. All of a sudden my bike slipped off the muddy road into a ditch and the bike, with me on top, fell down a 10-foot slope. I thought I was fine when I landed at the bottom, even though the bike had settled right on top of me, but I couldn't move the bike and I was shouting for Dan to come and help me. I used all my strength and pushed the bike off. Instead of moving it out of the way, the whole bike landed on my quadricep muscle, above my left knee. It almost crushed my leg. I honestly thought it was broken. Dan arrived within a minute and helped me out of the ditch. We drove back to camp. Of course, I was trying to hide my injuries from Cheryl, but she could see straight away that I was limping and wanted to know what had happened. I brushed it off, telling her I was fine and not to worry. The next morning I woke up and my leg was black and blue. Thankfully, nothing was broken; it was just a bruised muscle, but I was in agony.

A few weeks later – eight weeks before my World Championship fight – I was at Dan's house playing with his kids on their trampoline when I bounced in the air, came down and banged my two legs together. I cracked a bone at the side of my right leg just below the knee. I had to strap it up well when I went running, but it still hurt. Needless to say, I didn't tell Mat about these little incidents at the time!

In June, we went to training camp in St George, Utah. The advantage of training there was it was at a higher altitude than Vegas. It wasn't as hot in St George as it had been in Vegas, so that was also a welcome relief. We stayed in a lovely apartment complex and set up camp at a local boxing gym. I had four different sparring partners, ranging in size, and I did about 70 total rounds of sparring. I had sparred about 30 rounds with Alan at home before we drove to St George, so, in all, I'd sparred about 100 rounds. Training went well and we stayed there for three weeks. My legs were getting better every day.

I had been to see a Chinese herbalist because I was still having problems with my kidneys and he had given me medication which had worked wonders. I haven't had any problems since.

Our plan was to break up the journey, and so we stopped in Honolulu, Hawaii, halfway to Japan, and trained there for a week. We stayed on Waikiki Beach and while everyone was having a great time sunning themselves, I concentrated on the fight. I had brought Alan and Justo, my sparring partner, with me. Preparation went really well and my weight was good. When we left for Japan, everything was right on target. The whole team left Hawaii six days before the fight: Mat and his wife, Kim; Joe, Mat's brother-in-law, and his wife, Julie; Eddie and his then fiancée, Eva; Thell and his wife, Eunice; Dan and his wife, Janet; my brother Alan and Justo; Sean, an employee of Mat's; and Cheryl and me.

I'd had a light meal on the plane and when we arrived in Japan, I did a training session and checked my weight: I was about 8 lb over my fighting weight. I was a little stunned, but everyone else went into panic mode, including Mat. He started phoning around looking for diuretics. I thought about waiting for the pills, but instead decided training would be the better option to take off the excess weight.

On the Tuesday and Wednesday I trained as usual, twice a day. I was eating healthily and I felt good. On Thursday after my training session I was 8 st. 6 lb: right on the weight. I think it was high because I had been travelling and retaining water. Once that was gone, my weight was fine again. I felt strong and I had made weight the natural way.

On the Thursday afternoon I sparred with a Japanese fighter who was as tall as Yakushiji. The guy had come to prove something, so I went out and gave him a going over. I was supposed to do a public workout the next day and the Japanese media wanted me to spar, but Eddie said it was too close to the fight, so we just did a light workout. The Japanese people had planned everything to perfection. I had never come across such a well-mannered, gracious race.

While we were at the Nagoya Hilton, the staff treated us like royalty and took care of us magnificently. The first morning we went to breakfast in the private VIP breakfast room and placed our orders. Every day after that they had a selection of food that we liked waiting for us when we got there. The waiters were tremendous.

Everywhere I went in Japan a guy called Sumio came with me. He was only about five foot tall. He came running with us in the morning dressed in his suit with a briefcase in his hand. It was hot and very humid. I don't know how he did it. I would run around the park with Alan and Justo while Sumio stood watching us smoking a cigarette and then we'd all run back to the hotel. Sumio eventually realised it would serve him better to wear a pair of shorts and a T-shirt, but his briefcase didn't leave his hands!

One morning I went running about 5.30 a.m. I didn't wake anyone up; I just went out on my own. When I got back to the hotel, Sumio lashed out at me, insisting, 'You cannot go out there on your own.' It was then I realised he was with me for protection. I can only begin to imagine what was inside the briefcase. He was a great guy, though, and I'll never forget him.

A couple of nights before the fight someone banged on our hotel room door in the early hours of the morning. I knew it was scare tactics, but I thought nothing of it the first time. Then it happened again the next night. It startled Cheryl and me. When I looked through the peephole no one was there. I said to myself, 'They won't beat me like this,' and went back to sleep. Where was Sumio when I needed him?

On the day of the weigh-in I made weight easily. I sat down near the scale and started eating fruit while I waited for Yakushiji. He arrived in baggy shorts and when he got on the scale his camp started to panic. He shouted, in English, 'Oh, God' and then ran out of the room laughing. He was back within five minutes, in a pair of swimming trunks, and he made weight. I knew what they were up to. They were trying to play mind games with me, but it didn't work. I didn't worry about him because by the time he came back to weigh in, I'd had my liquids and eaten my fruit, so I was probably 3 lb heavier. I think it was just a dumb move and very unprofessional on their part.

The whole time we were in Japan, Cheryl and I were never off the TV screens. They loved us over there. We were even shown on television with a big, red heart around us. It was no different in the dressing-room. There were cameras everywhere. It was incredible. Who knows what they were saying about us, though. None of the print media from Ireland – north or south – travelled to Japan because I was the underdog and they probably thought I had no chance of winning. Obviously I was disappointed, but I had a job to do so I didn't let it bother me.

Dermot Lavery and Michael Hewitt from Double Band Films in Belfast were travelling in Japan with us, having followed my professional career since the beginning for a documentary entitled *Down the Street of Dreams*. Winning the Belt was the ending we were all hoping for.

Before the fight, Mat said if I won the fight, and he knew I would, I'd be in blast-off mode; if I lost, it wouldn't be the end of the world, we'd just sit down and regroup. But he was confident that I was going to win. Mat wanted to make sure I got the right fights and some good paydays, so I wouldn't just scrape through when I retired. I sat down with Dermot before the fight for an interview and I told him I wasn't scared of Yakushiji. I was never scared to get into the ring. If I was, I wouldn't step through the ropes. I said I'd missed the Olympic gold medal and I wasn't going to miss the World Championship. Comparing Yakushiji's style and my own, I knew I had the ability to beat him and the time had finally come to put my skill to the test.

I did the pre-fight medical the day before the weigh-in. They measured my bicep muscle, took my blood pressure, asked me a few questions about my health – through an interpreter – and then they wanted my height. The lady who was measuring me had to stand on a 12-inch box just to reach my head. I felt tall in Japan. Of course, there were about 50 cameramen and newspaper photographers watching my every move.

Bob Gibson had flown over from New Zealand especially for the fight and to support me. As I was leaving the hotel to go to the venue, he sang 'Danny Boy' and it reminded me of when he had sung it in Auckland in 1990, as I stood on the podium after winning my Commonwealth gold medal. A group of people had gathered to catch a glimpse of me leaving the hotel for the fight. It was fantastic. I had such great support. Cheryl's sister, Nicola, and her husband, Ian, had also flown over from Belfast. They arrived the day before the fight and were leaving the day after. Even though they were only coming to Japan for two days, they said they wouldn't have missed it for the world.

The fight was held on a Sunday afternoon, the major sports day in Japan, at the Aichi Prefectural Gym. I don't really like to fight on a Sunday – I'd had to in the Olympic Games as well – but I hope God understands.

Eddie and I had worked on several different strategies in camp, but it wasn't until I was in the dressing-room that he gave me the game plan. He told me to go out there and use my jab, and to double and triple it up. I had worked on this in the gym, but I didn't know it was going to be the plan. Yakushiji was a tall boxer with a good jab, so I doubted jabbing a jabber would work. But I thought I'd try it anyway.

As usual I prayed before the fight that I wouldn't get hurt nor would my opponent. Obviously boxing is a sport where I go into the ring to hit another person on the head, but there isn't a boxer in the world that would tell you he wants to seriously injure his opponent. I just want to get the fight over with as quickly as possible.

The walk to the ring was mind-blowing. U2's 'Mysterious Ways' was playing while its video was shown on jumbo screens. There were about 10,000 screaming Japanese fans. Yakushiji was making the fifth defence of his title and he wasn't about to give it up without a fight. He was rated as the number one fighter in my weight class. He was the guy to beat. He walked into the ring with Earth Wind and Fire singing 'Let's groove . . . it's all right', but for him that night it wasn't all right.

As the ring announcer introduced us, Yakushiji walked over to my corner and presented me with a huge bouquet of flowers. The Japanese people are very respectful, so I accepted the flowers, nodded at him and then handed the flowers to one of my cornermen. I just wanted the fight to start and wondered what all this was about.

In the first round, Yakushiji came out swinging and landed a few right-hands. The pace was fast from the opening bell. My jab was working. Eddie was so right. I caught Yakushiji with a good right-hand in the first and hurt him. I was thinking to myself, 'It can't be this easy,' and, boy, was I right.

In the second round Yakushiji used his reach to attempt to stay away from me. He was trying to use his long jab, but my game plan was to take that away from him. He threw a good left-hand right-hand left-hook combination that caught me on the chin. I put my hands out, gritted my teeth and said to him, 'Come on.' I fought straight back and hit him a good left-hook right-hand of my own. I backed him onto the ropes and landed hard shots to the head and body. I had him in trouble again. He caught me a straight left-right in the middle of my face, but I kept walking forward. My left jab was giving him trouble – even the Sky commentators noticed it – and I was following it with double left hooks to the body and solid lefts to the head. He was in trouble again before the end of the round and a right uppercut sent his head backwards as the round was coming to a close.

We were working at an extremely fast pace and from the beginning of the fight I knew he was going to have to be in great shape to keep up with me. To me, it looked as if Yakushiji's game plan was to knock me out. My double-jab right-hand caught him again in the third, but he fought back every time. I was moving my head well. I was impressed with my own defence.

Yakushiji was a solid puncher, though, and when he landed a shot, I felt it. Near the end of the round I pinned him on the ropes and threw an 11-punch combination without reply. Just when I thought he'd had enough, he came back with a nice left uppercut.

In the fourth round I was finding it easy to land punches to Yakushiji's head and body. I was throwing two and three piston-like jabs and landing them. He didn't know how to get away from my jab. He threw a left hook to my body, but I was able to block it with my right elbow. This round seemed easier to me because I was hitting him with more and more shots and he was finding it harder to land punches on me.

Round after round I used my jab to hit him to the head and to the body. Eddie told me to be careful early on in the round as he always started the first 30 seconds of each round fast and then began to slow down.

The crowd were strangely quiet for the first ten rounds. If Yakushiji caught me with a good right-hand, his fans would cheer, but the atmosphere was bizarre. I could hear singing from the back of the arena and I knew they were Irish fans. Of course, I could hear Cheryl yelling instructions at me too.

In the fifth round the pressure was starting to get to Yakushiji and my crossguard style was working well. It was during this fight that I realised I had finally perfected it. Later in that round I trapped him on the ropes and it was the first time he'd really stopped punching in the fight. I threw a double left jab and right hook that caught him perfectly on the chin. He was hurt and I thought he was gone. I stepped in and worked his head and body, but he showed the heart of a champion and fought right back.

I threw a good left-hook right-hand to Yakushiji's chin in the sixth. I was enjoying myself. I was having so much fun in this fight, although I knew all the pressure was on me to win. When Yakushiji threw a jab, I would throw a double jab back at him and confuse him. Up until this point, I thought his best punch was his right-hand, which had found its way onto my chin. He'd caught me with it a few times, but he'd never hurt me. I hit him with a good left-hand right-hand left hook to his chin and he backed onto the ropes once again. I knew I'd hurt him, so I stepped in. I threw another ten-punch combination without reply. But then he slipped off the ropes and got out of trouble. I hit him with a double left to the body and he almost doubled over. He seemed frustrated that he couldn't land his jab and that I was controlling the fight, but I knew I had to be in control if I wanted the Belt.

Eddie told me when Yakushiji jabbed, I had to roll underneath, work the body and then get back on the jab. My best work was done when I had Yakushiji trapped on the ropes, but he was slippery and able to move out of trouble. If I gave him any room at all, he could use his reach to keep me off. Some of the rounds were close, but I thought I had done enough to shade them. The later rounds were getting closer. He'd win a round, then I'd win a round. It was a back-and-forth battle, but the pace didn't slow. I would typically finish the rounds stronger than him.

With over half the fight gone, I was thinking I was closer to becoming world champion. Yakushiji started round eight fast but he wasn't landing anything significant. He tried to hold the centre of the ring and dictate the pace but he couldn't push me back. I was too strong for him. This was my time and I knew it. Yakushiji landed a good right-hand and I nodded at him, acknowledging he'd caught me, but I wasn't about to let him get away with it. I hit him a left-hand right-hand left-hook flush on his chin and he backed onto the ropes. Another 14-punch combination to the head and body stopped him in his tracks and he was in more trouble now than he had been in the fight so far. Showing his expertise in the ring, he came right back at me. It was at this point I knew I was going 12 rounds.

During the last few rounds I was so close to Yakushiji that I could hear him moan and groan as I landed body shots. Going into the last four rounds, Eddie thought I was ahead and told me to keep the pace going. I knew I wasn't going to get any favours since we were in Japan, so I had to make extra sure that I took it away from the champion. The referee, Joe Cortez, did a great job, but Yakushiji and I were experienced enough to know what to do in the ring. There weren't many clinches. It was a pretty clean fight.

At the beginning of the ninth round I just kept throwing punches. I couldn't afford to take any rounds off. I knew he'd be on top of me if I did. At the end of the round Yakushiji looked like he was ready to go again. I piled on the pressure and continued to use my jab. I was throwing thunderous left hooks to the body that were destroying him. A big right-hand landed on his chin with only six seconds to go, but he finished the round. I had a cut on my forehead going into the last two rounds that I didn't even know was there. I was also cut around the back of my head from a head-butt. But neither cut was serious enough to put the fight in jeopardy.

During the tenth round I heard the crowd come alive. It was the first time in the fight his fans had shouted continuously. They started yelling, 'Yakushiji! Yakushiji!', and I felt shivers go down my spine. There were only about 100 of my fans in the arena compared to over 9,000 of his, but they responded by shouting back, 'Pocket Rocket! Pocket Rocket!' They were actually making more noise. It was really exciting.

At the end of each round Yakushiji raised his hands in the air as if to say he'd won the round but most of the time he hadn't. After ten rounds, I knew I was well ahead. Eddie told me to stay out of trouble and box him in the final six minutes. I think, by this point, Yakushiji had realised I was out-jabbing him; by then, it was too late.

Going into the last round, I knew I had the fight in the bag but I was in the champion's backyard, so I couldn't relax until I heard the final bell. Yakushiji came out with both fists flying in round 12. I continued to move around and stay out of trouble, but I would have stood toe-to-toe if necessary. Yakushiji couldn't cope with my movement in the last 30 seconds, as I moved back and forward in front of him, and I could see I was upsetting him.

The bell rang, signalling the end of the bout, and we both raised our arms. I fell to the canvas on my hands and knees and thanked God. My entire team was confident of the victory, but we anxiously awaited the decision. The ring announcer read out the scores, but it was all in Japanese, so I couldn't understand what he was saying. I heard McCullough, then Yakushiji, so I knew it was a split decision. The final score was read out and the announcer shouted, 'MA-CULLA'.

I had won the WBC bantamweight championship of the world. Yakushiji never fought again.

One of the judges was Korean and we half expected him to give the fight to Yakushiji – which he did. Sadly, that's boxing. But it didn't matter because the other two judges did an honest job and saw that I won the fight. I was immediately surrounded. Mat was in tears in the ring. He was so proud. I hugged him and my brother, and then kissed Eddie and Thell. Then I walked over to Cheryl and lifted her into the air as if to say, 'We did it!' Two young kids from Belfast, who took a chance, had conquered the world.

The WBC official strapped the Belt around my waist. I kissed my hands and then planted that kiss on the Belt. They also presented me with five trophies as big as me and a certificate pronouncing me the world champion. At least I think that's what it says; it's in Japanese. Two of the trophies were taken from me in the ring to be displayed in a museum and the other three had to be shipped over to me.

There was almost another fight in the dressing-room when a WBC official came in to take the Belt from me, because it belonged to Yakushiji! They promised to send on my Belt. Even though I'd just won the title, I left Japan empty-handed.

The fight was televised in the UK by Sky and Ian Darke was one of their commentators. After the result had been announced, he told the viewers, 'He's got justice. He's done it the hard way in the other fellow's backyard. And that is one of the great performances by a British boxer. Wayne McCullough is the WBC bantamweight champion and how he deserved it.'

A group of Irish fans made their way from the back of the arena right up to the ring apron. They were singing, 'Wayne's world, Wayne's world.' When I stepped back, I could see there were Japanese guys singing with them too.

Mat hosted a party at the hotel afterwards with the officials, the referee and anyone else who was associated with the fight. Thell, Cheryl and I arrived late because we had to go to the hospital to get my cuts stitched up. At the party, Cheryl surprised me with a T-shirt that read: 'And the new . . .' on the front and 'WBC Champion of the World' on the back. I wore it with pride.

When we arrived back at our hotel room after the fight and festivities, there was an ice bucket on the table with a bottle of Guinness in it. It turned out the chef at the hotel was Irish and he'd sent it up to my room with a note of congratulations. I was able to meet him and thank him.

I knew I was paying all the expenses for training camp and so on, and Mat and I agreed they would not exceed $100,000; however, when the fight was over and it was time for me to get my cheque, the expenses amounted to well over $130,000. I was upset, but the team had flown first class and enjoyed a luxurious stay at a top hotel. We had brought home the world-title Belt, so at the time I thought every dollar spent had been worth it.

I did an interview with Dermot the morning after the fight. My face was busted up, my eyes were black and I was tired. I told him it hadn't hit me yet that I was the champion of the world. I said I knew it was going to be tough coming to the champion's home town, but I'd taken my trainer's advice and that's what got me through. We fought the right fight and came out on top.

I also told him I'd make my first defence of the title in November in Belfast. I wanted the fans to come out and support me this time. I felt as if I was Belfast's champion and I wanted to bring the Belt home and show it to my fans. Just because I lived in Vegas didn't mean I'd forgotten where I came from. I told Dermot that I would keep my two feet on the ground. 'I'm still a normal person,' I said. 'I'm still Wayne McCullough from Highfield Estate.' Dermot and Michael had taken a chance on me by following me to the top and it had paid off for them as well. We have all remained friends and often sit and reminisce about my achievements in Japan.

A Japanese lady who worked in the hotel had offered to record the fight for me and, just as we were leaving, she ran up and handed me the tape. Then she shuffled away. I was touched that she had remembered.

I became a superstar in Japan. I was in all their magazines – still am. They love me. Even though I'd beaten their champion, they still showed me a tremendous amount of respect. At the airport, while we were waiting for our flight, a group of Japanese Scouts surrounded me for autographs and photos. I sat in the middle of them and granted their requests.

Our flight from Japan stopped off in Canada on the way back home, and while we were waiting, a big guy came up to me in the airport and said, 'You're a great fighter.' I stopped and thanked him but thought nothing more about it until Justo informed me he was actually a famous baseball player. I was honoured that he had taken the time to approach me.

* * *

We didn't go to Belfast straight after the fight because I didn't want to go home until I got my Belt. It took about six weeks to arrive from the WBC.

Winning the world title was an emotional occasion for everyone involved and it is one moment in my life I don't ever want to forget. I should have been on top of the world. But I wasn't. I was the first ever WBC champion from Ireland but something was preventing me from being truly happy.

Eddie was thrilled with the result, and with what I had achieved in just over two years, but I couldn't have done it without him. Eddie paid me the biggest and best compliment anyone ever has in an interview for UTV. 'In my years of boxing,

I've worked with fellows like Joe Frazier, former world champion Ken Norton, Larry Holmes, Michael Spinks, Mike McCallum, Marlon Starling, Virgil Hill, Hedgemon Lewis. I've also had nineteen world champions. Wayne rates up there with the top five. The top five.'

11

THE HOMECOMING

Wayne McCullough was born to be great. From the Seoul Olympics he was singled out for stardom. I was lucky enough to be present in Barcelona when he won an Olympic silver medal. Soon after that I was privileged to promote his first professional fight in Ireland. In a lifetime if you can meet a great sportsman or a gentleman, you are fortunate. I met both at the same time, for those qualities were the hallmark of Wayne's character. He would later assume legendary status – the night he took the WBC title from Yakushiji. Just to know a man with his qualities is a privilege; to have shared in even a part of his life is an honour.

Brian Peters, Dublin-based boxing promoter

After paying my taxes and expenses – my manager received 25 per cent and my trainers 15 per cent – I was left with a little under $200,000 of my half-a-million-dollar payday from the World Championship. I could afford to enjoy some of the money I'd just earned and put the rest of it away.

When we got home from Japan, we bought another house. My first major cash purchase was a yellow Corvette sports car – for Cheryl – worth over $40,000. We were still young and enjoying life. We had left Belfast with two suitcases and a few pounds in our pockets and now, here we were, with a sports car and a quarter-of-a-million-dollar home. We deserved it.

Prime International replayed my world title win a couple of weeks later during a two-hour special. Rich Marotta and I were in the studio discussing the fight round-by-round. I was a big favourite with the fans in the States and they seemed to love my style of fighting.

Eddie and Thell were training at World Gym in Las Vegas by then. I went back there shortly after winning the title and everyone came up to me and congratulated me on winning the Belt. Boxers Mike McCallum, Montell Griffin and Justin Juuko, whom I'd known since the 1990 Commonwealth Games, were also training there. I was no longer 'Wayne' to them – I was 'Champ'. That hasn't changed.

I remember Mike telling me that my first defence would be my hardest. I didn't understand why it would be any more difficult than winning the Belt until he reminded me that every boxer wants to be a world champion. There is always someone out there who thinks they are better than the champion, and he would come to take my Belt. Obviously, I didn't want to lose my title in my first defence, so now there was added pressure on me to win in my next fight.

My first defence was set for 2 December in Belfast against Johnny Bredahl from Denmark. This bout was part of a new three-fight contract I had signed with ITV. I knew more viewers were going to get to see me on terrestrial channels and I was still getting exposure in the US, which was great. The fight was being promoted by Matchroom Boxing, Aiken Promotions and International Events, in association with Guinness. Matchroom needed a picture for the fight poster, but I still hadn't received my Belt, so Mike McCallum offered me his for the pictures. Mike was a light heavyweight at the time, so the Belt could have gone around my waist twice! I was honoured to use his Belt for my first promotional photos as a champion.

Cheryl and I flew to Belfast in September for a press conference to announce my next fight. My WBC Belt had arrived just a few days before we'd left. The press conference took place at the famous Europa in Belfast. I was doing a lot of PR to promote the fight and this time the response from the public was amazing. My first encounter with Bredahl was at the press conference, when he rudely ripped up a photo of me. I lost all respect for him after that. In my diary I wrote: 'Press conference. Met Bredahl. Very cocky guy. Smart remarks. Will knock him out cold.' It was the first time I hadn't liked an opponent.

Even though my friend Roderick had organised a car for me, the promoters had hired Mick Devine, chauffeur to the stars, to drive us to the press conference. Mick has taken care of us since, no matter where we are. He is the best driver anyone could ever ask for. He has even doubled up as a bodyguard at times, when I've needed him! Mick isn't just a driver or a bodyguard to us now, he is a very dear friend.

We only stayed in Belfast for a few days before going home, but I was still able to fit in my training and a couple of sparring sessions. Everyone got to see my Belt and that's what mattered to me the most.

A few weeks later Stephen Watson, a sports reporter from Belfast with whom I would work closely in the future, arrived in Las Vegas to shoot a documentary called *Rocket* for UTV. He stayed for about a week and followed me everywhere, getting a behind-the-scenes look at what goes on before a fight. During one of our interviews, I told Stephen that I had been putting some of my money away for the future. I knew boxing could end with one punch, so Cheryl and I were always careful not to overspend. In fact, I have never spent money before I had it: in boxing you have to live in the moment because you never know if a fight is going to happen until you actually step into the ring.

I arrived in Belfast a couple of weeks before my scheduled fight. I'd kept my promise to my home-town fans. I had dreamt all my life of fighting in Belfast's King's Hall – the home of big fights in Northern Irish boxing – and now that dream was coming true.

I did all my training and sparring in Vegas. Eddie and Thell were back and forth in training camp with Riddick Bowe. Mike McCallum was in the gym every day and he really encouraged me. Kenny Croom, whom Eddie had trained many years before, had been brought in to work with our team, so he practically trained me for this one. Kenny flew to Belfast a few days after I arrived. We did some of our training in my old amateur gym, Albert Foundry, but I was so used to the heat in Vegas that the cold in the gym was almost unbearable; I could hardly break a sweat. The manager of the hotel where we were staying permitted me to train by the indoor heated swimming pool every day instead.

The PR was non-stop. I was constantly on TV shows and did a lot of interviews for the local media. I was really looking forward to fighting in Belfast. People would stop me on the streets and tell me they had bought tickets. I was very excited and could hardly wait.

On the Tuesday night before the fight, the *Belfast Telegraph* Sports Awards took place at the Europa. It was the inaugural year of the event and because it was so close to my fight, I contemplated not going. Cheryl had already been informed that I was to be the recipient of the Sports Personality of the Year award, the major honour of the evening, and had been told not to tell me. She convinced me to go along. Jackie Fullerton, a Belfast TV sports reporter, announced the nominees for the award and a camera was focused on me. It was only then I realised I might actually be in the running. Jackie announced me as the winner and I was overwhelmed. The award takes pride of place in my home.

Two days before the fight I hurt my right hand in training. I didn't think it was anything to worry about, so I tried to put the injury to the back of my mind. The weigh-in was on the Friday afternoon, the day before the fight. I had worked harder this time to get down to the bantamweight limit. I was filling out and I felt as if I was growing beyond the weight class. The weigh-in took place at the UTV studios in Belfast, where Harry McGavock, a local MC, announced the weights as they were broadcast live on TV.

Bredahl was trying to taunt me by following me everywhere I went. He came over and stood right in front of me, then when I moved away he followed me, just to provoke me, but I ignored him. I think that annoyed him more. He wanted to get inside my head, but I was totally focused on the fight. I didn't let his mind games bother me. When Bredahl stepped on the scales, he shouted, 'New champion.' I just laughed at him.

On the day of the fight, Mat, Dan Milam and I went out in my car to pick up lunch. As I was driving along the road from the hotel, a car sped past us. A police car then whizzed past, which we thought was going to pull the motorist over. Suddenly, the police car slowed down and signalled for me to stop at the roadside. I knew I hadn't done anything wrong, so I pulled in to the kerb. I was driving the car Roderick had supplied for me and my name was emblazoned on the side. The policeman approached my window and asked me for ID, but I didn't have any with me – Cheryl always carries my wallet because I would lose it (or so she tells me) and she wasn't with me. So I told him my name and suggested he could have a look and see it printed on the side of the car. I wasn't being disrespectful, I was just trying to identify myself. I had been in every newspaper and on every TV show or news bulletin for two weeks, so I was sure he'd heard of me, but I was still only trying to be helpful. Then he asked me where I lived and I gave him my address in Las Vegas. It was the truth but he asked me again in an irritated tone. I told him once more that I lived in Vegas. My friends tell me I can be so naive at times and, looking back, maybe this was one of those occasions, but I was only telling him the truth.

Finally, he told me I had been speeding (I knew I hadn't) and that's why he had pulled me over. I was fighting later that night and was driving really carefully. He asked me where I was going and I told him. I had no ID, I couldn't prove who I was or where I lived, and he had no idea if I owned the car or not. But he didn't give me a warning. Instead, just as he was about to walk away, he said, 'Over to do a bit of boxing, then?'

'No, I'm here to play cricket,' I replied.

I wound up my window and drove off. Mat and Dan were astounded at the way the policeman had treated me when I had done absolutely nothing wrong.

My fight was scheduled to start at 11.30 p.m. It was being broadcast live on ITV around the UK. The King's Hall was packed to capacity with around 7,000 fans. I've never felt an atmosphere like it. Adrian Logan, commentating for ITV that evening, said, 'Never. Never have I witnessed a reception like this in the King's Hall for a boxer, and that really includes Barry McGuigan. This is very, very special for the Pocket Rocket.'

Bredahl had an undefeated record of 26–0, with nine KOs, coming into the fight. He was tall for the weight: he was a good 2 inches taller than me at 5 ft 9. Bredahl was both a former Junior and European bantamweight champion, so he was a live opponent.

I walked to the ring with U2's 'Desire' blasting through the arena, but I could barely hear it over the noise of the crowd. I knew I was home in front of my fans and they were all there to support me. Eddie, Thell and Kenny worked my corner and they were amazed at the crowd's reaction.

As I climbed through the ropes, Bredahl stood right in front of me. He was still taunting me. I danced back and forwards in front of him, while acknowledging the fans. Jimmy Lennon Jnr was the ring announcer. I had first met Jimmy in America in 1993 and he had announced most of my fights since my pro debut. To this day, we have remained close friends. I couldn't even hear Jimmy say my name, the noise from the fans was deafening. They were chanting, 'Wayne McCullough, Wayne McCullough,' and they didn't take a breath all night.

Bredahl did what I expected him to do in the first round – run and jab. When I caught up with him in the second round, I busted his left eye with a right-hand. I continued to stalk him while he continued to run away from me. I worked his body a lot when I had him on the ropes, but he kept slipping away. After the second round, Eddie told me to get close, work his body and then go to the head.

In the fourth round I literally ran him down, throwing punches when I trapped him. I was taking absolutely no damage because he was too busy running to throw any punches. When he did land a punch, I found out that Bredahl was the lightest puncher I've ever fought. He found it hard to keep up with my pace. I was getting faster every round, and I knew eventually he wouldn't be able to run any more.

Halfway through the fifth round I hit him with a left hook and a big right-hand to the chin, which sent him staggering backwards. When he regained his composure, he ran even more to try to get away from me. It seemed at this point that he was only there to survive. At the end of the round I pinned him in the corner and threw a 12-punch combination without reply, but again he slipped away. I just couldn't get him to stop moving. He was so tricky.

Cheryl was cheering and Mick was sitting right beside her, supporting me every step of the way. Cheryl was wearing her trademark, specially-designed earrings with my face on them!

Every round I was trying to get closer to Bredahl. In the sixth Bredahl was more negative, but even though I threw a double jab that put him on the canvas, the referee ruled it a slip. I pinned him in the neutral corner at the end of the round and pounded away at his ribs.

At the start of the seventh I knew I was getting closer to him and I was hurting him with every shot. He continued to run, but by now I was landing at will. The fans were singing, 'Here we go, here we go, here we go!'

In between rounds seven and eight Eddie knew I had got to him and told me to keep the pressure on. I was just getting warmed up. The referee warned him twice in the eighth round for not fighting back. I threw a 13-punch combination while Bredahl dipped low, trying to get away from them, but the referee stepped in and stopped the fight because he hadn't thrown anything back.

Bredahl wasn't badly hurt and he protested the stoppage. I didn't want the referee to stop it either. I wanted to knock him out cold because of the disrespect he'd shown me prior to the fight. But he had made it clear he didn't want to win. I went to his corner after the fight and he told me he wanted to go the distance. I told him the referee had wanted him to try to win.

I met Bredahl in Vegas when he challenged Paulie Ayala for the WBA bantamweight championship in 2000. I thought he beat Paulie because he fought a really good fight. I told his trainer I wished he'd fought me the way he fought that night: he stood right in front of him. If he'd stood in front of me, I'd have knocked him out earlier. I was pleased with my performance against Bredahl, but I knew I could have been better.

I woke up the next morning and felt as if I'd run a marathon. My legs were really hurting because I'd used them more in the fight than my hands. I was limping too, because of blisters on my toes from having to run after him. A fax was waiting for me at home. One page was a sketch of a boxer and the other read:

Wayne
What a fighter
What a prize
What a night
What a theme tune
What a shame
I couldn't see it live
God Bless you and keep you hard

Bono

* * *

My second defence was against Mexican Jose Luis Bueno on 30 March 1996. He was the former WBC super flyweight champion. He'd won on my undercard when I'd fought Bredahl, so we'd had a good look at him. Mat held a press conference in Top Rank in Las Vegas in January 1996 to announce the fight. He flew over some journalists from Ireland, north and south, as this was a double press conference: John Michael Johnson was there because I was pencilled in to fight him on the Julio Cesar Chavez v. Oscar de la Hoya undercard in June. I was a little worried about announcing two fights at once because I take one fight at a time – anything can happen in boxing. But I didn't question Mat.

I trained in Vegas for the Bueno fight, even though I was fighting him in Dublin. I was finding it more and more difficult to get my weight down, but I just kept working hard, thinking and hoping it would come off eventually.

Mat rented out Luttrellstown Castle, about 20 minutes outside Dublin, for my team. Four years later, former Spice Girl Victoria Adams would marry David Beckham there. Who knows, maybe I sweated off some pre-fight pounds in the room where they held their wedding reception.

It was a gorgeous location and we set up the boxing ring and heavy bag in the luxurious dining room. Staff were on hand 24 hours a day and treated us exceptionally well. Mat and his family came over from the States mainly for the fight, but the castle stay was a fairy-tale holiday for them. Only Cheryl and I treated it like a training camp. We had no choice.

Two years later I received a summons to the High Court in Dublin because the castle bill had not been paid. I phoned Mat and angrily asked him why the bill hadn't been settled. He told me not to worry about it and he would take care of it. Months later, he did.

Kenny travelled over from Vegas with me for this fight too. I brought a sparring partner in from England and he stayed in the castle with us. I ran around the castle's golf course every morning. It was really cold, so I bundled up to get a sweat going. When we trained in the gym, we had the heat on full-blast. We also lit the open fire so it was blazing away.

Eddie and Thell arrived a few days before the fight. One night we were all sitting at the dinner table and a member of staff came in to tell Eddie there was a phone call for him. Eddie asked who it was and was told it was his wife. Once he'd left the room, there was much debate. 'His wife?' Eddie didn't have a wife. When he returned, we asked him who it was. He told us it was Eva and that they had married the weekend before he came to Dublin, and he just hadn't told any of us. He sat back down with his trademark chuckle. Eva arrived a couple of days later.

I was eating healthily and trying to keep my weight under control, but the day before the weigh-in, Mel Christle, the Irish Sports Council representative, showed up at the castle and wanted me to weigh-in on his scale so he could check my weight. I told him I'd weigh for him after I'd worked out and, even though he wasn't happy, I went ahead and trained. I weighed 8 st. 8 lb after dropping about 4 lb in my training session.

After I'd won the title I told Mat that I wanted to make only one defence and move up a class, but I knew I was here now and I had to make weight no matter what. Everyone around me was drinking wine and eating cheese. This was the first time I was bothered by watching other people eating in front of me. It felt like I was dehydrating myself and hardly eating or drinking while everyone else enjoyed the high life.

On the morning of the weigh-in I got up and did about 12 rounds of shadow boxing and jumped rope. I got on the scales and I was 8 st. 7½ lb, still a pound and a half overweight. So I put on clean training clothes and did another ten rounds of shadow boxing. At this point I had nothing left in my body to burn off. After this second training session my weight had only dropped by half a pound. I was still over. Cheryl told me to stop, that I was killing myself, but I had no choice.

I went to the breakfast room with Cheryl and I felt as weak as water. I ordered a boiled egg. I peeled it, took out the yolk and ate the white – I could only afford to eat that part. No liquid crossed my lips. I went straight back up to the room and did another 12 rounds of shadow boxing and jumped rope. I was so dehydrated that my lips were sticking together and I was exhausted. I was down to 8 st. 5½ lb. I called Cheryl in to look at the scales. I wanted to make sure I wasn't seeing things. I was half a pound under the weight limit. I lifted my head up and said, 'Thank you, God.' I could barely walk from the bathroom to the bedroom, but I managed to lie down on the bed.

It was about 10 a.m. I still had roughly six hours to go before I weighed in. I went to the bathroom to squeeze out any last drop, but there was nothing left. I looked down at the toilet water and wanted to drink it. I was so dry it was driving me mad. Cheryl got me out of there immediately.

Mick picked us up and drove us to Tallaght shopping centre to pass a few hours. He was concerned about me and kept asking if I was OK. I could hardly open my eyes; I was walking like an old man. I spotted a fountain right in the middle of the centre and wanted to jump into it. Cheryl steered me away from it immediately, seeing the temptation in my eyes.

* * *

It was finally time for the weigh-in. I jumped on the scales, made weight and jumped off. They announced my weight as 8 st. 5½ lb.

I was so relieved. I'd never felt that way after a weigh-in before. I had about five litres of liquids to drink and it was gone in about ten minutes. I also ate about four or five chicken breasts. After drinking all those liquids, I was still dry. I couldn't believe it. After the fight, some commentators said that I must have made the weight easily because I was half a pound underweight, but they don't know what I went through to get there. I was the same weight from 10 a.m. that morning and I didn't touch any liquid or food. My weight stayed exactly the same for six hours. I had nothing else in my body to lose.

I can usually bring my weight down to about 8 st. 7 lb without a problem, but once I try to get below that I have a really hard time. I start losing my vision and I have no energy. That's exactly what happened that day, and the next day I still had to defend my world title. I put on 16 lb between the weigh-in and the fight, but I was bloated. It wasn't good for my body to gain so much weight so quickly and I still felt tired.

Dublin's Point Depot was packed to capacity with a sell-out crowd. Michael Flatley, Steve Collins, Bono and Larry Mullen came to the fight. I was honoured to know they were all there to support me.

Jimmy Lennon Jnr announced the fight. It was broadcast on ITV across the UK and Prime International in the States. The crowd was just as loud as the Belfast fans had been and I couldn't hear anything but chanting as I walked to the ring. I had watched tapes of Bueno's fights. He wasn't a big guy, but he was strong. He was a counterpuncher.

When I stepped into the ring, I was as white as a ghost. I've usually got a bit of a tan, but I was so dehydrated and bloated that I just didn't look or feel like myself at all. Bueno tried to counterpunch me in the first two rounds. I used my jab to get in close. In the second round I landed a straight jab followed by a right-hand to his chin. He grabbed me to buy some time and clear his head. I worked his body as he held on to me, but he survived the round. Referee Lou Filipo, who also played a referee in some of the *Rocky* movies, did a great job that night.

About a minute into the third round I thought I had him. I threw a left-right left hook to his chin and he slid along the ropes.

He was ready to go, but it seemed from that point that I had nothing left. I thought I was wearing cushions on my hands instead of boxing gloves and it felt as though he was hitting me with sledgehammers. My resistance was so low. I'm usually a good finisher, but I couldn't do anything to him. My face started to swell in the third round. I sat on the stool after the round and I knew I had nothing left. I was done. I prayed that I would get through it.

I remember nothing else from that point on until I woke up the next day.

* * *

Since I don't remember anything from the third round onwards, Cheryl has told me what happened. In the middle rounds she watched as my nose started to drip blood. Then, suddenly, it stopped. She says I did enough to win the fight, but the judges saw it as a split decision for me. Apparently, immediately after the fight I spotted Bono in the crowd. He was wearing his trademark sunglasses and I motioned to him to give them to me to cover my bruised eyes. He and Larry came into my dressing-room after the fight. Bono held my hand for quite some time, telling me how courageous I was, and before he left he handed me his sunglasses. He thought I needed them more than he did.

I was passing blood and then I started throwing up, so Cheryl got me ready to go to the local hospital. Mick took Kenny, Cheryl and me. I was starting to pass out in the car and they had to shout at me to keep me conscious. As soon as we stopped at the hospital, Mick ran me in with a towel over my head.

My blood pressure was out of control and even though I was lying still on a hospital bed, my heart rate was over 100 beats per minute. My eardrum was burst. The doctors said I was in shock and had to inject me with morphine to ease the pain in my face. I was trembling. Just recently Kenny told me he thought I was going to die that night. While I don't remember even being at the hospital, Cheryl has said that I walked past them to go for an X-ray and told them I was feeling OK.

Cheryl doesn't know why but they allowed me to go home in

127

the early hours of the morning. When we arrived at the castle, there was a victory party being held in my honour. Everyone started yelling and cheering when I walked in, but I just thanked them and went to my room to sleep. Cheryl woke me every half-hour, all night long, to make sure I didn't die in my sleep.

When I woke up the next morning, I asked Cheryl if I had won the fight. She told me I had. She also asked me to look in the mirror. I didn't recognise myself. It looked as if someone had pumped up my face. But it was strange because my body looked normal. Only my face was swollen. This was because of my blood pressure, not from excessive punishment from punches. Cheryl told me I'd met Bono and I was upset that I didn't remember, but I had his sunglasses to prove it. We took pictures of my face every day for about a week and, slowly but surely, we could see the swelling going down.

Bueno was supposed to leave for Mexico the next day but he couldn't because he was so sick. I decided to stay one more day in the castle because I was really embarrassed about how I looked. Now, when I look back at the fight, I wonder how I continued to fight after round three. I know it was answered prayer. I know I was fighting on instinct. I took a lot of shots against Bueno in the last nine rounds but I was still giving back enough to win the fight. Even in the last two rounds, when he was pushing me to my limits, I somehow managed to continue to hit him with good straight right-hands on the chin. The great trainer Ignacio 'Nacho' Beristain was in Bueno's corner. I see him at fights in Vegas all the time now and he always talks about my courage and heart. That was my last fight at bantamweight.

12

CONTROVERSY

Wayne is a world-class fighter, father and person. I am proud to call him a true friend and look forward to many years of friendship long after he retires.

Stuart Campbell, co-manager

After the Bueno fight, Cheryl and I flew to London with Nicola and Ian. I used this time to relax and recuperate before going home. We took in a West End show and did some sightseeing together.

As I was scheduled to fight as the chief supporting fight on the Oscar de la Hoya v. Julio Cesar Chavez card on 7 June at Caesars Palace, I went to my doctor when we got back to Vegas and had him check my ear because I still couldn't hear clearly. He said I definitely had a burst eardrum, so fighting in June was out of the question. I was disappointed – it would have been a dream come true for me – but my health was more important. I also spoke with Eddie and Mat about my weight troubles. They knew a little about what I had gone through but not all of it. We agreed that it would be sensible for me to move up in weight to super bantam.

Mat scheduled a fight for me for on 13 July in Denver. He'd arranged for Duke McKenzie, from England, to be my opponent. I remembered how I'd felt during my last fight in Denver, so this time I arrived there three weeks before the fight to get used to the altitude. I wasn't going to make the same mistake twice.

Although now I was having trouble with my trainers: I felt as if I wasn't getting enough work from them when I was in the gym. I like to train hard and even though I was a champion I still wanted to learn. I had become very depressed about the training situation a few days before I was due to go to camp. I remember sitting at home one night and having suicidal thoughts. I've been told this is usually a cry for help. I sat in my living room and looked up at the open beam separating the two living areas. I visualised myself tying my strong leather jump rope around the beam, putting a noose on it and hanging myself.

People may think I was selfish for thinking like this, but it came to the point where I felt I wasn't scared to do it. I had pictured it and planned it. The only thing that scared me was knowing that I could do it. That night Cheryl came out of the bedroom at about 2 a.m. and found me sitting in the dark. She probably saved my life. She knew she had to get me help as quickly as possible. If Cheryl hadn't come into the room, I would have gone through with it – I know that for a fact. God blessed me that night.

Cheryl told Mat she was worried there was something wrong with me psychologically. I flew to Denver and stayed with Mat for a week before I checked in to a hotel and he arranged for me to see a homeopathic doctor in Denver called Dr Kay. The doctor gave me medication and helped turn my thoughts around. Cheryl said I came out of his office a different person.

The fight against Duke McKenzie was to be the last in my contract with ITV. I had always admired him when I was younger. He was a former world champion in three weight divisions. But when McKenzie arrived in America, from what I have been told, he didn't have the correct paperwork and so went back to England. Mat told me he was going to offer him more money and was also going to fly him over by Concorde, but for some reason, unbeknown to me, he didn't come back. The matchmaker started looking for another opponent.

My purse for the fight under the ITV contract was going to be $450,000, which was remarkable for a ten-rounder. Mat told me that once McKenzie had pulled out, ITV would too, unless the matchmaker found an opponent they approved of.

Richie Wenton, who I'd known for a long time, was brought over from England. We were friends and had sparred each other years before in Belfast. This is business, though, and sometimes I have to fight my friends. I thought he was a good little fighter and a decent name for ITV, but I was told he wasn't suitable either. The matchmaker then said he had found a Mexican fighter from Guadalajara called Julio Cesar Cardona. Cardona had been preparing for a fight a week after mine, so he was ready. His record was 23–11 with 16 KOs. Apparently, ITV wouldn't accept Cardona either, so they pulled out. Overnight I'd gone from being offered $450,000 for this fight to getting $50,000.

So, I fought Cardona at featherweight. I think the fight turned out to be a lot tougher than the one against McKenzie would have been. I won almost every round of the fight on the scorecards. But it was hard to fight Cardona when I had prepared to fight someone else.

Even though I'd had psychological help, my mind wasn't really in this fight. Still, I got into the ring and acted like a professional. I did my job. I could have told Mat the fight was off, but I'm glad I didn't. It worked out well. CBS showed the fight live on a Saturday afternoon in a slot during their horseracing broadcast, so the audience for my fight was tremendous – Cheryl and I had applied for permanent residency in the United States and when we were brought in for our interview on 26 August, everyone had seen my fight that Saturday afternoon and knew who I was. It was amazing.

The McKenzie fight was supposed to be rescheduled for later in the year, but it didn't happen. Since I didn't have a fight date, I flew with Mat and Dan Goossen to the 1996 Olympic Games in Atlanta, Georgia, to scout some fighters for their new boxing promotional company, America Presents. It was a very successful and enjoyable trip.

* * *

Naseem Hamed was fighting at the Point Depot in Dublin on 31 August. I read in a newspaper that he had supposedly said Cheryl was scared of me fighting him, so I flew to Dublin to confront him. I arrived there the day of the weigh-in and met up with Mick Devine. Just as the weigh-in was finishing, I walked straight up to Hamed and shook his hand. He was surrounded by his entourage and Frank Warren, his promoter at the time. 'Don't dare say anything about my wife or my family ever again,' I said to him. He asked me what I was talking about, but I told him he knew what I meant. We almost got into a scuffle, but Mick pulled me away.

I know better than to believe everything I read in the papers. Maybe Hamed hadn't said anything about Cheryl, but at the time I thought he had and I wanted to make sure he wouldn't do it again. If anyone says anything about me, or my family, and they are wrong, I confront them. I fear no man. At the time, I was still the bantamweight champion and he was the featherweight champion.

He had put posters up around Dublin that read: 'Forget about McCullough. Come see the Prince.' I knew I was inside his head. Harry and his wife, and Alan and I went to the fight the next night and sat near the back of the arena. Fans began to recognise me and word started to spread around the arena that I was there. Sky TV located me and guided me to ringside, where I sat directly behind Hamed's dad.

Hamed was fighting Manuel Medina, but instead of the crowd singing his name, they were chanting, 'Wayne McCullough! Wayne McCullough!' It must have been frustrating for Hamed but the noise was out of my control. As my friends and family watched the fight, both in Belfast and the States, they couldn't believe the crowd was singing for me. I wasn't even taking part.

* * *

I was now the number one contender in the WBC super bantamweight ratings. Mat had managed to arrange a fight with the champion, 39-year-old Daniel Zaragoza of Mexico. Zaragoza was a three-time world champion and had been victorious at two different weight divisions. The fight was scheduled for 12 January 1997 in the Hynes Convention Center, Boston, Massachusetts.

In the middle of November, Harry and his wife came to visit for a few weeks. Eddie and Thell were in training camp with Riddick Bowe for his fight in December, so Harry worked with me. Harry, Mat and I went to Boston for a press conference to announce the fight. On our way home, we stopped off in Denver and I had another visit with Dr Kay. I wanted to make sure my head was clear of any negative thoughts.

I decided to have training camp at the Inverness Hotel in Denver and I arrived there four weeks before the fight. Thell came for a few days while Eddie stayed with Bowe in his camp and then they swapped over. We practically had the hotel to ourselves because it was the holiday season and they typically didn't have many guests at that time of year. The gym was set up in one of the hotel's function rooms until the last few days when we went to the Denver PAL (Police Authority League) gym. I'd brought in a couple of sparring partners and training was good. I had sparred well over a hundred rounds.

During our first few days in Denver, it was well below zero. The snow was up to my waist and I couldn't run outside, so I had to use the treadmill in the fitness suite. I had taught Cheryl how to hold the pads for me, so when Eddie and Thell weren't there she worked with me. One day I went out running in my ski suit in the snow. The snow was only about a foot deep and even though it was hard to run in, I wanted to do my roadwork outside. I had been miserable running on the treadmill. As I ran across the golf course connected to the hotel, I started to sink down into the snow. I ended up crawling on my hands and knees to make it out the other end.

When we got to Boston, it was even colder than in Denver. I didn't think that was possible. On our first night there Cheryl and I went outside for a walk. We got about ten feet before we turned back. It felt like someone was throwing ice-cold water over my body. I'd never felt cold like it.

The final press conference was held on the Wednesday before the fight. Robert Kraft, owner of the New England Patriots football team, presented me with a team jersey with my name displayed on the back. I was honoured. I met Zaragoza that day and he was polite and respectful towards me.

The fight was the first under Mat's new promotional banner, America Presents. On the day of the fight, Mat came to our hotel room and gave Cheryl a contract for me to sign. She kept it from me so it wouldn't be on my mind during the fight. It was a promotional deal, signing me up to America Presents.

* * *

In this first championship fight as a super bantamweight I made the weight easily. In fact, I was 2 lb under the weight limit. Zaragoza's record was 57–7–3 with 27 KOs; this was only my 21st fight. I knew he was more experienced than me, but I had Eddie Futch in my corner and with youth on my side, I knew I could beat him.

Zaragoza and I fought for an all-time combined record purse for the super bantamweight division. I got $505,000 and he got $500,000. Zaragoza was receiving his biggest purse ever – it was the first time he'd even stayed in a hotel suite. The fight was televised by HBO, which, for me, was huge. The Hynes Convention Center was sold out with mostly screaming Irish-American fans – all cheering for me. I wore the Patriots jersey into the ring and the fans loved it. When I stepped through the ropes that night, my WBC bantamweight Belt became vacant. I never lost my Belt, I gave it up voluntarily.

Eddie and I had watched tapes of Zaragoza and we thought if I stayed on the outside and boxed him, I would win easily. So I began round number one boxing him. I was sticking my jab in his face and it was working. He was a crafty southpaw, but I felt comfortable on the outside picking him off. I found out later that two of the judges didn't see what I was doing and weren't giving me any points. A lot of people thought I could only fight going forward, but I can box, as I did in the amateurs, and that's what I continued to do.

Obviously, I like to brawl, and Zaragoza and I got into it a bit during the fight, but ultimately I thought I was controlling the fight. After every round Cheryl would signal to me whether I had won it or not, and she had me ahead. I knew I was doing enough to take his Belt from him, even if the rounds were close.

Zaragoza's best weapon was his big wide looping left-hand and he caught me solidly with it in round two. He had his best round in the fifth when he landed a left to my solar plexus (the area just below the ribs on the right-hand side of the body) and even though I backed away from him to take a breather, he couldn't stop me. A fighter can be knocked out by a punch in this area and I didn't want that to happen to me.

In the first half of the fight I thought I could have been about two rounds up. I just continued doing what I'd been doing. Zaragoza was hitting me with wide shots, but I was the one in charge and was landing the better, more accurate punches.

We clashed heads in the eighth round and I got cut on the left side of my head in my hair. When I got back to the corner, Thell couldn't figure out where the blood was coming from. He finally found the cut and started working on it to stop the bleeding before the beginning of the next round. In the early rounds, I'd caught Zaragoza with body shots and could hear him moaning. By the later rounds, I thought I was going to stop him, but he stayed in there with me, taking all the punishment I was dishing out. Zaragoza's right eye was cut badly but his eyes seemed to get cut up in almost every one of his fights. He had a good cutman, who kept it under control. My left eye was swollen, but it wasn't bothering me.

During round ten, Zaragoza and I were in a clinch and I was so confident I looked out at Cheryl and winked. She was shouting, screaming and signalling at me to come forward and pressure him, but I was thinking, 'Why is she so concerned if I have the fight in the bag?' Little did I know that Cheryl had found out I was so far behind on the cards that I needed a knockout to win.

Eddie had told me that I was ahead going into the final rounds. He'd said, 'Just go out and win the last two,' and that's what I did. I had so much energy in the 11th and 12th rounds that I was planning to run right through him. I beat him up in those rounds and in my opinion they could have been scored 10–8. I still couldn't have won the fight on the judges' cards.

In the last round I caught Zaragoza with a left-hook right-hand combination and I knew I had him in trouble. I don't know how he stayed on his feet. As the bell sounded to end the fight, Jim Lampley, the commentator for HBO, described the atmosphere as having an 'unbelievable intensity'. He continued with, 'I just wish that you all could be here with us.' In the last round, Zaragoza threw an amazing 119 punches, but he had to because I had thrown 139. As we waited for the decision, I could tell it wasn't going to go my way. Zaragoza got the win by a split decision and kept his Belt. I found out after the fight that going into the 11th, I was six rounds down on two scorecards.

On our way back home, we had to change planes in Denver. I was stopped by a passenger in the airport, who said, 'That was a hell of a fight last night; you won it!' I thanked him, but it didn't make me feel any better about the decision. When I got to the airport in Vegas, Mike McCallum and a friend, Julie, were waiting for me. As a champion, I'd been surrounded by plenty of 'friends', but this time there were just two.

I watched the fight and listened to the commentators on HBO. It was as if I wasn't even in the fight. It sounded like Zaragoza was their favourite that night. The only commentator to show some consideration for me was Roy Jones Jr.

It was my first loss and it was definitely the hardest thing I'd gone through in my professional boxing career to that point. I just wanted to quit. Cheryl told me to go to hospital to get my cut stitched up, but I told her there wasn't any point – I was never going to box again.

Cheryl finally convinced me to go to the hospital the day after my fight with Zaragoza. My cut had almost closed, so I had to hold a wet cloth over it to reopen it. I didn't want to have a scar. I knew I should have gone straight after the fight, but I was too disappointed. I only needed two stitches. I took it easy for a few weeks after the Zaragoza fight and did only a little training. I was eating my usual favourites – chicken, meat and biscuits; pretty much anything I wanted because I wasn't training for a fight. But my back teeth were hurting.

I made an appointment to see my dentist and after he'd examined me he told me he had good news and bad news. 'The good news is your teeth are fine,' he said. The bad news? 'Your jaw is broken.' I had a small hairline fracture on the right-hand side of my face. There was also a crack through one of my wisdom teeth. I thought he was kidding since I'd been eating and it wasn't bothering me that much.

I went to see an oral surgeon, who extracted two wisdom teeth and wired my jaw shut. I had to keep the wires on for five weeks. After three weeks I had to get them tightened, which was really painful. For the first couple of days, talking was also very hard. It felt as though my teeth were glued together. After a while I could talk as well with my jaw wired as I had without it.

Everything I consumed had to be liquidised and I sucked it through a straw. No matter what I 'ate', I couldn't keep my weight up. I'd put on a little weight after the fight, but by the time I got the wires off I must have only weighed about 8 stone. If I'd kept them on any longer, I might have disappeared.

When I watched the tape of the fight, I was able to pinpoint exactly where in the fight my jaw had been broken. It happened in round two when Zaragoza caught me with a big looping left-hand. So I'd fought for ten rounds with a broken jaw.

13

THE ROCKET RETURNS

Wayne is a throwback: he is dedicated to his family, his sport, his friends and his many fans around the world. Today there are crowns being worn by different fighters every other month, yet Wayne will for ever be thought of as a champion because he has always fought and lived like one.

Ron 'G-man' Gerrard, journalist, straightjab.com

In early April 1997, Cheryl and I flew back to Belfast. While I was there, I bought my mum and dad a house. I don't think it was ever fully appreciated; I felt they expected more. I love my mum and dad, always will. I took care of them when I started to make money because I wanted to. I looked after all my family members. I would send them money at Christmas and their birthdays. I also bought Harry a new car. I wanted to say thank you to him for the time and effort he'd spent training me for over 14 years.

I haven't seen my parents since one day in June 1998 when, while standing in the house I bought them, I was accused of not doing anything for the family. My sister, Christina, was the only one who stood up for me that day. I kissed my mum and dad on the cheek, told them I loved them and said I was going back home to Vegas. A week later there was a fictitious story in a tabloid from one of their so-called friends relating to Wynona. As a dad who idolises his precious daughter, for me this was the final straw. I phoned them in 2004 in an attempt to resolve things, but my mum and dad both hung up on me during separate phone conversations.

* * *

Back in late spring 1997 Mat flew in from Denver to stay at our house. We all went to see U2 in concert at Sam Boyd Stadium and were able to go backstage and meet the band. Bono and I chatted about my fight in Dublin in '96 and I told him I was delighted to finally meet him – and remember it this time. However, my business relationship with Mat was not going so well. I felt things had changed after the Zaragoza fight. Mat kept asking me to sign the contract he had given to Cheryl that night. I had just thrown it in a drawer because boxing had been the last thing I'd wanted to think about. But then I'd soon realised that I still loved the sport and decided I would box again after all.

I didn't understand most of the contract Mat had given me, but he was my friend and so I finally signed it in June without any legal advice and posted it to him in Denver. I soon began to think that the contract I had signed did not have my best interests at heart. I bumped into former world champion Johnny Tapia and his wife, Teresa, in Vegas and he said his attorney, Stuart Campbell, was coming in to town and that we should sit down and talk to him. I thought it couldn't do any harm and surely the more advice I got, the better.

The press in Belfast had a field day trying to destroy my relationship with Mat. Even though we were not seeing eye-to-eye on business matters, we were still very good friends. The press pitted us against one another and I did not like that. They made false accusations about Cheryl and me, and Mat, as my friend, supported us. I didn't ask him to do that. He just did, knowing how much the press had hurt me over the years. From the minute I'd left Belfast back in '93 some of the local press were expecting me to fall flat on my face. They didn't think I'd ever make it in the States. But I had become a legitimate world champion in two years, five months and seven days. At this point in my career, I had also just fought for my second world title.

My goal was now to get the rematch with Zaragoza. I wanted to avenge my loss. I couldn't fight right away because of my broken jaw, so I didn't mind that Zaragoza defended his title in April in Japan. I was willing to wait however long it took for the rematch to happen.

Zaragoza went on to lose his Belt to Erik Morales in September 1998, so I never did get the chance to fight him again.

* * *

I met Stuart Campbell in the autumn of 1997 and when he looked at my contract with Mat, he shook his head in disbelief. Stuart renegotiated a new contract for me with America Presents and both Mat and I were happy. Mat was now my promoter, Cheryl had taken over as my manager and Stuart had become my co-manager. The revised contract was still unsigned, as we were working through the final points, but Mat scheduled another fight for me on 10 January 1998. A couple of days before the fight I read in a newspaper that my fight had been cancelled: I had been training every day and no one had told me.

I was furious, to say the least. My friend, Frank, and I flew to Los Angeles on the day of the fight and as I walked into the arena there were posters announcing that I was fighting. The place was packed – with Irish fans. I met Tom Brown, working with America Presents now, outside and he asked what I was doing there. I joked that I was fighting. He told me my opponent was out back, so I said 'Get him into the ring!' We laughed.

During the fights I worked the room, stopping by all the Irish fans who were there to see me in the ring. They asked why I wasn't fighting and I pointed towards Mat. I told them to go and ask him. I didn't know why I wasn't fighting, so I couldn't explain it to them.

I talked to Dan at the fight and asked him what had happened. But he didn't have an explanation for me either. Mat was there, but he avoided me all evening. Finally, as we were walking out, I bumped into him and he asked if I was joining them for something to eat. I told him I was going home.

Since receiving a big payday against Zaragoza, I'd put most of my money into investments, which tied it up for five years. I'd kept enough money liquid to live on for about a year, but since I didn't fight in January 1998 and I hadn't made any money in over a year, finances were tight. Cheryl and I were down to our last few dollars. I never complained or told anyone about our lack of money. We would go to the store and buy ten-cent noodles. We liked them anyway and they tasted good.

* * *

Stephen Watson called me soon after the contract troubles with Mat came to light and said he was interested in coming to Vegas to film another documentary about the situation. He arrived with a crew in February. The documentary this time was to be entitled *Leaving Las Vegas?*

Mat agreed to fly in from Denver to try to get everything sorted. Cheryl and I picked him up at the airport and took him to the Hard Rock Hotel. We spent most of the day discussing matters in his hotel suite and finally signed the new contract. Mat gave me the first instalment of my signing bonus.

Cheryl was pregnant at the time and was due to give birth in March, so I told Mat I didn't want to fight until April. My first fight under the new contract was set for 17 April at the Mohegan Sun in Uncasville, Connecticut. After the Zaragoza fight Eddie and Thell went their separate ways and Eddie retired a short time later. I was still with Thell, but I thought I wasn't getting the attention I needed in the gym; I thought I'd learned enough from Eddie to know what to do on my own.

Eddie passed away in 2001. Eva, his wife, phoned to tell me the news and I was devastated. We had become very close in his last years. My little daughter loved going to visit him. I did too, because he would sit and tell us stories about all the old-time fighters he had sparred or worked with. He always compared my style to Henry Armstrong's, with my perpetual motion. Eddie trained 20 world champions. I was his lightest.

Eddie was the reason I came to Las Vegas. In boxing circles he is known as 'the best trainer that ever lived' because he was a great technician. He would dissect my opponents and give me a game plan that worked every time.

The day before my fight against Javier Medina in 1994, USA network had interviewed Eddie about his bond with his boxers. He said, 'I've always been able to communicate very well with my fighters. I've always wanted them to understand me and I've always wanted to understand them. The relationship is not merely athletic, it's person to person. I consider them my friends and I treat them like my friends. You always want to do the best for your friends. That's the way I feel about them.'

I haven't forgotten anything Eddie taught me and I still feel his presence when I am in the gym. Someday I will follow in his footsteps and pass his knowledge on. Eddie was a loyal, honest man and I will never forget him. He is the reason I became a world champion.

* * *

Cheryl went into labour in the early hours of 30 March and baby Wynona was born later that evening. My fight was only 2½ weeks away so I had to keep training.

* * *

Thell, Cheryl, Cheryl's mum and Wynona all travelled to Connecticut with me for my April fight. My friend Dennis picked us up at the airport. I'd met Dennis in 1995; he is a huge boxing fan. He has travelled around the world at his own expense to see me fight and has become one of my closest friends. Stuart flew in from Oklahoma and met us at the airport. The promoter made some excuse about why there was no transportation for us – I was only the main event, after all – so we all piled into Dennis's five-seater hire car with our luggage and my fight gear. I don't know how we did it.

I was still ranked number one by the WBC in the super bantamweight division, although I fought this fight at featherweight. I was told that the opponent I was scheduled to fight had apparently crossed the Mexican border and run off, so they'd brought in another Mexican, Oscar Salas, to fight me instead; however, the boxing world is small and after the fight Salas and I talked. He told me he'd been training to fight me for six weeks!

Salas was a tough guy, but I won every round on all three scorecards. It was hard to fight someone I hadn't prepared for, but, once again, I did what I had to do. I could have pulled out at the weigh-in but, being a professional, I fought on.

I had another fight scheduled for 19 May, four weeks later, against former world super flyweight champion Juan Polo Perez from Columbia. The fight was set for Corpus Christi, Texas. When I asked for a tape of him to watch before the bout, I was sent a tape of him fighting in 1990. If I'd sent him a tape of me fighting in 1990, it would have been of me as an amateur, fighting in the Commonwealth Games. This fight with Perez was the only one Mat didn't attend. We'd had a minor falling out over expenses. Understandably, I was thinking about him. When I was in the dressing-room, I was wondering if he had turned up and if he was sitting in the arena. He wasn't.

Thell was working with another fighter who fought right before me. It was getting closer to my fight and Thell wasn't there to warm me up. Stuart offered to hold the pads for me, but I didn't want to get sweat on his suit, so I sent him out into the arena for Cheryl. She came to my dressing-room in her sparkly dress and shoes. Of course, USA network, who were televising the fight, thought this was fun and filmed it. It went out live all over America. When Thell came into the dressing-room, I told him I was ready to go, so we left for the walk to the ring.

The Perez fight was a struggle for me. I went through the motions. I didn't want to hurt him. I didn't want to be in the ring. I wanted to walk away. I was thinking about Mat too much. I was bitterly disappointed that he failed to come to the venue, and in the circumstances I had difficulty motivating myself to fight for his promotional company. I realised then that I was boxing to please Mat, not to please myself.

I won seven rounds out of ten, but the judges scored it a split decision. I didn't really care. I had another cut on the side of my head (if I'm going to get cut, I'd rather it would be on the side of my head instead of above my eyes). Dennis, Richard – another

143

friend from Texas – along with Cheryl and Stuart, accompanied me to the hospital in Corpus Christi and sat there for most of the night while I waited to get my cut stitched up. To this day, Stuart, being an American, thinks it is the funniest thing to say 'Your head's cut', which is Belfast slang for you're talking nonsense! He never uses it in the right context, but it's always funny. While they were all sitting in the waiting room of the hospital, I was on the toilet. We had used water from the tap in the corner bottles and it didn't agree with me!

I looked awful during the Perez fight, even though I'd won. I was mentally unfit for it. Most people thought I was done then. But every cloud has a silver lining and I believe my struggle with Perez paved the way for the Hamed fight. In 1995, Hamed had knocked out Perez in two rounds.

14

POCKET ROCKET AND THE PRINCE

Wayne McCullough is one of the greatest Irish fighters of all time. In my opinion he's certainly the toughest. He has an outstanding chin, incredible stamina and a heart like a lion. He's been involved in some of the best fights anywhere in the world over the last decade and it has been my good fortune to have had the chance to comment on them. His bouts with Yakushiji, Zaragoza, Hamed, Morales and Larios were noted for their pace and ferocity. I am one of hundreds of professional boxers who marvelled at his implacable attacking style. Wayne McCullough is a fighter's fighter.

Barry McGuigan, former world champion
and TV commentator

Nothing had happened on the fight scene since the bout with Perez and I was becoming more and more miserable by the day. The summer months were passing me by and I still hadn't got a date to fight. I'd been praying day after day for something big to happen.

In early August Cheryl got a phone call from Stuart to say that the WBO featherweight champion Naseem Hamed had made an

145

offer for me to fight him. She asked for details and was told that it had been tentatively scheduled for 31 October 1998 and the venue would be the Convention Center in Atlantic City.

I was still in bed when she burst in the door. She woke me up and said I had been offered the fight with Hamed. It was the first morning in a long time that I jumped out of bed. I asked if she'd said yes – she had. She still hadn't told me where it was, when it was or how much I was getting paid, but I didn't care. I wanted to fight Hamed so badly I would have fought him for free. Well, maybe not for free . . .

I was having trouble again with the palm of my left hand and I had been praying to God every night to take the pain away. One night I woke up and it felt as if the pain was being lifted from my hand. I know God was working on me. My hand was perfect after that.

Things weren't going well in training. Kenny Croom hadn't been on the Vegas boxing scene for a couple of years, but I had been able to track him down. I asked Thell if he would work with Kenny and share the training fee for the Hamed fight if I brought him back. I loved working with Thell, but if he wasn't in the gym every day, no one was there to work with me. With Eddie gone, I'd felt as if there was something missing in the gym in the lead-up to the last two fights.

I had done a lot of pad work with Cheryl over the summer, but I knew, with the Hamed fight coming up, I needed a trainer who could be there for me. Cheryl is excellent on the pads and one of the best I have ever worked with, but she'll tell you herself she isn't a boxing trainer. She knew I needed someone who would be committed to getting me through the Hamed fight.

Thell didn't work with Kenny, so Thell and I parted ways – and, of course, Cheryl got the blame. But I make my own decisions. I went ahead and brought Kenny in to work with me.

In early September, Kenny and I flew to New York for the press conference to announce the Hamed fight. We trained in my hotel room. I shadow boxed and then Kenny would hold the pads for me. Mat didn't show up for the press conference and that bothered me. I thought he didn't care.

Hamed was characteristically hyping up himself and the fight.

He told the press it was my biggest payday and that I should spend the money wisely. I made sure he knew I'd been paid more than this twice before. He wouldn't let me get a word in but that was normal for him.

I set up training camp at Sugar Ray Leonard's Nevada Partners boxing gym, which was run by the referee Richard Steele. I didn't ask for private sessions; anyone and everyone was in the gym. I didn't mind; I had nothing to hide.

I got great sparring. Sergio Sanchez, whom I'd sparred with many times before, turned southpaw to spar me. He could mimic Hamed to a 'T'. Don Juan Futrell, a tricky southpaw boxer, also sparred with me. A couple of weeks before the fight I brought in the fighter who'd had Hamed on the canvas several times when they'd fought: my buddy, former world featherweight champion Kevin 'Flushing Flash' Kelley. Kenny visited Eddie to ask for his advice on the fight. He told him to keep Hamed moving to his left and not to let him land the big right hook. He said if I was able to do this, Hamed would look like an ordinary fighter.

I was being interviewed daily. I got calls and emails from journalists around the world. HBO came to Vegas and filmed a piece on Cheryl and me to show on fight night. This bout was huge. I'd never fought an actual featherweight before and Hamed had knocked out 18 opponents straight in his last 18 fights, so I knew it was going to be tough. A lot of the media said Hamed could punch like a heavyweight and even though I knew he could hit hard, I thought probably not that hard. Still, in my mind, I prepared for the worst.

We flew to Philadelphia on the Monday before the fight. It took us all day to get there. We travelled for about 12 hours and had to change planes on the way. Then we had to drive to Atlantic City. There is a non-stop flight, but this was the itinerary the promoter's travel people had provided us with. Mick Devine came over from Dublin to look after us. We were supposed to stay in Bally's Hotel, but Hamed and his team were staying there, so we decided to go to the Tropicana instead to save on any possible aggravation.

We went to the press conference on the Wednesday and it was like a media circus. About 99 per cent of the media gathered there agreed with Hamed that he was going to knock me out. When Hamed got up to speak, he said he was going to seriously hurt me and that it would be my last fight. In my opinion, in this business, boxers shouldn't say things like that. It is a very dangerous sport and we all know the risks. That shouldn't be what boxing is about. I can honestly say I have never wanted to 'seriously hurt' any opponent. That is just wrong. Of course, almost everybody in the room laughed along with him. I am a nice guy, sitting there minding my own business, but they took this for weakness.

I had to grit my teeth a few times. My Belfast-ness nearly came out. I wanted to rip his head off because of what he was saying, but I kept my composure. It was the best thing I could have done. Hamed tried to beat me psychologically, but I believe I had him beat a few years back when he fought in Dublin. I know he likes to get into a slanging match with his opponents, so I just sat there and smiled at him. I wouldn't play his games. Cheryl and Nicola did – even though they had told me not to stoop to his level; they couldn't help themselves that day.

Going into this fight, my track record spoke for itself. I'd never been off my feet, amateur or pro, so I don't understand how everyone could think Hamed was going to be the first person to knock me out. I wondered who had the better chin. I'd never been knocked down, but Hamed had, several times. Personally, I don't think Hamed fought the same class of opposition as me in my early career. When he did step up against Kevin Kelley to defend his WBO featherweight title, Kelley had him down and almost won the fight. Although Hamed came back to knock him out in the end, I think Kevin showed him up in that fight.

I was scheduled to do a public workout at Bally's Hotel on the Thursday afternoon. I wasn't planning to work out in front of all his people anyway, but that didn't matter because when I got to the workout at my time slot, Hamed turned up too – trying to play more mind games. Kenny and I left and just went back to my hotel suite to work out there instead.

This caused a commotion in the media: they reported that I wasn't training in the week of the fight. But all my hard work had been done. All I needed to do was keep my weight under control. I can work out in any space: my hotel suite was perfect, I didn't need a gym. Anybody that knows me, knows I'm always training and I'll always be physically ready for a fight.

Cheryl's family, Harry and my brother, Noel, and his son all came over for the fight. Christina and Sam weren't able to come because they'd just had a new baby, Dylan. Stephen Watson was filming *The Prince and the Pocket*, a documentary with clips of me training in Atlantic City, at the weigh-in and of Naseem at the press conference, which was televised in Belfast after the fight. Larry Hazzard, the New Jersey Boxing Commissioner, told Stephen in an interview, 'If anybody thinks the Prince is in for an easy night, they'd better think again.' He had seen me fight in the past and knew I was a tough warrior. Hamed was a really cocky guy. 'Wayne McCullough is a fighter I can do what I want with in a fight,' he said to Stephen, 'and I'll do it and I'll prove it to you.'

The weigh-in for the fight took place in a small arena and most of the audience was made up of either media or Hamed's fans. None of my fans could get in. That didn't stop them standing outside cheering and screaming my name. The boardwalk in Atlantic City was full of Irish pubs. They all had posters in their windows saying 'Support Wayne McCullough', so I knew the arena would be filled with my fans on the night.

Michael Flatley flew over from England to see me fight. He came to my hotel suite before we left for the arena to tell me how much he supported me and how proud he was of me. Michael is a huge boxing fan. He remains one of my best friends. Wynona was only nine months old and even though I took her to the fight venue, she stayed in my dressing-room with boxer Robert McCracken's wife, Karen. Robert had fought earlier in the night, and won.

Mat and Dan Goossen were at the fight. America Presents had been paid a lot of money by Hamed's promoter to permit me to fight under another promotional banner. Things were still a little strained with Mat, but I tried not to let it affect me like it had in the past. Cheryl and Stuart got credentials to get into the arena but there were no actual seats allocated to them and they ended up squeezing in beside the ringside physicians.

Michael and some of my other friends surrounded me as we walked to the ring to U2's 'Mysterious Ways', while the fans sang along. About 10,000 people were screaming for me. The atmosphere was electrifying. Since it was Hallowe'en and the fight was being billed as 'Fright Night', Hamed made his entrance to the ring through a mock graveyard. Other than his family and friends cheering for him, he got booed. After taunting some of my fans on the way, he was forced to run to the ring and it ended up being one of his quickest ring walks ever. I hadn't been totally motivated for my last few fights, but I was more than ready for this one. Hamed actually had the nerve to predict that he was going to knock me out at 2 minutes 28 seconds of round three.

Former world champion George Foreman was commentating for HBO that evening. He had been in Barcelona to watch the Olympic Games in 1992. 'I saw the love of the motherland. It made you feel like you were from Ireland,' he said. 'Everyone wanted him to win for Ireland. If he can recapture just a little of that excitement, we can have a good fight tonight.'

When the referee, Joe Cortez, brought us to the centre of the ring, Hamed said, 'Come 'ere, Wayne.'

'I'm here,' I replied.

I think this shocked him because his response was a timid 'Good.'

On the other side of the pond, Sky were televising the fight live in the UK. Barry McGuigan was one of their commentators along with Gary Jacobs and Jim Watt. Barry gave his 'keys to victory' – what we both needed to do to win – and then his prediction: 'I don't think it's as cut and dried as everybody thinks, although I do expect Naz to stop McCullough in the middle rounds.' Hearing that from my hero, and friend, hurt more than the punches I took that night.

Jim Watt was more gracious. 'McCullough is not a fool,' he said. 'He knows how hard Naz punches. I'm sure he'll pay more attention to his defence in this fight.'

Then, when asked by presenter Paul Dempsey if he thought Cheryl and Wynona being in the dressing-room played a part in my preparation for the fight, Gary Jacobs unbelievably replied with 'Shocking, shocking, shocking! His mind should be totally focused on the job. Fine, OK, his wife and his baby can be there, but not sitting in front of him in the dressing-room. He's getting ready to go and do a job.' Cheryl and Wynona have every right to be there. Also, Cheryl is not only my wife but my manager. And it certainly doesn't affect my performance. I gave the Hamed fight my all. Cheryl has been there from the start, and Cheryl and Wynona will both be there to the end.

* * *

Round one began with Hamed throwing wide right hooks, but I had prepared for this. He was a really awkward southpaw. He hit me on the chin, but I just shrugged my shoulders as if to say, 'Is that all you have?' When I went back to my corner after the first round, I said to Kenny, 'It's true, Kenny. He really does hit like a horse.' Since I'd prepared my mind to take his biggest shots, they weren't as bad as I thought they would be.

Hamed continued to try to knock me out in the second round, throwing big, wild shots but most of the time he was off balance. Even when he was throwing punches that missed, the HBO commentators would tell the viewing audience that he was landing. It was like he couldn't do anything wrong. George Foreman was the only commentator who was giving me a chance.

After the first couple of rounds, I saw blood coming from Hamed's mouth and I knew that I could hurt him. In the third round, with about 36 seconds to go, Hamed was trying to make his prediction come true. He threw a right uppercut followed by a left uppercut that caught me square on the chin, but I wasn't going anywhere. I stepped in and with his third-round 2:28 prediction ringing in his head, I threw a left hook that grazed the back of his head and his glove hit the canvas – a knockdown! I thought it was hilarious. I had him down at the exact time he said he was going to knock me out. Needless to say it wasn't called a knockdown and the fight continued. I hit him another right-hand on the bell that shook him up.

As I went back to my corner, I lifted my two hands in the air as if to say, 'I'm still here.' I told Kenny I was ready. After the third round Hamed started to run away from me. He knew he wasn't going to knock me out, so what else did he have? He had hit me with his best shots and I was still there. My game plan was to get close enough to him to work his body, but every time I got near he would pull me down from the back of the neck. What annoyed me the most was that he didn't receive a warning for it. My doctor diagnosed me with minor whiplash after the fight as a result of Hamed pulling me down.

In the fourth round I was trying to slow him by throwing left hooks to his body. Round after round, I was calling him on, asking him to stand and fight me. But Hamed was still looking for the one big shot, although he knew from early on that I wasn't going anywhere. I landed a good right hook near the end of the fifth round and Hamed backed off again. When Hamed landed a big shot, Larry Merchant of HBO commented, 'These punches have knocked a lot of other fighters down.'

In the sixth round, Hamed continued to move around, doing nothing, and then throwing one big shot. Seemingly even on the punch stat he was landing more shots, but that was a joke. After six rounds I thought I was doing well, but I knew going into the fight that I would have to knock him out to win because he was the favourite; he had sponsors and a big TV deal.

In the seventh round he was really negative, moving around doing nothing. He started doing the Ali shuffle and dropping his hands. Kenny told me before the fight that if Hamed started to mess about, I just had to put my hands up and back off him. HBO commentator Jim Lampley told the audience that Hamed had looked away from me and threw a punch that landed on my chin. In fact, Hamed had missed. I don't know what Lampley was looking at – maybe *he* was the one looking away.

As the seventh round drew to a close, Hamed held my head down and I thought this was my chance to work his body. Even though I was only throwing light body shots, my head was on his chest with his hands on the back of my neck and the referee allowed him to do it.

Hamed was extremely hard to hit. He looked easier to hit on tape. When he was moving around doing nothing but running away from me, it was frustrating; but I needed to keep my composure. In the eighth, Hamed wasn't willing to invest in the fight. The commentators were saying he was moving around too much. George Foreman said I was very strong.

The few fans supporting Hamed were now quiet and my fans were going crazy, chanting my name. In the ninth round I got close to Hamed and when he was pinned to the ropes, I landed a right-hand on his chin. I was doing my best work inside. 'This is what the Pocket Rocket needs to do,' said Lampley, 'make Naseem fight.' But that was easier said than done.

Hamed landed some good left uppercuts in the ninth, but I continued to stalk him and move my head, and slip under a lot of his shots. He was practically running away at the end of the ninth. My fans were totally amazing throughout the fight and their support kept me going.

In the tenth I stayed closer to Hamed and made him work more. He landed a good left-hand to the chin. But not to be outdone, I landed a double left-hand to his. He nodded at me, acknowledging that I'd hit him.

Throughout the fight Hamed was throwing back-hand jabs, which are illegal in boxing. I felt he'd got away with every dirty trick in the book. He landed a good straight right in the tenth – probably his best in the fight – and I put my hands up to him to say 'good shot'. I caught him with a sharp left-hand just as the bell rang to end the round.

I went out in the final two rounds and stepped up the pace. At this point, my nose was bleeding and his lip was cut. My left eye had a little lump on it, but I didn't let it bother me. After the 11th round I thought I was ahead but I knew the judges probably wouldn't have seen it that way. In the last round I pushed Hamed around the ring and I was able to get really close to him for the first time in the fight. The commentators said it would be a moral victory for me to have gone the full 12 rounds, but I wanted more than the moral victory. When the five-second warning from the timekeeper sounded, signalling that the end of the fight was coming up, I put my two hands in the air and did the Ali shuffle. Hamed copied me. The crowd exploded with excitement. I'd done enough to take the title from him, but I knew I probably wouldn't win on the cards. The final two rounds were clearly mine, but I didn't get them on the scorecards.

I hoisted Hamed into the air to show my appreciation for him. The commentators acknowledged that I was a good sportsman. They started making excuses for him, saying he had arrived in America late due to visa problems, but he arrived the same night as me. He had flown over from England by Concorde. My journey from Vegas to Atlantic City had taken longer than it had taken him to get there from England.

On the Sky telecast, Barry noted: 'It was a lousy performance by Naz. He wasn't on form tonight and I thought Wayne boxed very well, very bravely. Put up a good performance and kept the pressure on him and done the best he could. He was just under-powered and was unable to hurt Naz. But Naz was certainly not impressive tonight.'

Jim Watt was compassionate towards me: 'It's not often we have two winners in the one fight, but I think that's what happened tonight. Naz has won the decision, but Wayne McCullough has won the credibility. Put up the fight of his life. The difference is Wayne McCullough is used to having hard fights, and we forgot what a tough little number he is and how much pride he takes into the ring with him. We didn't give him credit for being the warrior that he is.'

When I was lifted up on my doctor's shoulders, the crowd gave me a standing ovation that nearly lifted the roof off the Convention Center. However, when Hamed was lifted up in the air, the crowd started to boo. He was quickly taken from the ring, unlike the champion he still was. There were reports of rioting and fans burning T-shirts with Hamed's face printed on them outside the arena, and whilst I don't support violent behaviour of any kind outside a boxing ring, this puts into perspective the mood among the fans that evening. There was a lot of respect between the two of us once the fight was over, and when we hugged in the ring after the fight, he told me I had unbelievable strength.

At the pre-fight press conference Hamed said he was in the best shape of his life. I'm glad he admitted to that beforehand because I didn't want him coming up with any excuses afterwards – he must have been in good shape to have been able to run away from me for 12 rounds.

The judges' scores were ridiculous: 116–112 (eight rounds to him and four rounds to me); 117–111 (nine rounds to him and three rounds to me); and 118–110 (ten rounds to him and two rounds to me). The scores were so varied. They were absurd and the fans showed what they thought of the decision with the booing. I was the first fighter ever to go the distance with Hamed in a world championship fight.

I told Stephen that I'd been hit harder before: Rabanales, Zaragoza and Bueno had all punched me harder. But Hamed was super-strong. I even had blisters on my toes from running after him, just like after the marathon with Bredahl some three years earlier.

I wanted a rematch. I deserved a rematch. His promoter, Frank Warren, even said we should do it again. I believe Warren would have kept his word and staged the rematch in Britain, but it never materialised and Hamed never fought for Warren again. The staff at the hotel had organised a party for me after the fight. Michael Flatley joined my family and friends and they made me feel like a winner.

Hamed had come to the States to win over the fans, but he hadn't worked out that I'd lived there for five years and had already built up a huge support. A lot of the fans had come from Boston, New York, Chicago and the surrounding areas, and almost everyone there supported me. A future edition of *KO* magazine shouted the words 'EXPOSED' across its cover, with a picture of Hamed and me. I had exposed him.

After the fight I was slapped with a lawsuit by my former trainer Thell because I had used Kenny in the fight. It was eventually settled, but I have never worked with Thell again.

I met Hamed again when he fought Marco Antonio Barrera in Las Vegas in 2001. His trainer phoned me and asked me to come to the MGM Grand to meet him. We got pictures together and he signed the gloves we fought in. I supported Hamed 100 per cent when he fought Barrera – he's a great guy when the cameras aren't on him!

Eddie's technical plan was right. I had made Hamed look ordinary.

15

PUSHED TO MY LIMITS

The Pocket Rocket is from a rare breed of men. That small percentage who truly understand the benefit of sacrifice and hard work. He is a good friend and a great fighter.

Kenny Croom, boxing trainer and friend

Along with Gary Jacobs' comment on fight night, *Boxing News* reported that it was tasteless that my wife and daughter were at the Hamed fight. I saw the editor, Claude Abrams, at a boxing match at the Hilton in Las Vegas a few weeks later and confronted him about the article. I said it was my choice to have them there and that I shouldn't be criticised because they mean more to me that anyone else in this world. He apologised for the article and I respect him for that – it takes a bigger man to say he's sorry.

* * *

Cheryl and I flew back to Belfast to celebrate Wynona's first Christmas at the end of 1998. The Hamed fight had been weeks before but the fans remembered the effort I put in and everywhere I went I was surrounded. I couldn't believe the response I got from the fans in Belfast. Cheryl and I would go out shopping and

I would end up standing signing autographs all day. I loved it. To me, fans make a fighter. Without the fans I would be nothing. Eventually, Cheryl would leave me at home while she went out Christmas shopping because she just couldn't get anything done!

* * *

My stock rose after the Hamed fight, even in defeat, and America Presents secured me a fight with Mexico's Erik Morales for the WBC super bantamweight championship on 8 May 1999. Training camp was held at Prince Ranch boxing gym in Las Vegas and Greg Hanley, the owner, let me train there for free. America Presents arranged for a boxer called Rudy to spar with me and I brought in another couple from California. On his first day of sparring, three weeks before the fight, Rudy stepped behind me and punched me near my spine. My left arm and leg went numb and I almost collapsed. But rather than stop, I turned southpaw and started throwing huge right-hands to try to knock him. I was so angry at him for using such a dirty tactic. He did it again and then held on to my left arm and tried to break it.

'What the hell are you doing?' I shouted at him. But I got no answer.

Everybody around me was furious. Kenny told me to stop sparring. I couldn't have gone on anyway. Kenny was rubbing my back, trying to help me, but I was in agony. Cheryl took me straight to my doctor, Sam Colarusso. He told me Rudy had missed my spine by about half an inch but had ripped a muscle on my back. Apparently, if he'd hit my spine, I could have been paralysed.

I couldn't run, the pain was unbearable, so I sat on an exercise bike twice a day from 15 April. I was hoping that I could still fight Morales. I didn't tell anybody what had happened. On 22 April, two weeks before the fight was scheduled to take place, I threw a punch for the first time since my injury. Cheryl held up the pads for me. After that first punch I broke down in tears. I was in so much pain and I knew the fight was going to be off.

Cheryl immediately called Morales's promoter, Bob Arum, to tell him what had happened. She asked if, instead of cancelling the fight, he would consider postponing it. I really wanted to fight Morales. Bob agreed and he kept his word. Morales fought in May and, following his victory, plans were put in place for us to fight in October 1999. I took time off to allow my back to heal. We flew to Belfast in May for a few weeks, and I started light training and was back to normal training by June.

In July, Dermot Lavery visited us in the US with his wife, Denise, and their son, Daniel. We went to the drive-in movies, which would, for most people, be an enjoyable night out. Not for me – disaster struck again. A dust storm erupted and I got some dust in my eye. It was really sore and when I rubbed it to try to get it out, I made it worse. I eventually had to go to accident and emergency, where the doctor told me I'd scratched my cornea.

Nevertheless, I wanted a warm-up fight before I fought Morales. My promoter was worried that I would get cut or injured in the fight, so they didn't want me to take it, but if I hadn't fought I'd have been out a year before stepping into the ring. I needed to get the rounds in. America Presents therefore arranged a fight at the Hard Rock Hotel in Las Vegas on 31 August 1999. I fought Len Martinez from Lincoln, Nebraska. Len's record was 17–5–1 with six KOs. As usual, I'd sparred over a hundred rounds for this fight and even though it was a warm-up, I treated it as if it were a world championship bout.

Len was a tough little fighter who never quit. I hit him some great body shots and some uppercuts to his chin that knocked his head back, but he kept coming back for more. Referee Kenny Bayless deducted a point from me for throwing a low blow but apart from that I won every round. It was a good win for me. Len gave me the rounds I needed to step up and fight Morales.

Len was delighted to go the distance with me. After the bout he said, 'I gave it my best. I went ten rounds with Wayne McCullough.' Len and I have stayed in touch by phone and email since that fight. We've become great friends. Cheryl's parents were visiting when I fought Martinez and the next day I went out and played a round of golf with her dad.

* * *

The fight with Morales was scheduled for 22 October on the undercard of the Naseem Hamed v. Cesar Soto fight at the Joe Louis Arena, Detroit, Michigan. When I arrived at our hotel, Morales was also checking in with his team. I know Morales's cutman, Miguel Diaz, from Vegas and I went up to him to say hello. I also shook Morales's hand but he had a shocked look on his face, as if to say, 'We're not supposed to do this.'

Morales had knocked out nine opponents in a row. He was 34–0 with 28 KOs, so I knew I was being brought in as the opponent. I was just happy to get the opportunity to fight him after being forced to pull out of the first scheduled fight in May. At the pre-fight press conference he stood up and stated he was going to do to me what Hamed couldn't do – knock me out. I just laughed at him. He said, '*Tú también puedes reír, si quieres,*' which his interpreter translated as 'You can laugh if you want to.' So I did. I was used to people telling me they were going to knock me out, so he wasn't saying anything I hadn't already heard. We both made weight easily.

Cheryl got a seat right behind Morales's corner this time. Miguel saw her and asked what she was doing on that side of the ring. He said she should be on the other side and they both laughed.

In the first round, Morales came out to knock me out. But he couldn't even push me back. He's only about an inch taller than me, but I fight small so he looked much taller. Near the end of the round he hit me with a good left uppercut right-hand on the chin. I banged my two gloves together. 'Hit me harder,' I thought to myself and pushed him back to the ropes. I hit Morales a cracking right-hand while he was on the ropes. Even though we traded shots and it went back and forth, I took the first round off the champion on the scorecards.

In his corner after the first round, Morales's dad, who is also his trainer, told him to keep his distance and stay away from me. Their plan had changed and now they wanted him to box me from the outside. They knew I would take everything he had so he wouldn't have lasted the whole fight had he traded with me from the beginning. A minute and a half into the second round Morales hit me a left-right combination to the chin followed by a left uppercut. I stepped back and did a little dance, banged my gloves together again and pushed Morales back.

Morales was, by far, the hardest puncher I've ever faced in the professional boxing ring. Round after round his power didn't diminish. When he hit me hard, I knew I could either go down or stay up and fight back. I chose to stay up and fight back.

I threw a good left-right to Morales's head in the third and my body work was great. He threw two right-hands at the end of the round and I did the Ali shuffle! Kenny told me in between rounds that I needed to push him back with my jab.

In the fourth round Morales continued to use his long jab and reach advantage. He hit me a right-left combination and I did another dance. I always came back and this time I landed a right-hand to his chin. He threw another good right-left combination to my chin, but I came straight back with a right of my own. He followed it up with a right to my body, but I fired back. Every time he hit me hard I threw a combination of my own and that kept him confused. In the fourth round he landed an overhand right that burst my eardrum. I had a ringing in my ear for the remainder of the fight.

In the fifth he lay on the ropes and I worked his body and then came up to throw punches to his head. The HBO commentator said he'd never gone through this kind of toe-to-toe battle. They said he was getting hit with more shots than he usually got hit with. Morales's face was starting to swell. He hit me twice on the back in the fifth round and I had flashbacks to Rudy's punch, but I put it to the back of my mind.

I was trying to throw a big looping left hook to his chin to stop him from landing his right-hand. I was cut on the left side of my head, on my sideburn. When I went to my corner, my cutman, Ray Rodgers, found the cut and got to work on it. Ray had been working with me since the Hamed fight in 1998. He is a great cutman and an even better person.

At the start of round seven, Morales and I stood toe-to-toe. We both landed good shots to the head and body. By the eighth round Morales was breathing heavily and his face was getting worse. I landed a good right-hand that sent him backwards to the ropes. I jumped on him but he came straight back at me. At the end of the

Taken just after I won the WBC
Belt in Japan in July 1995

Accepting a personalised football
shirt from the New England
Patriots owner, Robert Kraft

With Eddie Futch at his
89th birthday party

With Naseem Hamed in Las Vegas

Taken in 1999 after the
epic battle with
Erik Morales

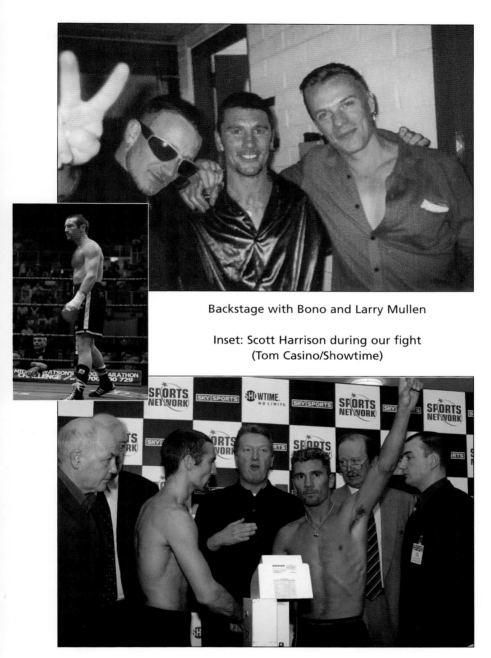

Backstage with Bono and Larry Mullen

Inset: Scott Harrison during our fight
(Tom Casino/Showtime)

At the weigh-in with Scott Harrison (Tom Casino/Showtime)

My long-time sparring partner, Brian Clements

Matt (left) and Craig – my sparring partners!

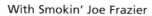

With Smokin' Joe Frazier

My co-manager Stuart Campbell with me and Michael Flatley

My family with Mike Tyson

With Kenny Croom in London

With Kevin Kelley at the Boxing
Writers Association of America dinner

Landing a right-hand on Oscar Larios's chin (William Cherry/Press Eye)

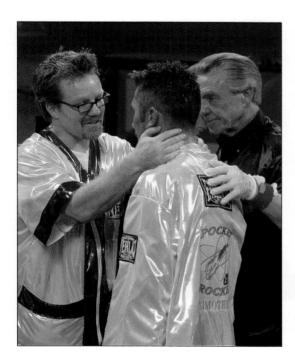

With Freddie Roach and my cutman, Ray Rodgers, after the first Larios fight (William Cherry/Press Eye)

With Freddie in his Wild Card Boxing Gym, Hollywood, California
(William Cherry/Press Eye)

Cheryl, Wynona and me (William Cherry/Press Eye)

round George Foreman said: 'That round had to go to McCullough.' I knew I was staying in there with Morales, I just didn't know how many rounds, if any, the judges were giving me.

We started the ninth round standing toe-to-toe, trading blows in the centre of the ring. My left jab was working well, but I didn't use it as much as I should have. My burst eardrum was giving me trouble. It was knocking my balance off, but, as usual, I wouldn't let anything stop me.

In the tenth round, Morales landed an overhand right to my chin. I shrugged my shoulders again as if to say, 'Big deal,' and fought straight back with a triple jab. Near the end of the round I threw a right-left combination which landed flush on his chin. He grabbed me. We neared the end of the round trading blows with his back on the ropes. I threw a left hook to his head followed by a left hook to his body. I'd made a lively comeback right at the end. Morales was literally lying on the ropes at this point. 'The Pocket Rocket did a lot of damage in the last minute of that round,' was HBO commentator Jim Lampley's summing up.

In between rounds 10 and 11, Morales was practically lying on his stool in the corner, but right at the beginning of the 11th round he hit me with a straight right-hand, so I knew he was still dangerous. A left-right to the head and a right-left to his body backed him onto the ropes again. Morales's punch power was amazing. Even though I knew he was dead tired, he was hitting harder with every punch in every round. With a minute to go in the round, he threw a left-right combination to my chin. With 30 seconds left, I fought back. I threw a 12-punch combination to finish off and let him know I was still there. I was cut above my left eyebrow but I hadn't realised. Ray took care of it for me.

I started the 12th round by throwing an overhand right that landed perfectly on Morales's chin and shook him. The crowd went wild. Morales kept fighting even though he was worn out. I landed a lot of right-hands in the last round instead of actually taking them. He threw everything he had at me and I was still running after him. We finished the fight just as we'd started it: toe-to-toe war on the ropes, both landing good shots. 'Stand and cheer everybody. You don't see many like that,' Lampley announced.

Ian Darke, commentating for Sky, said: 'This, for me, has been one of the best performances of Wayne McCullough's career and I've seen most of them. On another night, an effort as valiant as this would have taken him to a famous win, but this guy he's up against is class . . . Every fight fan from every country would have to take his hat off to those two fighters. That was like fights you read about from the old days. Incredible stuff. How did McCullough get through it?'

Morales won the unanimous decision. Two judges scored 116–112 (eight rounds to four) and the third scored 118–110 (ten rounds to two). I didn't expect the scores to be so wide. I thought the fight was closer and that I'd maybe only lost by a round or two. I was hoping for a rematch, but I didn't imagine he would give me one.

Cheryl has always been my biggest supporter and even if I lose a fight, she makes me feel like I'm a winner. After the Morales fight she presented me with one of the best gifts ever: a Rolex watch. She knew it was something I'd wanted for a long time. We flew to Belfast a few days later, where she organised a party at Belfast's Waterfront Hall in my honour. She had invited friends and family and before the end of the night she took us all outside for a spectacular fireworks display. It was so unexpected. I was speechless.

Every time I see Morales at fights in Vegas we talk through an interpreter. We've become good friends and have a lot of respect for each other. In round number two, when he hit me and I did a dance, he told me he thought I was crazy! I told him he was right! My stock after the Morales fight had gone up, just as it had after the Hamed fight, and I had broken Morales's knockout streak as well. I had fought competitively and everyone acknowledged that. But for some reason America Presents didn't set up another fight for me right away.

Later, on a website, Morales was asked for his three toughest fights. My fight came in at number two. He was quoted as saying: 'It was a physically demanding fight. McCullough took a lot of hard punches and gave it right back. He was very tough that night and I really felt it. I've always thought of this as one of my greatest wins.'

16

LIFE OR DEATH

Wayne may well have been kept secret in Ireland prior to his 1992 Barcelona Olympic silver medal success, but after that he was an internationally renowned star. Unfortunately for us over here, Wayne decided to pursue his career in the United States and what a fantastic career he has had. We have, however, been fortunate to have had him over a few times and he conducts himself as much as a gentleman outside of the ring as a warrior that he is inside. Personally, our relationship got off to something of a rocky start when the board initially would not grant him a licence to box here, arising from brain-scan queries, but once these were resolved he became a licence-holder of the board, and both he and his lovely wife Cheryl have treated me and all our officials with the utmost courtesy.

Simon Block, General Secretary of the BBBC
(British Boxing Board of Control)

I sat out of the ring for a year, but Kenny and I continued to work out in the gym every day. Cheryl's goal was for me to get a fight, but I started to focus my energy elsewhere. I had decided, since I had left school without qualifications, that I should do something educational. I chose fitness and nutrition. I figured I already had a head start on this since I'd been boxing for about 22 years. But I was wrong. I learned so much and I enjoyed every minute of it. In March 2000 I became certified in fitness and nutrition, and Cheryl began to think of ways to start up my own personal training business. I already had a boxing gym in my garage – a ring, heavy bag, speed bag and a ground-to-ceiling ball – so it wouldn't be that much of a stretch. One day we were chatting with a friend of ours, Tina, who mentioned that she wanted to lose some weight after having her first child. Cheryl had found a guinea pig!

She started working out with me, training three days a week – mostly boxing training – and the other days she would run on her own. I guaranteed her that she could lose the weight if she did what she was told. Some days she came over and was trying to work lighter than I wanted her to, so I'd shout, 'Come on, slacker' at her. That would make her work harder.

She had a target weight and, combined with healthy eating, she hit her goal well within the time frame. Her husband was impressed. She's just had another baby and is now back working out again.

* * *

I wanted to fight again in Belfast, so we went to meet Dan Goossen in his office in Vegas. It was the first time we'd had a heart-to-heart with him. Even though I didn't have a contract with America Presents at the time, they knew I was loyal and would stay with them. I told him what I wanted and left him to do his thing.

Dan, as usual, came through for me. He worked out a deal with Sky and he showed me the figures up front. He made me an offer that I was happy with and the fight was made. We secured a local promoter in Belfast and scheduled a fight for 20 October 2000 in the Ulster Hall. I was so excited. This was to be my first fight on home soil since 1995. I trained in Vegas for this fight.

The day before we flew to Belfast, Cheryl found out that ticket sales weren't going well. The arena only holds about 1,500 people. I was disappointed and I didn't want to go. What was the point if the fans weren't coming out to support me? I had campaigned to get a fight in Belfast and now it wasn't going to be a sell-out. Cheryl reassured me, saying, 'Wayne, you haven't fought in over a year – it's been five years since you fought in Belfast. The people don't believe that you're going to fight over there. They have to see you in the flesh. Once you get to Belfast the tickets will sell out and they'll be sending people away.'

We left for Belfast the next day and I arrived at the airport on 6 October to a hero's welcome. There were kids from a local boxing gym with posters and banners supporting me. There were friends and family there to greet us and even the press turned up.

I did my final preparation in a local boxing gym. I was on TV and in the papers every day, promoting the fight, and within a couple of days the arena had sold out. I attended the Northern Ireland v. Denmark match. At half-time Stephen Watson interviewed me for the BBC. I got to meet my boyhood football heroes George Best and Billy Hamilton. The week before the fight, I was invited on to UTV's *The Kelly Show* to promote the fight card. The fans couldn't wait to see me back in a Belfast ring.

On 12 October I did all my usual medicals for the fight. I had blood taken and then went to the Department of Neurology at Belfast's Royal Victoria Hospital for an MRI scan. Once a year every boxer who fights in Britain has to have an MRI scan, so this was routine. The MRI cost me £170. When I did the scan, I asked the technician if she could give me the results, but she told me they had to send them straight to the BBBC. I wondered why that was the case since I'd paid for it myself. I presumed everything was fine because I had a licence in Nevada, so I just let it go. I later found out that I had every right to be given the results.

I felt great. I knew I was going to be fighting in front of a sell-out crowd in my home town of Belfast and I was really looking forward to it. On the afternoon of 18 October, the last day of training and six days after going for the scan, the promoter of the card was hounding Cheryl, telling her he needed to see us. Since he didn't say what he wanted on the phone, I finished training before we went to his office. This was the day before the weigh-in and, after my final workout before the fight, my weight was fine, but I was tired, which is typical before a fight. I just wanted to get home, get something to eat and go to bed.

We drove to the promoter's office and Cheryl went inside to see what he wanted. I waited in the car with Wynona. Cheryl was back out within a minute. It was dark outside, but I could see the promoter and his girlfriend walking towards the car. I could sense something was wrong. The promoter came to my car window and Cheryl got back into the car.

'It's not life threatening,' Cheryl said. 'There was a problem with your scan.'

I asked her what she was talking about. Apparently, I wouldn't be allowed to fight on Friday. In fact, I would never fight again: one more blow to the head could kill me. I supposedly had a cyst on my brain. The promoter asked me to come into his gym and sit down and talk, but I just wanted to go. I was in shock. I drifted off into a world of my own.

Cheryl phoned Stuart Campbell and filled him in with what was going on, then we went to Cheryl's sister's house, where we stay when we're in Belfast, and told Nicola and Ian. Cheryl phoned my sister Christina and asked her and her husband to come over so we could tell them face-to-face. Then we told Cheryl's mum and dad. Of course, everyone was devastated. There were a lot of tears that night as the house filled with concerned family members. Cheryl phoned Mat in America and, surprisingly, he already knew. I thought I should have been told first.

I was beginning to think 'Thank God they caught it in time,' but then I also worried if I would die if, say, two-year-old Wynona accidentally kicked me on the head. As I walked upstairs to my bedroom that night, I hit my head on a picture on a wall. I was waiting to fall down and die.

Cheryl phoned Dan and they discussed getting a second opinion, mainly for peace of mind. They organised for me to go to Dublin the next morning and have a second scan done. Meanwhile Cheryl also phoned Marc Ratner, the executive director of the Nevada State Athletic Commission. The first thing he asked her was if I was OK. He was concerned about me as a person first and as a fighter second. Marc told her to get me back to Vegas and the commission would arrange for me to see some of the best doctors in the country.

Cheryl was still trying to convince me to go for the second opinion. I had almost given up. I wondered what the point was – would the results not be the same? I didn't want to put myself through it again. But I hadn't actually heard what the doctor needed to tell me nor had I seen anything in black-and-white, so I decided to go to Dublin the next day, if only to hear what the risks were. I got up at 4 a.m. and did 12 rounds of shadow boxing. It was the day of the weigh-in and I assumed if I got the all-clear in Dublin, I would still fight.

Roderick had provided me with a people-carrier and Cheryl rounded up everybody who wanted to drive with me to the Charlemont Clinic in Dublin. The journey is pretty much a blank for me, but I knew my team was there to support me. As far as I knew, the press hadn't heard anything about my situation; however, as we were sitting in the waiting area, *Sky News* was on and they were already reporting that I had failed a brain scan and that my fight was cancelled. I was astounded.

I got the results almost right after the MRI was carried out, unlike the first one in Belfast. One of the nurses from the clinic took us to Adelaide and Meath Hospital in Tallaght, where Dr McInerney sat down with me and explained what was going on. He had already seen the report from Dr Flynn in Belfast, even though I hadn't. He told me Dr Flynn thought I had an arachnoid cyst in a space between the brain and the skull – the cyst wasn't actually on my brain, something that was widely reported. The MRI films were right in front of us and he was pointing at the area where the cyst was supposed to be. He told me he didn't see any problems and he would allow me to fight. Before we left the hospital, he had two colleagues look at my MRI films and they gave me the all-clear too. Dr McInerney's report read:

> I cannot definitely demonstrate any abnormal fluid collections and no arachnoid cyst is demonstrated. The cerebrum and cerebellum show no significant abnormality except possibly slight diminution in volume of the frontal lobes.

We took the scans with us and started the drive back to Belfast. I was even more confused now. A press conference was scheduled for 6 p.m. at the Holiday Inn in Belfast to coincide with the weigh-in. When we got there, I sat in a separate room with Stuart and Cheryl, the America Presents matchmaker Tom Brown, my own doctor and one representing the BBBC. I told the BBBC doctor that I had a clear scan in my hand and I passed the films across the table to him. He said he couldn't read them as he was only a GP, so Cheryl picked up the scans and we left the room. The doctor left the hotel before the press conference even started. Was the fight back on or not? I presumed it was.

We went into the function room where the media were waiting. It was packed with journalists, family and friends. The cameras started clicking as soon as I walked in. The atmosphere was gloomy and all eyes were on me as everyone held their breath, waiting for the news. I sat down and the questions started flying at me and for the first time not about a fight. I didn't know where to look. I didn't really have an explanation or any answers for the press, because I didn't have them myself. I still hadn't seen any reports from the first doctor who had 'failed' me, so I honestly didn't know what to tell everyone. All I could say was that I had been told that I couldn't box again. After I said those words it finally hit me and I broke down in tears. Cheryl comforted me and the media went wild.

The weigh-in took place after the press conference. John Campbell, the Northern Ireland Area Council representative, allowed me to weigh in, even though he told me I probably wasn't going to be allowed to fight. John called out my weight and at this point I was still thinking the BBBC were going to change their minds and let me get into the ring. Although, looking back, I don't know if mentally I could have fought after the roller coaster of emotions I'd been on.

The fight card went ahead as planned, just without me. The BBBC told us they still had doctors in London going over my scans and I wouldn't be allowed to fight until their reports came through. A lot of fans wanted their money back, which was understandable since I was off the card, and their requests were granted.

On the morning of the fight, Cheryl, Sam, Stuart and I went to see Dr Flynn, the doctor who had 'failed' me, at the Royal Victoria Hospital. Stuart demanded to see the reports and we all wanted some answers. He was very forthcoming with his information and understood my situation. We discussed going back to America to see a neurosurgeon. He told us that would be the best thing to do since they would be more qualified in neurosurgery to give me answers. He didn't tell me I could never fight again. His report read:

> This study demonstrates a small extra-axial fluid collection (2x1 cm) in the anterior and inferior aspect of the left middle cranial fossa. It is of CSF signal on all sequences and represents a small arachnoid cyst.
>
> The remainder of the brain study appears normal.

I left Dr Flynn's office with hope. Maybe I wouldn't die with a blow to the head after all. Boxing was the last thing on my mind. I just wanted to know if I was going to live long enough to see Wynona grow up.

I had bought several extra tickets for the fight at the Ulster Hall for friends and family. I didn't ask for a refund. Cheryl and I went to the fight anyway to show our appreciation to the fans who had attended, but the arena was half-empty. That evening Cheryl and I were asked on to *The Kelly Show* again to talk about what had happened and where I was going to go from there, but I didn't know. I'd got to know the show's host, Gerry Kelly, over the years and I became a regular on his show each time I returned to Belfast. I could tell he was really concerned. I was emotionally drained with the events of the past 48 hours.

Cheryl spoke to Simon Block, general secretary of the BBBC, by phone on the Saturday night, the night after the fight was due to have taken place. He said he was going to Mexico the next day, but he'd be in Las Vegas in November and we could chat then. He promised her that my scans would be sent to their doctor in Oxford so he could report on them.

A couple of days later Cheryl, Wynona and I went to Donegal with Nicola and Ian. He and I played golf and I tried to relax. We even managed to joke that I should be wearing a crash helmet in case of flying golf balls. During our stay we got a call from a Belfast journalist who told me someone was trying to sell a story to his paper stating I had failed a brain scan in America before I came to Belfast. I thought to myself, 'I went away for a couple of days to clear my head and they won't leave me alone. I don't know if I am going to live or die, and someone is trying to make money off me.'

Cheryl told the journalist I wouldn't have done that. I'm a very honest person and if I'd failed a brain scan, I wouldn't have taken the risk. Plus, I'd be up for an Academy Award for the performance I put on at the press conference. No man wants to cry in public. Later that week, I played golf with the journalist's editor. I showed him my Federal ID card from Nevada, stating I was licensed to fight. His editor assured me the story would go no further. I later found out who tried to sell the story. What hurt me most was when I was at the lowest point in my life, people were still trying to beat me down with money as their main motivation.

On 29 October we flew home. Dr Margaret Goodman, the Nevada Commission physician, and Marc Ratner had organised for me to see one of the world's top neurosurgeons, a Dr Neil Martin, Professor of Neurosurgery at UCLA. Cheryl's mum flew over the next weekend. We picked her up at Los Angeles airport and on the Monday morning went to see Dr Martin. The first thing I asked was whether I could die from a blow to my head. He laughed, but not in a bad way. 'Whoever told you that was way off,' he said.

Dr Martin gave me a neurological examination to check my reflexes. He informed me he was going to have a meeting with three other neurosurgeons from across the country and it would take a few weeks to finalise their reports. We drove home and waited.

* * *

Simon Block was in Vegas for the Lennox Lewis v. David Tua fight at the Mandalay Bay hotel on 9 November 2000. I caught up with him because I wanted to meet face-to-face and ask him why I had not seen the other doctors' reports. I didn't get the answers I thought I was going to get and I got a little irritated. We parted on good terms and he assured me he would have the reports sent to me when he got back to England.

About this time we moved into a new custom-built dream home. Nestled in a suburb of Las Vegas, it was everything we'd ever wanted. But now, with my brain-scan scare hanging over our heads, neither Cheryl nor I were interested in the house. From that day I don't think either of us were truly settled there because it held so many memories of an unpleasant time in our lives.

In between times, Stephen Watson had arrived in Vegas to make a documentary called *The Fight of His Life* about my situation. When he asked how I felt about my medical problem, I told him how hard it had been for me. 'I thought I was dreaming,' I said, 'but there was nothing I could do about it.' This was the truth. It was now out of my control. No matter what I said or did, the BBBC would not change their mind.

I was hoping to get the report back from Dr Martin before Stephen left, however he had wrapped up filming and they were getting ready to leave for Belfast by the time it finally came through. I phoned to tell him what the report had said and he rushed back to my house with his crew to film my reaction to the news.

It was the evening before Thanksgiving, Wednesday, 22 November, when Dr Martin phoned our home at 11.20 p.m. Cheryl almost didn't answer; normally, she'd be asleep by then. She went into her office and listened silently to what Dr Martin had to say. Even though Thanksgiving is one of the biggest holidays in America, Dr Martin had gone into the office to get the reports and fax them to us. I couldn't have been happier. His report read:

> Examination: General exam: Fit, healthy young man, with no remarkable findings.
>
> Neurological exam: Alert, oriented, articulate. Memory intact. No cranial nerve, motor, sensory, or cerebellum deficit. Gait normal.
>
> Assessment: Small incidental asymptomatic CSF density area in anterior aspect of middle cranial fossa, most likely arachnoid cyst.

171

Medical Implications: I have reviewed this case with three microsurgical colleagues highly experienced with traumatic brain injury and sports-related microsurgical issues. We all agree that this small apparent cyst represents no significant threat in the context of normal activities and no treatment would be recommended. In the absence of the issue of boxing, a follow-up MRI scan in one year, while optional, would be a reasonable plan.

It appears that the cyst has been present since at least 1995 and has not changed or been associated with any brain injury over a period of time during which Mr McCullough has had approximately 10 professional fights. In fact, the cyst may well have been present since birth.

Arachnoid cysts of the middle cranial fossa, when much larger than in Mr McCullough's case, have been reported to be associated, in some cases, with subdural (intracranial) hemorrhage. The small size of this cyst suggests that it would be associated with very low, and probably insignificant, risk of hemorrhage. However, because of our lack of experience with similar lesions in contact-sports participants, we would not be able to certify that this finding represents no risk in the context of professional boxing.

In conclusion, with respect to boxing, we believe that this small cyst represents only a very small, and probably insignificant risk. If Mr McCullough decides to continue fighting, it would be advisable to have follow-up MRI scans done before future boxing matches, to be sure that no change has developed in the cyst, or in the adjacent brain.

While this report was very positive, Dr Martin hadn't ruled out all risk, so I still wanted to see the BBBC doctors' reports before I made my decision about whether to fight again.

Finally, six days later, on 29 November 2000, the BBBC faxed me the report from Peter Richards, their doctor in Oxford. When I saw it, I was speechless.

1.Wayne McCulloch [*sic*]

There is a small CSF collection at the tip of the temporal lobe on the left. I personally would have considered it a prominent subarachnoid space rather than a true arachnoid cyst, but as it has been named an arachnoid cyst by three of the country's leading neuroradiologists, I would have to defer to them in that judgment. However, the reported cases of haemorrhage associated with arachnoid cysts have been in much larger ones and I would consider, with a cyst of this size, that Wayne McCulloch is not at any greater risk of an intracranial haemorrhage than any other boxer and would have no concerns about allowing him to continue with his boxing career.

Thoughts swirled in my head. Was I cleared by the BBBC as a result of this report? Would I get my BBBC licence? Could I go back now and fight in Belfast? As it turned out, this was to be just the beginning of a long dispute with the BBBC. Cheryl and Simon began exchanging letters after we had received Peter Richards's opinion. On 30 November 2000, Cheryl sent a letter asking the current status of my boxing licence application. On 1 December, Simon responded:

I must advise you we are not in receipt of and have not considered any application from Wayne McCullough to hold a full boxing licence within our jurisdiction. An application was sent to us on Wayne's behalf for him to be granted an Alien Permit. As we know and have discussed it was not possible for the Board to grant this permit. That effectively concludes the matter as far as the Board is concerned. However, if it is your husband's intention to make a formal application then prior to doing so he needs advice from a Licensed British Manager or Agent about the various formalities involved.

Cheryl replied that same day, asking him for the 'formalities' necessary to start the process of applying for a BBBC licence. Simon replied with:

I have posted you today an application form for a professional Boxer's Licence which Wayne must complete in full.

I also fax herewith and have enclosed with the application form an advisory letter which is primarily aimed at a young Boxer turning professional for the first time. Wayne may find this helpful when he makes his application.

I have not addressed any medical requirements in this letter but it may well be, if it is possible to take any application further, that these will have to be addressed in due course.

For the avoidance of doubt I would stress that neither myself nor the British Boxing Board of Control is inviting Wayne to make an application for a Boxer's Licence but if he wishes to do so then it will receive the proper consideration.

So I sent in the application form and all the necessary medical requirements. After getting the report from Dr Martin and Peter Richards, I was sure my application would be granted and I could get on with my career. On 15 February 2001, Dan received a letter stating that the stewards of the board had considered my application but they were unable to grant me a licence because I would be 'unable to be passed fit to box' under their jurisdiction. When Cheryl wrote to Simon asking why my licence had not been granted when his own board doctor passed me fit to fight, he responded as follows:

With regard to Mr Peter Richards, the Stewards have great regard for his opinion but at all times the decision on whether or not to grant a Licence or a Permit rests with the Stewards not with any other person.

In March, Stephen Watson came to Vegas to visit us. Stephen and I went to the Mandalay Bay to see Evander Holyfield fight John Ruiz. That night we met a lot of celebrities. I introduced Stephen to many world champion boxers. During one of the fights we spotted movie star Tony Curtis. He was only about 30 feet away from us. He shook his fist towards us, so I looked behind me to see who he was looking at. Stephen did the same but then he realised he was looking at me. I shook my fist back at him and he smiled. A few weeks later I saw him again at fights in Las Vegas and approached him for a picture. 'Anything for you, Wayne,' he said. It was so hard to believe that he is a fan of mine!

In June I was invited to the World Amateur Boxing Championships in Belfast. I co-hosted an evening TV show for a week on BBC and commentated for them during the day. I enjoyed every minute of it. I had also started writing for the Seconds Out website and I was sending them daily coverage from the championships. Even though I had no prior experience in journalism, I felt I took to it like a duck to water.

I met Simon again in November at the Mandalay Bay when he was in Vegas for the Lennox Lewis v. Hasim Rahman II fight. We chatted again and I asked him if he could send me the reports from October 2000, even though 13 months had passed since. He thought I had received them and said he would send them straight over when he got back to England. He kept his word.

* * *

On 23 November 2001, the reports from October 2000 were finally faxed to me. I read them in disbelief. The first, from consultant neuroradiologist Dr Kendall on Tuesday, 17 October 2000, read: 'MRI Brain: There is a cavum septae pellucidae. No significant abnormality. The skull vault is of normal thickness.' The second, from Dr Thakkar, likewise a consultant neuroradiologist, dated Thursday, 19 October 2000, read: 'A small middle fossa arachnoid cyst is noted. Comparison with previous films, if any, would be helpful to complete the evaluation.' Finally, dated Monday, 23 October 2000, Dr Moseley wrote:

> Images were obtained in axial, coronal and sagittal planes. There is, as reported by Dr Kendall, a small arachnoid cyst in the left middle cranial fossa. I would doubt whether this was of significance as regards an increased risk of haemorrhage, but that possibility cannot be entirely excluded. I very much doubt that there are

adequate data on the prognostic significance of a cyst of this size.

On 23 October 2000, my MRI films were then sent on to Peter Richards for a final opinion, and his opinion was that I was at no higher risk of a haemorrhage than any other fighter.

Stuart followed up with a letter to the BBBC soon after we received the doctors' reports, advising them that there was no medical reason why I should not be able to box in the UK. He wrote that they were stopping me from making a living. Many letters were exchanged between Stuart and the BBBC, but I didn't know how much more I could take. I was having a mental breakdown.

A friend recommended I get some professional help. She suggested I see Dr Matez, a hypnotherapist whom she had once consulted. In the beginning I wasn't really interested because, to be honest, I didn't care if I lived or died. I didn't care about anyone or anything. I was at the lowest point in my life. I wasn't suicidal, but if I'd died, I wouldn't have cared. I know this was selfish, but I couldn't help what was going through my mind. I knew I needed to do something before things got any worse.

When I thought about hypnotherapy, I pictured a doctor swinging a pocket watch in front of my face. To me, therapy was such an American word and I associated it with storylines on TV shows and movies I'd seen, but it was not like that at all. Dr Matez talked me through what was going to happen. I sat on a recliner in a dark room and put earphones on while I listened to Dr Matez talking to me from another room. I was really relaxed and I told him things I've never told anybody. I talked about the BBBC doctors and their medical reports, and he listened. He asked what my main concern was. I expressed my fears about boxing. I told him I couldn't get into a boxing ring. I imagined the ropes around the ring as bars and when I walked up the steps of the ring, I just couldn't get through.

After my first session he told me I was going to have a very vivid dream and that I would remember it when I woke up. I still wasn't convinced this was going to work, but I knew I needed to give it a go. That next morning I woke up and remembered every single thing from my dream the night before. I wrote it down and told Dr Matez in my session the next week.

His interpretation of my dream was that, among other things, I was vulnerable and looking for a new start. I knew he was right. He told me I was holding back and that I was scared but there was nothing to be afraid of. It wasn't going to be any different in the ring now than it had ever been before. He also said the day I got the news, a part of me died. I was reliving that day over and over again in my mind. He said he could help me get past it. And he did.

I visited Dr Matez once a week for six weeks and I can honestly say he cured me. I thank God every day that he was sent into my life to help me get through it.

* * *

Early in 2001 America Presents secured a fight with Willie Jorrin for the WBC super bantamweight championship. The plan was to bring him to Dublin. Cheryl sent my scans and reports to Professor Philips, who reported on them for the Boxing Union of Ireland. His conclusion read:

> It would appear that the imaging performed on Wayne McCullough going back to 1993 shows evidence of a small left temporal fossa arachnoid cyst and small cavum septum pellucidum which have not increased in size as far as we can determine by comparison of CT scans and MRI scans. While these images cannot be precisely compared it is nonetheless my opinion that there have been no obvious changes in these findings going back to 1993. In addition there is no evidence of any injury to the cerebral parenchyma in any of the CT scans or MRI scans. It is likely therefore that the small arachnoid cyst has been present for many years and may have been present since birth. While cavum septum pellucidum is a finding in boxers it may also be a developmental abnormality with no significance.
>
> I have read the medical report by Dr Neil Martin, neurosurgeon in the United States, dated 3rd of November 2000. Based on those clinical observations I would

conclude that Wayne McCullough is a fit and healthy boxer with no clinical evidence that he has ever sustained an injury to his brain.

In summary, therefore, it is my conclusion that none of the findings on the MRI scans can be definitively attributable to his boxing activities. In addition the findings have not changed over the years as far as I can ascertain going back to 1993. Wayne McCullough has been examined by a highly reputable neurosurgeon known to me in the United States and he has found him to be fit and well. It is my recommendation therefore that Wayne McCullough be considered by the Boxing Union of Ireland for a boxing licence. If he wishes to proceed I would be happy to examine him on your behalf in order to confirm Dr Neil Martin's findings. I would recommend that Wayne McCullough have an MRI scan and neurological examination after every major professional fight. If any change was detectable on the MRI scans or any abnormality was found on clinical examination, he should not continue to be licensed.

However, since I had applied for a BBBC licence again, and they had denied me, we couldn't get a TV network in the UK to broadcast my fight while I was under suspension by the BBBC. I had now missed out on another world-title fight.

Dan told me I would probably have to fight in the States until we could get the problem sorted and the BBBC suspension lifted. He scheduled a fight against Alvin Brown from Kansas for January 2002. I applied for my Nevada boxing licence and, after undergoing all the necessary tests, was given a clean bill of health and a licence.

I was set to fight Brown on the undercard of Joel Casamayor, whom I had fought in the Olympic final, and Acelino Freitas. Showtime was broadcasting my fight and I was so grateful to them because they were the only TV network in the world that would touch me. I was a bit nervous going into this fight because, even though I knew I wasn't going to die, those words from the promoter back in 2000 were still in the back of my mind.

It was my first time in the ring since I'd fought Morales in October 1999. I was really excited. Especially to be fighting in Vegas, as it had been my home town since 1993. The Nevada Commission had taken great care of me, not only as a fighter but also as a person.

Alvin Brown had a decent record: 17–4 with six KOs. He was brought in to see if I could still compete at the top level. If I'd struggled with him, everyone would have said the layoff hurt me. For him, this was his big chance. He would have a worldwide audience and if he could beat me, a former world champion, he would be on top. I saw Brown at the weigh-in and shook his hand. I don't hate any of my opponents, I'm just going out to do my job.

I hadn't stopped training since the brain-scan scare in 2000. Just before the start of the fight, I hit myself hard on the chin with both hands. Boxing again was now a reality. Steve Albert, the Showtime commentator, said, 'Sometimes in boxing the word "tough" is overused but never is it more applicable than with the Pocket Rocket Wayne McCullough. All you had to do was witness his last fight with hard-hitting Erik Morales. He may be too tough. He's given his share, but he's taken a lot of punishment as well.'

The opening bell rang and I walked straight out and threw a three-punch combination. I was slipping the punches well, but Brown was swinging wild shots, probably thinking that with my layoff he could catch me cold. He'd been active while I had been sitting on the sidelines.

I hit Brown with a left and a right 30 seconds into the fight and I wobbled him. He looked like he was ready to go down. I was hitting him with my left hook to the body and it was working beautifully. I was immediately back to my old ways, throwing loads of punches and walking forward. I stunned him with a good right-hand that sent him back towards the ropes with a minute to go in the first round. I knew my body work was really hurting him and I had thrown well over a hundred punches at this point.

With about thirty seconds to go of the first round, he hit me with two solid overhand rights and then a left. Bobby Czyz, a former world champion commentating on Showtime, said I 'barely flinched', but instantly I thought, 'He hit me a good shot but I'm still here.' That was the last time I thought about my MRI scan. I threw over 150 punches in the first but, as always, I was just getting warmed up!

I started just as fast in round two as I had in round one. Brown tried to move around a bit more, but I was stalking him and wouldn't let him go anywhere. I hit him with a straight jab and a right to the body. He fell up against the ropes but stayed on his feet. The body shots were hurting him more and more. But he was still in there. He hit me another two right-hands, but I just shrugged my shoulders at him. I didn't move. 'He's got a granite chin,' Albert said. It wasn't the first time I'd heard that but I was trying not to keep proving it.

Brown was trying to keep up with me, but he was fading. He landed another big right-hand, but I came back and hit him with two rights of my own. My punches were so much more effective than his. I threw a long left hook to his chin and he dropped to the canvas. He got up, but he was unsteady. I went after him, stepping in to throw a punishing left hook to his body, followed by a right to his head, and he wobbled. A left to his body put him down again and he was counted out at 2:43 of round two. Up until the point of the stoppage, I had thrown 113 punches. I was just getting started.

I prayed to God before the fight and asked if boxing was still for me to let me know when I got into the ring. When I stepped through the ropes for the first time in 27 months, I felt peaceful and at home. I put all the anxiety behind me. I was looking ahead to competing in bigger fights. I was sharp as a razor against Brown and I looked like I'd never had a layoff.

I received my first pay cheque since October 1999 and it felt good to be making money again. Cheryl was sick for a couple of weeks after the fight and, as she normally takes care of finances, she didn't get around to depositing my cheque from America Presents immediately. When she did, it bounced. I eventually got most of my money from that fight, but I didn't get it all.

* * *

In March, our friend Laura Serrano and her husband, Oscar, were planning a trip to Mexico to visit family and friends. Laura was a world champion and is one of the best women fighters I know. They came to see us before they left and to pick up my gloves from the Zaragoza fight and have him sign them. I also asked her to get me a photo of him to hang in my boxing gym. When they returned from their trip, she had the gloves but said he didn't have any photos the day she met him, so she had taken a photo of him instead. She handed me the photo, with him pointing to the plaque he received for taking part in the WBC Fight of the Year 1997. It was the bout in which I had fought him. I was shocked, to say the least. I had never seen any such plaque.

I phoned Mat and he said he got it in 1998 at the WBC convention but hadn't sent it to me. When I finally received it, the plaque was in three pieces.

America Presents folded later that year, so I was on my own again. Even though I didn't have a licence in the UK, I had a win behind me, and that made a difference.

Mat was a big part of my life at the beginning of my career. The last time I saw him was in 2004 when he drove to Vegas with his kids for spring break. We hadn't spoken in over a year before that. I had wanted to stay in touch, but he'd changed his numbers and moved house.

* * *

Cheryl had been in talks with Frank Warren from Sports Network, a UK-based boxing promotional company, and he was interested in signing me up. We worked out a deal and, pending the approval of my licence, I was going to be fighting for them.

I reapplied for my BBBC licence. We sent all the information – MRI scans, doctors' reports, blood work – to the BBBC and advised them that I was going to be fighting on 8 June 2002 in the UK. Cheryl, Wynona and I flew over to Belfast to finish training for the fight. I knew there was no medical evidence to suggest I couldn't fight, so I was confident they would grant me a licence and allow me to box. I met with the Northern Ireland Area Council in late May and they recommended I be granted one; however, on 31 May 2002, Simon responded to my application with this:

> I am obliged to confirm that it will not be possible for a decision to be made with regards to your application for a Boxer's Licence prior to the end of next week.
>
> The London Imaging Centre have confirmed with me this morning that they have received the plates dispatched from America and these will now be reported on by a Consultant Neurologist. Following receipt of their report almost certainly we will require a further report from a Consultant Neurosurgeon and a Consultant Radiologist. As these consultants will require sight of both the report and the plates it is not going to be possible for these to be reviewed and reported on prior to the end of next week.

Obviously I couldn't fight on 8 June. I was disappointed and wondered why it was taking so long. I knew that even when the other doctors mentioned in Simon's letter gave their opinions, the Board's decision would be final. Finally, the reports came through. The first, from Dr Thakkar, whose name I recognised from one of the reports from my first MRI scan in 2000, noted:

> Comparison is made with the previous examinations of 12.10.00 and 11.12.01.
>
> MRI Brain 01.05.02 (U.S.A.)
>
> No interval change. In particular the small middle fossa arachnoid cyst noted on the left side of has remained unchanged in size. The post contrast axial scan shows at least one vessel crossing the arachnoid cyst (image 6). This finding was also present in the previous examination of 2001. No new features.
>
> MRA of the Intra Cranial Vessels: Normal appearances.
>
> Conclusion: No interval change. Left sided small middle fossa arachnoid cyst remains unchanged in size and shape.

After this an almost identical report came through from Peter Richards, which read:

Dear Simon,

Thank you for sending me the scans of Wayne McCullough. My comments are from the perspective of a neurosurgeon and should not be considered as formal neuroradiological reports.

I have available to me three MRI scans, one from the Royal Hospital dated 12th October 2000 and two from Las Vegas dates 11.12.01 and 5.1.02 respectively. I do not have Mr McCullough's fighting record.

The MRI dated 12.10.00 shows a small cavum septum. This has not changed in the scans of December 2001 and January 2002. In addition, there is a small CSF collection at the tip of the right temporal lobe. Again, this had not changed in size in the following two years. As I have indicated before, I would have labelled this CSF collection as a prominent subarachnoid space, whereas I note Drs Kendal, Moseley and Thakkar have noted it to be a small arachnoid cyst.

Whilst prominent subarachnoid spaces would be considered variants of normality, arachnoid cysts would be considered abnormal. However, I would consider whichever way you label this CSF collection, it is at the borderline of normality. I do not consider Mr McCullough at any greater risk than any other boxer of subdural haemorrhage as a result of this small CSF collection. I do not consider it equivalent to the risks associated with large arachnoid cysts of the temporal tip.

The MRI scan from Las Vegas in January 2002 includes an MR angiogram. I can see no abnormality on this.

I therefore have no concerns about Mr McCullough continuing to hold his boxing licence on the basis of these scans.

We were told it still had to wait for a response from Professor Lees, Professor of Neurology in London. Whatever he said was to be the final report on my case and would determine whether or not I would get my licence in the UK. By this stage, Robert Smith, the assistant general secretary of the BBBC, had taken over my case. Professor Lees wrote:

> I feel that, provided Peter Richards is happy with him boxing, then I am too.

But Peter Richards had been happy for me to box in 2000.

When Professor Lees' report came through, Cheryl and I looked at each other. We were shocked beyond belief. All we could do was laugh. Just like the other reports I had received, I was waiting to see if one of the reports said I shouldn't box again, but there wasn't one. Robert Smith phoned Cheryl on 24 June 2002 to inform her that I had been granted my British licence. He also said the BBBC would be issuing a press release to announce it. This read: 'The Board has granted to boxer Wayne McCullough a licence as a professional boxer following changes in the way in which the Board seeks independent consultant advice in respect of brain scan queries.'

Simon Block and Robert Smith worked on my case for over two years and without their help I would never have received my licence. I know they didn't make the medical decision in the beginning. I have no hard feelings towards the BBBC having missed out on work, even though I was in the prime of my career. But I can't turn back the clock.

It was one of the happiest days in my boxing career, as I knew I would be able to fight on British soil again. It also confirmed that there was nothing wrong with my brain scan to begin with. I had probably fought my whole career with the cyst in my head, not on my brain. Arachnoid cysts are typically congenital and it was more than likely I was born with it.

Cheryl and I had to get help to understand all the medical terminology in the reports, but it was all worth it in the end. It had been the biggest fight of my career, but I came out on top.

* * *

Sports Network would be promoting my fights now that I was licensed to fight in Britain. We had worked out a good deal and I signed a two-year contract in April 2002. My goal was to fight in Belfast again and that was what they were working towards.

My first fight with Frank Warren was scheduled for 14 September 2002 in Bethnal Green's York Hall, the most famous boxing arena in London. I had asked Frank to set up two fights within two months so that I could keep busy, and he had. My second fight, barring injuries, was pencilled in for 2 November in Belfast. Most of my sparring was done with Brian Clements and Kevin Kelley in my gym. Another fighter, super featherweight Arturo Quintero, also helped me out. I was ready. I was in great shape.

Cheryl and I had been invited by our friends William, a professional photographer, and Toni to attend their wedding just outside Belfast so we left Vegas earlier than usual for an out-of-town fight. We thought it would be a good opportunity to spend three months in Belfast. We wanted to see if we could adapt to living there again, as we'd contemplated moving back. We got everything organised and then dropped our adorable boxer dog, Champ, off with friends. We stayed with Nicola and Ian in Belfast and I trained at a local boxing gym. About four days before the fight we flew to London to stay at the Britannia International in Canary Wharf. Everything was running smoothly. York Hall was sold out and the fans were terrific. They had come out to show their support. I'd been away from British boxing since 1995, when I had fought Bredahl in Belfast. My good friend Larry Mullen flew to London and walked me to the ring. Steve Collins was also at ringside cheering me on.

Right before I left my dressing-room, Sky TV's Ed Robinson came in and interviewed me about getting my licence back and fighting in a British ring. 'I just want to go out there and enjoy myself,' I told him. 'I love getting into the ring. I can't wait to get in there tonight.'

I walked in to U2's 'Beautiful Day' and, for me, that's exactly what it was – a beautiful day. I could barely hear Michael Pass, the ring announcer, say my name because of the cheers. And I knew where Cheryl and Stuart were because Frank Warren always gave them front-row seats!

The fight was shown live on Sky and delayed on Showtime in the USA. My friend Dennis flew over from San Francisco and my doctor, Sam, had flown over from Vegas. Since the Hamed fight, he'd been giving me a massage on the day of every fight.

I was up against Johannes Maisa from South Africa. His record was 17–3 with 11 KOs. I wasn't as nervous for this fight as I had been against Alvin Brown in January; it felt good to be fighting in Britain. Maisa's game plan was to try to out-work me and push me back. He started the fight trying to push me towards the ropes. He was fast, but sloppy, so I just started boxing on the back foot like I had in my amateur days. With a minute to go in the first round, I knew he had no power and he wasn't going to give me any trouble.

The second round was more or less the same as the first. Maisa tried to force the fight but I boxed and moved. I think he thought I was going to trade with him and he was surprised when I didn't. With about a minute to go in the second round, I hit him with a left to the chin and I wobbled him. He looked ready to go, so I stepped in. I caught him with another left hook that rocked him once more. I was picking my shots and taking no punishment. I had him trapped on the ropes with 30 seconds to go and I hit him a great right-hand on the chin. He stumbled back but was saved by the bell.

In between rounds Kenny told me to keep boxing and not to trade with Maisa. Not that he could hurt me, but Kenny didn't want me to take any unnecessary shots.

Maisa hit me with a nice right-hand in the third. But I got back on to my jab. As he tried to force me to the ropes, I hit him with a right uppercut flush on the chin. I was picking my shots but still throwing an average of 150 punches per round. As Maisa got slower, I got faster.

In the last minute of the third, I hit him a right to the head followed by a left to the body. I knew the body shot really hurt him. He slid along the ropes and I landed another right-hand to his chin. He dug deep and stayed in there. Just before the bell, I hit him a left-right to the head and he looked up to the ceiling as if to say, 'I need some help.' The commentators saw it too, remarking, 'Maisa knows he is in a very deep ocean.'

I started the fourth round still taking my time, moving around the ring, picking my shots. I pinned him on the ropes and threw a left hook to his body. He almost fell through them. I threw a big right uppercut that landed square on his chin. He was taking a lot of punishment now. I threw a right-hand that landed on his chin. Commentating from the press row, Ian Darke said: 'McCullough looks as if he's enjoying this . . . [it's] almost as if he's venting his frustration at all the time he's had to be away from the business he loves.' Poor Maisa!

A big left and right to the chin rocked him again and he stumbled back to the ropes. I threw over 30 punches before the referee Richie Davies stepped in to save him. The fans were on their feet, giving me a standing ovation. Darke commented, fans 'know world class when they see it'.

A friend of mine got up onto the ring apron and gave me a big hug and a kiss. I brought Wynona into the ring. I'm sure it didn't go down too well with some people, but it's what I wanted. She was so excited and loved the attention.

It was good to get the fight over with because I knew I had another one coming up six weeks later. Frank Warren had arranged for my next fight to be back in Belfast and I applaud him for that. I was looking forward to it. The fight was going to be held at Maysfield Leisure Centre and, compared to the last time I fought at Maysfield, Warren said he could have sold out the arena four times over. All the tickets were gone a few weeks before the fight.

My friend Darryl acted as security for me at the fight. Kenny, Ray, Sam and Brian flew back over from the States to work my corner. My brothers-in-law, Ian and Sam, walked me to the ring. Dennis had flown over in his second trip to the UK in two months to support me. Stuart brought his wife, Tiffany, over and she loved her first visit to Belfast. She still talks about the wonderful time she had there. Sharon and Caroline from The Corrs sat ringside with Caroline's husband. I kissed Wynona in her grandmother's arms on the way to the ring. The atmosphere was breathtaking. I was home and I was happy.

I was fighting Nikolai Eremeev from St Petersburg in Russia. He had a record of 18–5–2 with seven KOs. We fought at featherweight, even though he had mostly fought at a higher weight class. Boxer Alex Arthur came from Scotland to support me, with his girlfriend. He had stopped Eremeev in six rounds at super featherweight, so I knew Eremeev was going to be tough.

Eremeev moved around well in the first round. He was using the whole ring. He couldn't punch very hard, but I found it hard to catch up with him. After about a minute into the round, I was able to get closer. I threw a right uppercut, followed by a right-hand to his chin that sent his head backwards. He quickly found out that I could punch and he started to back off. I threw 117 punches in the first round.

In the second round I jumped straight on him. He was still trying to move, but he couldn't get away from me. Every time I hit him to the body I was hurting him. He was a good, smart boxer and I could see why he had given a lot of other boxers trouble. I threw a left hook to the body with a minute to go in the second round and he covered up and moved away. I stalked him with rights and lefts to the body. They were hurting him and he was tiring. I finished the round with an overhand right to his chin. I threw 135 punches in the second round, but I was raring to get back in for the next one.

He faded in the third and my pace was faster. He was struggling. I threw two big left hooks to his body and a left-right to his head. He threw a jab in my face and turned away. It was only a matter of time before he was going to go because I was landing right hooks at will. I threw a 12-punch combination as he ran around the ring, trying to get away from me. I hit him a right-hand that sent his head backwards. He looked confused. Eremeev had a little success when he threw a left-jab right hook that landed on my chin and I knew he was still in the fight, so I had to be careful all the time. Eremeev was in trouble and it looked like the referee, Marcus McDonnell, was going to stop it. I threw over 30 punches without reply and he fell to the canvas right at the bell. I'd thrown 150 punches in that round and I knew Eremeev had felt almost every one of them. I told

Kenny after the third that I could get him in the next round, but he told me not to get reckless and to be cautious.

With a minute to go in the fourth, I threw a left-right to his body. He bent over. I followed it up with a ten-punch combination. He threw a straight jab to get out of trouble, but I knew he wasn't going to last much longer. He showed guts and stayed in there, even though he had taken a lot of shots. I was so dominant. I stepped in with 20 seconds to go and landed a big right uppercut that sent Eremeev stumbling towards the ropes. I was back on top of him when I saw his cornerman step onto the ring apron waving a towel. Neither the referee nor Eremeev could see his cornerman, so I signalled to the referee that they wanted it stopped. I could have ignored the cornerman, but I didn't want to hurt Eremeev any more. The fight was stopped at 2:55 of round number four.

Eremeev was pretty busted up at the end. My face was clean. The fans loved my performance and I got another standing ovation. I loved the support from my fans this time. My homecoming was complete.

17

RE-LAUNCHING ON BRITISH SOIL

Wayne Pocket Rocket McCullough is definitely a part
of the brotherhood of boxers: a fraternity of fighters
who look out for each other. He has the heart of a
champion in the ring and in his personal life. I am
proud to be his friend.

Alex 'The Bronx Bomber' Ramos,
founder of the Retired Boxers Foundation

In October 2002 Kenny and I had gone to Glasgow to watch
Scott Harrison fight Julio Pablo Chacon for the WBO
featherweight title. I was working for Sky TV as part of their
commentary team. Harrison won, and Kenny and I liked what we
saw.

After my fight against Nikolai Eremeev in the November of
that year Cheryl entered into negotiations with Sports Network
to challenge Harrison for the Belt. We finally agreed that I would
fight him on 22 March 2003 in his home town of Glasgow.

We had planned to go to Belfast for the three weeks before the
fight and set up training camp there, but a week before we left
Vegas I became ill. I kept training twice a day, but in between
training sessions I'd have to go back to bed, which is unusual for
me. I was totally exhausted. Cheryl told me to rest from training

for a few days because I was so weak and pale, but I couldn't afford to take any time off. My World Championship fight was just around the corner.

Cheryl had arranged for us all to stay and train at the Holiday Inn in Belfast. The hotel staff couldn't have done any more for us. I set up my gym, including a boxing ring, in one of their conference rooms, so that everything I needed was on site. I'd borrowed the ring from my friend Mickey Hawkins, and Roderick had a car for me as usual. Kenny was training Olympic gold medallist Audley Harrison at the time, so during our first week, Audley came over from London to work with him.

I still felt a bit weak and for the first few days I took it easy. Usually when I'm in Belfast I put my head on the pillow at night and I'm out like a light, but this time I wasn't able to sleep. I'd be awake most nights until about 4 a.m. and I was getting up again at 9 a.m. to go running. Then I'd eat breakfast, even though I didn't feel like it. My eating and sleeping habits were all over the place. I felt as if nothing was going right and I didn't think it had anything to do with jet lag.

When I sparred with Brian Clements, I was exhausted after only two rounds. I had a burning sensation across my back and down my arms. I didn't know what it was. My team were worried because they know how I train: I can usually go on for ever. I went to see my local GP and he gave me a B12 injection to give me some energy. That will usually pick me up, but this time it didn't. I was taking a tonic and drinking every energy drink I could get my hands on but nothing was helping me.

Cheryl could see that my training was suffering, so she phoned a friend who lives in England. He came to Belfast in a bid to cheer me up. One morning, before we went out running, I was putting on my baseball cap and it took me almost a minute to reach my head. When we went running, along Belfast's Botanic Avenue and around past Queen's University, the same thing happened. It was like I was running in slow motion. Kenny could see that I was struggling in training, but what could he do? I just ploughed on.

I did a lot of publicity for the fight in Belfast. On one occasion, I sparred two journalists who wanted to feel what it was like to be in a boxing ring. We had a good laugh, but my body was ready to break down. Every day fans would turn up at the hotel to meet me and watch me train. They were sometimes unexpected but always very welcome. One day Robert Dunlop, brother of the late legendary motorbike racer 'King of the Roads' Joey Dunlop, came to visit. He also travelled to Glasgow to support me. Darryl came in every day to use my gym. Kenny would work with me and then hold the pads for him. The atmosphere in training camp was light-hearted and fun, and although I think everyone could sense there was something wrong, no one said anything to me.

One afternoon Cheryl and I took part in a conference call with Harrison and Frank Maloney. I had been accused of saying nasty things about Scott, but when I asked what those bad things were I was told I'd said I was going to win. I was puzzled: wouldn't every fighter say that? Did they want me to say I was going to lose? Maloney also criticised Cheryl for holding the pads for me. He said if Cheryl held the pads for Scott, he would break her arms. Didn't he know that pads are mostly held to perfect technique? Cheryl had held pads in my gym for Kevin Kelley, who's a bigger puncher than Harrison, and he didn't break her arms; in fact, he loved it.

About ten days before the fight, the burning in my shoulders and back got worse. After a round and a half of sparring, I was done. When I got back to our hotel room, Cheryl looked me straight in the eye and said, 'Wayne, I'm pulling you out of the fight.'

'No, you're buckin' not,' I said. 'I can't let anybody down.'

'Look at you. You're exhausted. You have no energy. How can you possibly fight next week like this?' I told her I'd be fine. 'Then I wash my hands of it.'

Looking back, I know she was right. I should have withdrawn from the fight, but I overruled her guidance as my manager and I paid the price. On my last day of sparring a few journalists came to the hotel to watch a public workout. I looked and felt terrible and the journalists knew it. I had wanted to appear as if I could knock down walls, but it was the complete opposite. I'm sure they thought I was just old and done, but they didn't know what was going on behind the scenes.

On the Tuesday morning prior to the fight we arrived at Belfast airport to catch our flight to Glasgow. We were delayed due to fog and had to sit in the airport nearly all day. When we arrived in Glasgow, there were a few journalists waiting for us at the airport. That was the last thing I needed. I just wanted to get to the hotel, train and lie down. But I would never refuse to do an interview, so I talked to them.

John Campbell, of the Northern Ireland Area Council, had checked my weight the week before the fight. But when we arrived at the Holiday Inn in Glasgow, a Scottish Boxing Council representative was waiting for me. The first thing he said to me was 'You've got to come and weigh in.' I told him I wasn't going with him because I had only arrived and 4 p.m. was my training time. I said I'd go after training. But according to him, I had to go with him there and then. I protested, telling him I'd weigh in when I was ready. I was in no mood to argue with him and no one had mentioned to me that I would have to have my weight checked before the official weigh-in. I was irritated at this point and walked away. He had no option but to back down.

The driver who picked us up at the airport told me I could use his room to weigh in, since he also had a scale. I weighed in after I'd trained and my weight was fine. I was already annoyed after being stuck in the airport all day and this was just the icing on the cake. If the Scottish representative had been nicer to me, I would have weighed in for him, but he had caused a commotion and that just made me mad.

The press conference took place at the fight venue, the Braehead Arena in Glasgow. I have to say it was the most depressing I've ever attended. There was no fun, no hype, nothing. Kenny tried to joke around, but no one was taking the bait. Kenny, Cheryl and I just sat joking with each other, but most of the journalists were expressionless. I was glad to get out of there and do my interview with Showtime, who were televising the fight in the USA.

The weigh-in took place at the Glasgow Hilton the day before the fight. I felt so much better, but I knew I wasn't 100 per cent. Compared to what I was like in Belfast, I felt good. I weighed one pound under the featherweight limit. Harrison looked drained and gaunt. As we did press photos, my sparring partner Brian Clements shouted, 'And the new . . .' My fans were going crazy, yelling and screaming.

After the weigh-in a group of us went out to eat. I filled up with pasta and drank lots of liquids. But when I went to bed that night, I was still below the featherweight limit. I couldn't seem to put on weight. I knew there was definitely something wrong with me because I can usually gain about 6 lb or 7 lb after a weigh-in. My doctor arrived and gave me another B12 injection. Ray, Stuart and Tiffany all arrived over from the States, as had some of my friends: Jim and Tim Molloy (originally from Belfast), Jeff Klein and Dennis. Mick had come over from Dublin and our family had come over from Belfast. The excitement was building.

On fight day, Cheryl, Wynona and I took it easy. We stayed together all day and I relaxed. I was confident and I was trying to convince myself I was 100 per cent, but I knew I wasn't. Before I went to the fight the hotel lobby was full of fans who had gathered to cheer and support me. Mickey, my long-time sparring partner and friend, from London, had also arrived. We got to the venue and I did my pre-fight drug test. Kenny warmed me up and I got dressed into my Grant ring outfit. I was ready to go.

I walked in to U2's 'Beautiful Day'. My supporters were fantastic. Harrison's fans were jeering and making hand gestures at me. It was the first time I'd ever walked to the ring in such a hostile atmosphere. Even Ian, who is normally really reserved, got into a fracas with security after being provoked by Harrison's fans who were so rude to my entourage during our walk to the ring.

Over a thousand people had come over from Belfast to support me. It was the first time I'd seen the Braehead Arena filled to capacity. I knew my fans wouldn't let me down. At least half of the arena was behind me.

Referee John Coyle brought us to the centre of the ring for our instructions and I wondered if Harrison was the same guy who'd weighed in the day before. He was massive. It didn't help that I'd hardly put any weight on either. We had weighed almost the same at the weigh-in, but when I watched the fight on TV Harrison looked like he was about three weight classes above me.

At the opening bell Harrison came straight out headhunting, trying to land big right-hands. I was trying to use my jab on the outside and move around the ring. I landed a double jab right-hand in the first minute of the fight but it had absolutely no effect on him. I tried to push him back with a four-punch combination, but he wasn't moving. He was super-strong and I knew I wasn't going to be able to push him about the ring like I'd done with other opponents. Harrison threw an overhand right that landed around the back of my head near my left ear. He was looking for one big shot. He landed an obvious low blow but didn't get warned for it. With 30 seconds to go, he landed another right-hand. I dropped my hands, shrugged my shoulders and said to him, 'Ain't so bad.' I did a dance and then put my hands back up, but at this point I started to think I should use Plan B and box him instead of fighting him because he was just so much bigger than me.

Our friends, Johnny and Teresa Tapia, were sitting beside Cheryl. When I went back to the corner after round one, I could see Cheryl and she mouthed to me, 'Are you OK?' I nodded yes but mouthed back 'Phew' as well. I just couldn't believe his strength. I'd been in the ring with Morales and Hamed, but Harrison was far stronger and larger than any other fighter I'd ever fought.

In between rounds Kenny told me not to stand in front of him so much and to go and feel him out. He wanted me to jab and feint, while keeping my hands up. I always throw over a hundred punches, but I had only thrown about 80 in the first round. That was slow for me and I knew I'd have to pick up the pace.

In round two Harrison was looking for overhand rights and lefts. I continued to move around to my left and right, and my jab was working well. I didn't necessarily come to box Harrison but I had to. In my opinion, I won the first two rounds. I was working well to his body, throwing rights and lefts. The ring was tiny at only 17 ft by 17 ft and that suited him since he was such an aggressive fighter. I threw a sweet left hook to the body, but it didn't seem to bother him. Coming in to the fight, Harrison probably thought I was going to stand toe-to-toe with him, but he was just too strong for me and I had to try to stay away from him. I tried to land an overhand right of my own because I saw that he carried his left-hand a little low. I can't talk, though, because my left-hand was low too.

He threw another low blow a minute into the third round and
again he wasn't warned. My jab was still giving him trouble. It
looked like his plan was to land the right-hand because he was
able to land it over and over again, and I just couldn't get out of
the way. Each time he threw the right-hand it would land on my
left ear. At the post-fight press conference he said he'd been
working on that punch.

Even though he was catching me, I would come straight back
at him. He slapped me with an illegal overhand right with the
open glove that caught me on the ear again. The slap was so
blatant that the referee had to warn him for hitting me with the
inside of the glove. But he had done damage to my ear and it
began to swell. Every shot he landed was a big one, but I wasn't
about to give in. With about ten seconds to go in the third, I
landed a huge left to his chin. Amazingly, he didn't flinch. We
traded toe-to-toe until the bell sounded to end the round.

I looked at Cheryl before I sat down in the corner and in our
special code she instructed me to move my head from side to side,
keep my chin down and my hands high. Kenny told me to get
inside with the jab and then work Harrison's body. He told me to
counter his right-hand, but my chin was doing that for me!

The pace was still quite slow in the fourth round. My body
and head shots were having no effect on him. He was walking
straight through them. A minute into the round I threw a quick
left-right that stopped him in his tracks, for one-hundredth of a
second! By this point the area underneath his eyes was starting
to bruise. He landed a good left hook and then an overhand
right that caught me flush on the chin. I backed off and when he
threw a right and a left hook, I ducked under both. I did the Ali
shuffle and shrugged my shoulders, but I think that just
annoyed him. Harrison stopped punching for a few seconds and
I was able to hit him with my jab. I was pushing him back for
the first time in the fight. I threw two right-hands that caught
him clean, followed by a right-hand and a left hook. I was
coming on a little in this round. With 30 seconds to go, one
more right-hand stopped him momentarily. I don't think he
knew what to make of me at this point. I finished the round just
bouncing around the ring.

In between rounds his corner told him I couldn't box going back. But if I hadn't known how to box going back, there's no way I would have made it through this fight. He came out in the fifth, throwing everything he had. The crowd were shouting 'Wayne McCullough! Wayne McCullough!' but Harrison ploughed on. He hit me with another low blow and still didn't get warned. I was trying to land the left-hand underneath, but he took them well.

Finally, with about a minute to go in the fifth round, he threw another low blow, but this time he finally got a warning. Harrison threw a left-right left-right combination that landed on my chin. I backed away from him and moved around. He hit me another right-hand on the jaw. I threw two left hooks but they had no effect. Another four-punch combination hit me, the last one landing on my ear again. I had my chin up too high and at this point I was really struggling. I was so weak. I had no energy.

At the start of the sixth round Harrison landed a huge right uppercut that made my head look as if it was about to fall off my shoulders. I stepped back with my hands down, clowning around, making him miss, but he came back with a double jab followed by a right-hand. His punches were stinging shots, but I'd been in with bigger punchers. It was Harrison's strength that was affecting me. He felt 100 times stronger than anybody I'd ever fought.

I threw a left hook to his body and dropped my left-hand. At that same instant he threw a huge right-hand followed by another right-left right-left combination, which all landed on my chin. I stumbled back towards the ropes, but I fought straight back. I knew he believed he was on the verge of stopping me but I thought to myself, 'You're not putting me down.' With a minute to go in the round, he stopped. I'm sure he was wondering what else he could do to knock me out.

'Hey, Pocket, Pocket. I need you to go to him with your hands up. Roll your head,' Kenny said in between rounds. Cheryl asked me again if I was OK and I told her I was. I could see her and Teresa chatting between rounds. Two women fight managers chatting intensely can't be a good thing!

In round number seven I tried to push him back with my jab. I threw another right-hand, but my punches were having no effect on him whatsoever. After such a bad sixth round, I really expected him to come out and try to stop me, but he couldn't do anything to me in the seventh. With only a minute to go, I stepped in with a sharp right uppercut underneath that caught him clean. It didn't faze him. I was stunned. What would I have to do to hurt him? My movement was definitely giving him trouble, but he was still able to catch up with me and land big shots. Harrison stepped in and landed another right-hand on my ear with the inside of his open glove.

He started the eighth round by throwing another big right-hand. I backed off to get away from him. My ear was bending away from my head as he continued to hit it with the open glove. Then he landed a big right-hand to my chin and I had to back off again. I was able to stay out of trouble for a few seconds anyway. The Showtime pundits were commenting: 'A fight like this and a fighter like McCullough is a referee's worst nightmare because he keeps fighting back.'

Harrison was still trying to knock me out, but I kept on throwing back. He came after me and landed another right-hand open-glove shot on my ear. I wasn't hurt, but I just couldn't get him off me. He pushed me away and I flew across to the other side of the ring. The referee was staying close, but he could see that my eyes were clear. He saw the fight up close and personal and he knew my style of fighting. I came back with a good body shot at the end of the round but Harrison had done the damage by then.

This was my worst round so far and Cheryl asked me again if I was OK. I nodded to her that I was fine. If she'd seen anything in my eyes, she would have stopped it. One of the commentators for Showtime said: 'It's hard to take the credit away from Harrison, but when you see this kind of action and you see these kinds of shots, you just have to ask: is Wayne McCullough's heart bigger than his entire body? How many fighters could take this kind of abuse and not only take it but punch back as hard as he possibly can? Amazing.'

Kenny asked me in the corner if I was all right.

'Yeah, I'm OK. I'm just getting hit.'

'You gotta stop getting hit then!' was Kenny's response. We just laughed. I'm sure after battering me around the ring in the eighth round Harrison thought I was done. His face was battered and swollen.

I got back on my jab at the beginning of the ninth. Harrison landed another right-hand on my ear and it looked like it was going to rip my head right off. Johnny started yelling at me: 'Move to your right, Wayne.' I was trying, because if I moved to my right, then I would get away from his big right-hand. Harrison threw another punch that went around the back of my head and the referee said to me, 'Don't turn around, son'!

It seemed as if Harrison was taking round nine off, or that he'd punched himself out, but I wasn't complaining because it meant he wasn't hitting me. I landed a left-right to his chin and thought I might be back in the fight. I was still trying to win. I thought I might have been able to stop him because of his cuts. People asked me why I took that sort of punishment when I didn't have the punch to knock him out, but what if . . .

In round number ten I was moving well. He landed a left to my chin but nothing followed it. Even though I was well behind, afterwards the commentators said I had shown 'incredible heart'. Then, all within ten seconds, Harrison hit me with two huge right open gloves on my ear, which was now completely swollen and throbbing. And again, a third open-glove punch landed on my ear. I knew there was something wrong with my ear, but I honestly didn't realise it was as badly hurt as it turned out to be. The referee had been looking on, but Harrison didn't get warned once. I was so frustrated. Harrison seemed to get stronger in every round and as the fight went on I thought his muscles were getting bigger – I must have been hallucinating!

The advertisement painted on the centre of the ring had become slippery as a result of water and sweat dripping off our shorts, and we were both sliding on it. After he'd kicked my backside for ten rounds, I pointed at the advertisement as if to say to him, 'Watch you don't slip there.' I'm such a nice guy; too nice for my own good sometimes.

At the end of the round, the commentators noted: '[McCullough's] reputation precedes him and that is what is getting the respect of [referee] John Coyle. That, I think, is a big point of why he hasn't stopped this. At this level a referee should know the styles and the histories of the fighters. You won't treat Wayne McCullough the same way you treat a four-round club fighter, and Coyle is not [treating him that way].'

I knew I needed a knockout going into the last two rounds. My fans were singing, 'Here we go, here we go, here we go,' and I could feel them urging me to keep going. I was using my jab and moving around in the 11th round and Harrison had slowed – a little. At this point, Steve Albert of Showtime commented on my ear: 'The viewers at home can clearly see the left ear of Wayne McCullough is not where it was when this fight started. It has been rearranged. You usually see that with noses but tonight with an ear.'

In between rounds 11 and 12, Kenny encouraged me on. 'Pocket, last round coming up. I gotta gamble with my life. OK, baby. I gotta put my feet up under me. My chin on my chest and I gotta go out there and try to make something happen.'

At the start of the twelfth round I was back on the jab again. I only had three minutes to go and I was still trying to win. Harrison threw a ten-punch combination, but he only landed two of them, as I was effectively bobbing and weaving. I was still trying to land body shots, hoping that he would go down. I threw a double jab to his chin and a right-hand to his body. His glove touched the canvas. I heard Cheryl shouting 'Woo hoo!' and the crowd was on fire. The commentators were saying, 'McCullough is still trying to win.' But what did they honestly expect me to do, give up or quit? I jumped on him, thinking – more like hoping – I'd hurt him. The crowd was singing 'Wayne McCullough! Wayne McCullough!'

Harrison had a quiet last round but his strength hadn't diminished. With 30 seconds to go, we stood toe-to-toe. I was never once fazed by him: I was annoyed and frustrated that he could land so many shots and that I couldn't get away from them. The Scottish crowd were now standing and applauding me after showing such disrespect to me on the way to the ring.

As the final bell rang, I hugged Harrison and told him if he came to America, I would come out and support him. He'd been the best man on the night. Johnny got up onto the ring canvas and hugged me. Cheryl and Stuart were both in the ring. Cheryl wanted to get me to the hospital right away, not only for my ear but also because I had taken so many shots.

I always say I'm a 15-round fighter, but I wouldn't have wanted 15 rounds that night. Harrison won an obvious unanimous decision. Jimmy Lennon Jnr was the ring announcer. He told Cheryl it was one of the hardest decisions he'd ever had to announce.

I went back to my dressing-room and there were quite a few tears. I walked into the bathroom and closed the door. I thanked God for getting me through the fight. Then I threw up.

I went to the press conference in the arena, and was trying to joke with Harrison and the press, but I could feel myself wilting. My nose started dripping blood and I didn't know why. Cheryl got up and said, 'That's it,' grabbed me and we left.

As we were walking back towards my dressing-room, I started to feel light-headed but stopped to sign autographs for my fans. I felt as if I was walking on cushions. I hadn't drunk any water since the fight. I was too upset to think about taking care of myself. I felt like I was ready to collapse. Mick grabbed me and Sam threw me over his shoulder. I whispered to him, 'Take me to the hospital.' At that point I thought I was dying.

Cheryl said when I looked at her she was scared. My eyes were fixed and piercing. She was thinking the same as me. Frank Warren's security guard grabbed me from Sam and put me on a chair. It was mayhem, sheer panic, but I was virtually unaware of what was going on around me.

An ambulance arrived and the paramedics put me on a stretcher and the ringside physician was waiting for me in the ambulance. I felt as if I couldn't breathe; I was faint and I know I was drifting away. I looked at Cheryl, who was less than three feet behind me. I wanted to tell her I loved her and I would always love her, but I couldn't get a breath. I thought it was the last time I was ever going to see her.

18

RISKING IT ALL

Courage isn't the absence of fear, it is the dominance of it, and long before I became involved with boxing in a professional capacity I respected the Pocket Rocket's ability to master his fear more than any other fighter in the world. Both inside and outside the squared circle, Wayne McCullough epitomises the fighting spirit that makes boxing such a magnetic sport.

Anthony Evans, assistant editor, SecondsOut.com

I was immediately taken into accident and emergency when we arrived at Glasgow's Southern General Hospital. I was connected to monitors and a drip. I was totally dehydrated. They were pumping me full of potassium, which was apparently to regulate my heartbeat. If this hadn't been done immediately, my condition could have been fatal.

I have a vague recollection of the drive from the arena to the hospital. I remember just wanting to go to sleep, I felt so relaxed. But the doctor kept me awake, telling me that we were getting closer to the hospital. I felt as though I couldn't breathe. The doctor who was accompanying me from the arena was asking me to blow out and when I did he told Cheryl I was getting air into my lungs. I had a pain in my chest but I couldn't describe it; I'd never felt anything like it before.

Most of the team had come with me to the hospital, but when they realised I was being admitted overnight they left as some were flying back to the States the next morning. Kenny had to go to work with Audley and had other commitments in Vegas.

There were a couple of journalists hanging around to get the inside scoop about why I had been taken to the hospital. They were told I had been admitted for dehydration and observation, and that I would be released the next day. A nurse had connected me up to an ECG machine, which I assumed was just routine. But after determining that my heartbeat was irregular, the staff immediately transferred me to the coronary care unit. I remember feeling a cold breeze as I was taken out of A&E into the ambulance.

I was admitted into a ward full of people who were much older than me and were suffering from heart disease. The nurses in the ward connected me to a heart monitor that constantly checked my heart rate. I was also connected to a machine that checked my blood pressure every hour. They had strapped it on my arm, which was already sore and swollen from the fight. When it was removed, my arm was like Popeye's!

Every time my heart rate dropped under 50 beats per minute, an alarm would sound on my machine and the nurses would come running in. They'd check on me and switch it off. I've since been told that, as a fit athlete, it would be quite typical for my heart rate to be low.

Cheryl sat on a chair next to me all night, resting her head on the bottom of my bed. Nicola also stayed in Glasgow and took care of Wynona. They were sleeping in the family waiting room. The nurses gave Wynona scrubs to sleep in and lots of bits and pieces to play with. She was having a great time, unaware her daddy could have been lying on his deathbed.

Apparently there was a man at the other end of the ward who moaned all night. Someone else threw up, and Cheryl went to find a nurse to sort him out. I slept through it all. I was exhausted and was finally getting some much-needed rest.

The media were still hanging around trying to get a story, so the next morning the nurses moved me into a private room away from prying eyes. I wondered why they were putting me in the room when I was going home. I was really sore and disappointed after the fight. Cheryl had filled me in on what I couldn't remember from the night before; however, she was keeping the press cuttings away from me, so I couldn't read what the press was reporting about me. Little did they know I was in hospital close to death.

The nurses did another ECG on me to see if my heartbeat had regulated itself, but it hadn't. A doctor drained my ear and applied a bandage all the way around my head to hold it down. I still thought I was in hospital to have my ear treated and to deal with my dehydration, and I was going to be released any time.

The doctor on duty, a Dr Murdock, came into my room and sat down on my bed. It didn't look good. He told me I couldn't go home that day. I asked him why and he told me there was a problem with my heart. He went on to tell me that a virus – most likely the one I'd picked up in Vegas – had attacked my heart. He said I had a myocardial injury, which is bruising of the heart muscle, and because my ECGs were still irregular I would have to stay in hospital for at least another day to see if they could get my heart to regulate. I asked him if I could have had a heart attack during the fight and he answered yes. I was shocked. I knew I'd been feeling run down, but I had never imagined I was that ill. I already felt weak and, with this news, I just sank back in the bed. I wasn't able to really get my head around what the doctor was telling me.

Just before Dr Murdock walked out of my room, he turned to me and said, 'Are you going to fight again?' I didn't have an answer for him, so I told him I'd go home and rest up before making any decisions. I was still in shock from the news he'd just given me. 'If you get a scare like this, I would chuck it,' he said.

When Cheryl came back into the room, I told her what the doctor had said and she was devastated. I told her it probably wasn't as bad as it sounded, but I don't think either of us believed that. Stuart and Tiffany were still in Scotland. They were checking in every few hours to find out what was going on and Cheryl was filling them in.

The doctor was expecting my previous ECG reports to be sent from Dr Margaret Goodman so he could compare them to my current reports. He needed to see if there had been a change since my last one. When he received them, there had been a change since 1999, so he decided to keep me in hospital until my ECG returned to normal.

As we'd gone straight from the arena to the hospital, we had no clothes or toiletries. Our friends, William and Toni, had taken our luggage home with them on the boat as we were unable to get to our hotel after the fight. We all thought I'd be home the next day, so we didn't keep anything in Glasgow. Cheryl was still in the dress she'd worn to the fight and I was dressed in my matching hospital robe and slippers, so I told Cheryl to go out and get us some clothes. I also asked that she bring me back something nice to eat – you know what they say about hospital food. Nicola, Cheryl and Wynona went out and Brian, who had come to the hospital with me, stayed in my room and we talked about the fight and watched TV. The nurses brought in cups of tea every hour. I loved it. The tea was the best I'd tasted in a long time.

Cheryl had read reports that the media were speculating I had something wrong with my brain – going back to the BBBC scare of 2000 – but the doctor hadn't needed to do a brain scan because he said there were no signs of brain damage when I'd arrived at the hospital.

My friend, Paul Weir, a former two-time world champion whom I've known since 1990, came to visit me in the hospital with his wife, Laura. He'd phoned several times on the night I'd been admitted and visited me the next night with goodies. It was hard being cooped up in a small room. It was my first overnight stay in a hospital in my whole life. After the first day they took the drip out of my arm and told me I could get out of bed and walk around the room. They told me not to do too much, but I was bored. All I could do was walk around my tiny 10x10-foot room or sleep.

The whole time I'd been in the hospital Michael Flatley had been phoning me from the States. He must have phoned at least ten times. We weren't really supposed to have our mobile phones turned on but if Michael Flatley is phoning me, I'm answering! Martin O'Neill, former Celtic manager, also stopped in to see me. He sat with me for over an hour and we chatted about everything under the sun. A little while later I visited him in London and he gave me a motivational speech. Martin calls me after every fight now. He is an awesome person and I'm honoured to call him a friend.

By the Tuesday after the fight my ECG still hadn't returned to normal but the doctor put it down to me having an 'athlete's heart' and allowed me to be released. His only requirement was that I didn't fly back to Belfast; I had to take a boat. I also had to postpone my flight home to Vegas for two weeks. He told me to go for a stress test when I got back to America to make sure everything was in working order.

I thanked all the nurses as I left. One of them asked me for a 'Wayne McCullough' T-shirt so I took off the one I was wearing and gave it to her. When I walked out of the hospital with Brian, it felt good just to have fresh air on my face. I still felt a bit light-headed, but I was happy and thankful to be alive after what I had gone through.

Wynona was brilliant throughout the whole ordeal. Even though she didn't know what was going on, she didn't question why she had spent three days in a hospital. She just accepted it as something we had to do and behaved very well.

My brother-in-law Ian travelled back from Belfast again to drive us to the boat the next day. Nicola, Ian, Cheryl, Wynona, Brian and I all stayed at Paul's house that evening. I don't know how we would have got through it without his hospitality. Ian was driving us to the port in Scotland to catch the P&O ferry to Larne in Northern Ireland and after a few wrong turns we made it there. On board, Cheryl and I were offered use of the captain's cabin. There were tea and biscuits waiting for us. It was Wynona's first time on a boat and she loved it.

Later that week, Cheryl arranged a small get-together for me with some of our friends and family at the Holiday Inn. It was also Wynona's fifth birthday so we had a double celebration with a cake and balloons for her.

The first thing I did when I got home was go for my stress test. The doctor needed my heart rate to reach 150 beats per minute so he could see if my heart got stressed while I did exercise. I started off walking but after ten minutes they realised I would have to run to raise my heart rate. Finally, after 17 minutes, my heart rate was 151 bpm and the machine beeped. The doctor did follow-up lab work and everything came out normal. They couldn't find any evidence of heart disease and I was given a clean bill of health. I saw Dr Goodman again and her report gave me the go-ahead to continue with my boxing career. It identified that there was no obvious structural heart disease and the risks were not unusual.

* * *

Frank Warren did what he promised he would do for me: he took me to Belfast to fight and got me a world championship bout. For that, I want to thank him. I believe Frank is one of the best promoters in the world today and we parted on amicable terms.

19

BACK WHERE IT ALL BEGAN

> If I was going to build a fighter from scratch, I would start with Wayne McCullough's heart, determination and his chin. I'd finish by giving him George Foreman's power. This fighter would retire undefeated.
> *Dan Goossen, Goossen Tutor Boxing Promotions*

I rested up when I went home. Well, I mean I trained lightly every day for a few weeks. I was contacted by TWI Productions, who wanted to know if I'd be interested in taking part in the remake of the 1970s hit BBC show *Superstars*. It was going to be filmed in La Manga, Spain, in May 2003. I was delighted that they had even thought of me and I agreed to compete. Some of the production team flew to Vegas to film a piece for the show since I was travelling the furthest to participate.

When we got to La Manga, we shared an apartment with Ricky Hatton, the IBF light welterweight champion. He has always been one of my favourite fighters and I support him every time he fights. Cheryl's family joined us, as she was celebrating her 30th birthday during the trip and they had decided to make a holiday out of it. Typically, the boxers hadn't done well in previous episodes of *Superstars* and nothing changed this time either. I was the smallest guy in the competition – but that's nothing new.

I was looking forward to the strength tests. I had practised the squats and dips, and I knew I could win that event. For squats, we had to get down on all-fours and jump over a marked line on a board to register one squat. We were given one minute to do this. Just before the competition some of my teammates mentioned that it might be easier to slide on the board instead of jumping. That sounded easier and quicker than the way I'd practised, so I thought I'd try it. Everyone before me had jumped and they hadn't done many squats. If I wanted to win this event, I knew I'd have to do more than them. So I started to slide.

I got to about 40 seconds in, when I felt like one of those cartoon characters whose toes are on fire. I kept going. I finished the event and rolled over in agony, pointing to my toes. My socks were soaked in blood. I suffered the pain and walked off the stage gracefully. The doctors came and carried me over to the first-aid tent to start working on my toes. I'd taken the skin off both big toes and suffered third-degree burns. They were raw right down to the nerve. I can't describe how tender and sore they felt, and I still had to take part in the dips competition. For this one, I would be standing between two bars and, using my arms, I would push myself up and down while the referee counted how many dips I did.

My feet were to be off the ground the whole time, so I thought it couldn't be that bad since I was using my arms and not my toes! I did the dips and won the strength competition over all my teammates. I still had to take part in an 800-metre run and a mountain bike ride. I remember thinking I could barely walk, so how was I going to run or cycle? Everyone expected me to pull out of the competition but, not known for my quitting, I decided to keep going.

Dr Richard put some numbing solution around my toes and bandaged them up. He told me I'd be OK for the run but he'd told Cheryl I'd probably start feeling pain after about 200 metres. I felt confident at the start of the race because I enjoy running and my toes were numb. At the 200-metre marker, I began to feel pain, but Dr Richard had told me I'd be OK, so I didn't understand why this was happening! The pain was so intense that I had to run the rest of the race on my heels. I finished a very disappointing last, with bloodsoaked socks, but at least I finished.

The bike ride went much the same way. It certainly was an uphill struggle as I had to cycle up a steep mountainside for 800 metres and try to make it to the top. I held a strong second place until a fumble with my gears slipped me into third, again with blood on my socks. Under the circumstances, I was unable to secure a place in the final but at least I provided the entertainment value!

From Spain we flew to Belfast, where I was scheduled to host a documentary called *Bits of Belfast: Up the Shankill*, commissioned by the BBC. The focus was on the good times on the road. In November 2002 I'd filmed a pilot that was accepted by the BBC. It was the first time I'd presented a TV programme and I loved it. It was very emotional returning to my roots and visiting areas I hadn't been to since I was very young. I learned so much about the area during filming: it was eye-opening and heart-warming all at the same time. The programme was ably directed by the award-winning Mickey McGowan.

Filming was spread over two weeks and I literally took a walk 'up' the Shankill Road. I met a lot of different people, who loved reminiscing about the old times and chatting about some of the area's newer features. One of them was a man called Albert Haslett, a poet, who has written a poem about a journey along the road. He knows the Shankill Road like the back of his hand. Everybody was very open about their lives and the different events that have taken place there. It was the first time in 30 years that I'd been back in Percy Street at the same spot where I was born. The documentary has been repeated a few times and each time the viewing figures are fantastic. I am thrilled to have been part of it.

Once we had arrived home Cheryl tried to schedule a fight but nothing was materialising. I kept training on my own every day with Cheryl holding the pads. Throughout the year I worked on my technique in the gym. I wanted to be ready should something come up. I was two weeks away from a match at any given time, but I just couldn't secure a date without a promoter. Everybody seemed to think I was done. I hadn't made any excuses after the

Harrison fight, so no one knew how ill or close to death I'd been. People had put it down to old age. The headlines were screaming that I should retire.

We started 2004 in a new house and we knew it was all going to work out. Cheryl started looking for a promoter for me but no one wanted to touch me. I got a couple of offers from American promoters, but they weren't what I was looking for. In July, I issued a press release stating I'd fight for free. The response I got was astounding; a lot of promoters took it literally. What I'd actually said was, if I didn't perform, they didn't have to pay me. I knew I was going to perform.

Since I wasn't fighting, I was driving Cheryl crazy. There are only so many times the grass needs mowed in one week! I felt as though no one was interested in me any more. After what I had given to boxing over the years, I was honestly hoping someone would help me get back into the ring. Outside of the ropes, I live clean; I don't abuse my body. I knew I wasn't old. I knew I shouldn't retire. And it really hurt me to think that journalists – some of whom had never stepped into a boxing ring themselves – could write the things they did about me. Someone, somewhere, would help me. I just had to find the right person.

* * *

Cheryl suggested I think about personal training again, but I didn't know where to start. I wasn't really looking, but one day while we were out I met to a guy from Thunder from Down Under, a group of male dancers who perform in Las Vegas. He mentioned he had a couple of friends who were interested in learning how to box. I told him to give them my number, but I thought I'd never hear from them again.

Next day a guy called Craig phoned, saying he was the friend who wanted to box. Cheryl set up a time for him and his friend, Matt, to come and work out. I didn't really want to get into personal training because I still wanted to fight, but at least it would keep me out of Cheryl's way!

I liked Craig and Matt from the beginning. They are Australian, so I felt as if we had something in common: we'd all come to this country to make something of ourselves and have all succeeded. They were really interested in learning how to box. Since they had muscles popping out of their muscles, they thought they were fit, but I put them through half of a training session and they were exhausted. Craig is about 13 st. and Matt is about 14 st., but they are both built like brick walls. They started training twice a week and they loved it. Afterwards we'd sit and chat about fights we'd seen at the weekend. Eventually I knew they were good enough to get into the ring to spar – but who with?

It was right around this time that I was offered a job at *Ring Magazine*, the bible of boxing. The editor, Nigel Collins, got in touch and asked if I would like to be their Las Vegas correspondent. I jumped at the chance. I had been writing for the SecondsOut website since 2001 and now I was going to be writing for the most prestigious boxing magazine in the world. I was honoured. My first report was published in July 2004. Today I get more recognition for my writing than I do for my boxing.

* * *

Cheryl had been in touch with Dan Goossen about promoting me. There had always been a special bond between Cheryl, Dan and me, mostly because I had my professional debut on one of his boxing shows in Los Angeles. Dan had always been up-front with me.

We saw Dan at the MGM Grand in Las Vegas and chatted for a while. He came up with a long-term deal for me, and so on 3 August 2004 I signed with Goossen Tutor Boxing Promotions and the Rocket was ready for re-launch.

Kenny Croom and I had remained friends, but he was busy with his other fighters, so Cheryl arranged for me to train with Freddie Roach at his Wild Card Boxing Gym in Hollywood, California. Freddie and I go back many years. I met him in 1993 when I moved to America. He was working with Eddie and the one thing I remember about him that has stuck in my head is that he passed me a skipping rope. Of course, being a typical boxer, he doesn't remember! Freddie had his hands full with James Toney and

Manny Pacquiao, both world champion fighters, but he said he saw something in me and decided to bring me into his stable of fighters. Freddie was also working with a friend of mine, Irish featherweight Bernard Dunne, but he has since moved back to Ireland.

Since Freddie's gym is in Los Angeles, I knew I'd have to go there for training camp. I was already in shape, so I only went to his gym for a few days before my scheduled fight on 23 September. I just wanted to get used to him before I stepped into the ring. We clicked right away.

My first fight with Goossen Tutor took place at the Pechanga Resort in Temecula, California. My opponent was Mike Juarez from Omaha, Nebraska. Even though he might be seen as a journeyman in boxing circles, he'd fought world-class opposition: he had been knocked out by Junior Jones in seven rounds and by Erik Morales in three.

Juarez had a record of 23–14–2 with nine KOs, so he was a veteran with ring experience. A lot of people still felt that I was done. I told myself beforehand if I struggled with him, then maybe I was, but if I got him out early, I'd be able to step up to the next level again.

A friend, Scott, had been following my re-launch in the ring for a glossy magazine article. He tagged along with me into the dressing-room and couldn't believe how precise everything was. Freddie wrapped and taped my hands before the fight – there was an exact way to do every little thing. I was now sponsored by Everlast and they provided me with incredible ring outfits for each of my fights.

There was a fantastic crowd in Pechanga supporting me. A lot of my friends had driven from Los Angeles. Romolo's sons, Frank and Tony, drove in from Vegas with Frank's sons. This was my first fight in 18 months, but I wasn't apprehensive – just excited. Juarez tried to cause an upset in the first round by coming out all guns blazing, but I was hitting him with left and right hooks to his body and right-hands to his head. The Fox network commentators, Barry Tompkins and Max Kellerman, kept referring back to the Harrison fight. As far as I was concerned that part of my life was over and this was my chance to move on. To me, Sean O'Grady is what a professional commentator should

213

be like. Maybe it's because he's an ex-boxer himself and seems to understand how to commentate on a fight.

A clash of heads in the first round opened up a tiny cut over my left eye. It was the first time I'd been cut so early in a fight. I could feel the cold blood running down my face, so I tried to step up the pace. I jumped on him and landed two great right-hands to his head. I knew my body work was hurting him in the opening round, but he was still trying and had come to win. I won the first round easily, but the commentators said it was a tough round for me and that I'd lost it. They weren't even close. I met Barry Tompkins later in the year and we talked about his criticism of me during the fight. He apologised for what he had said. I've always respected him and I didn't want anything to stand in the way of our friendship.

Justin Fortune, who fought Lennox Lewis in 1995, and Freddie Roach worked my corner. Freddie was so cool and calm. He reminded me so much of Eddie in my corner. Freddie kept everything under control.

The press reported this as my comeback fight, but I had never retired. Max Kellerman was reported as commenting, '[Wayne is] one of my all-time favourite fighters . . . The Pocket Rocket. This is his comeback fight. He throws tons of punches to the body and the head. He just wears you down. He's had tons of world-class experience and he also takes a tremendous punch.' I'd taken some time off, but I certainly didn't see it as a comeback from anything.

Juarez tried to trade with me in the second round but I landed a left hook to his chin that sent him back to the ropes and I knew he was hurt. Juarez called me on – obviously he wanted to take some more punches. I stayed on him. I was hitting him with every shot. He fought back gamely but I knew he was done. I feinted a right and then threw a right-hand to his chin. I had him hurt and he almost fell flat on his face. Before he went down, I hit him with another left-right combination and he fell against the ropes. A right uppercut left hook put Juarez down and out on the canvas. He was down for a couple of minutes. When he got up, I went to his corner to make sure he was OK.

The commentators were still criticising me, but I got rid of my opponent the way I was supposed to. I took fewer shots in this fight than I ever had before. I felt great. It was my first fight back with Dan and I had performed. I got the win by KO and everyone was happy. After the fight, I went to the doctor's tent and got my cut stitched up. My friend and co-manager, Stuart Campbell, who has travelled around the world with me and fought for me through thick and thin, was delighted when I got the win over Juarez. We'd all worked hard to get to this point and he knew there was only one way to go – up.

* * *

Dan worked tirelessly after the Juarez fight to get me back into the ring. I was now ranked in the top ten WBC super bantamweight ratings. I was really happy to be back with Dan. We'd started off together and I knew I wanted to end my career with him. Dan is not only my promoter, but also a very dear friend. He and his family mean so much to us.

Dan scheduled another fight for me in December, so we went back to Los Angeles to train with Freddie. Later we got news that the bout had been cancelled. Still, Dan was working on something far bigger for me.

20

ROBBED – AGAIN!

When I was asked to work with Wayne McCullough, I knew I could take him to the top. We fought for two World Championships together and Wayne never gave up. He has the true heart of a champion.

Freddie Roach, the best trainer in
the world today and a friend

In the middle of December, Dan told me he was going to make Oscar Larios, the WBC super bantamweight champion, an offer to fight me on a Goossen Tutor show in February. Dan worked diligently throughout Christmas putting the fight together. Cheryl and Stuart were kept in the loop every step of the way. By the beginning of January, the fight was signed and Dan had come through for me again.

There were still doubters calling for me to retire. Even though the Juarez fight had been recorded for Fox TV, it hadn't been televised, so no one had seen how good I'd looked in that fight. Why would I step in against the best super bantamweight in the division if I wasn't ready? It certainly wasn't for the money – it was for the opportunity to be back on top of the world.

Right before I went to training camp, I went to get another cortisone injection in my left hand. It felt good, but not great. We talked about the possibilities of surgery to repair the damage in my hand, but it wasn't something I'd consider with my World Championship fight right around the corner.

I went to Los Angeles on 9 January for training camp with Freddie. I'd been out of the ring for almost two years before I fought Juarez in the September of 2003 and even then I'd only fought two rounds, but Dan knew I was ready to take on the champion and I wasn't about to pass this one by.

Training camp went quite well, although it could have been better. I kept a training diary and I posted it on my website every evening for my fans. The response I got was amazing. People from all over the world would email and tell me they felt as if they were part of my camp because I was giving them inside information they would usually never get to hear about. Since I was just a visitor at the gym, when I sparred one of its fighters, the permanent boxers would stop what they were doing and encourage my opponent. That didn't bother me, though; I've always been running into the wind.

Cheryl and I loved staying in Los Angeles: her for the shopping and me for the training. We stayed in West Hollywood, an area we thought was beautiful. We had everything we needed right on our doorstep. Each morning I'd leave the hotel early and go for a run. I was able to go along Santa Monica Boulevard to Beverly Hills and back without crossing any roads.

Less than a month before the fight, in the middle of January, I hurt my left hand again. I was sparring and hit it off my sparring partner's head. A pain shot through my hand and up my arm and I was worried that I had really done damage this time. I continued to spar over the next few days, but it got so bad that we had to go home and see my doctor. It wasn't really a question of *if* I should get a cortisone injection, more like when. My doctor took care of me again. Before we went back to Los Angeles I tested my hand out on Craig and Matt's heads – I had finally found them a sparring partner! We drove back to Los Angeles and finished camp. I didn't get as much sparring done as I'd wanted to because of my hand and I had to rest it a lot. We had fun in Los Angeles, but I was ready to box.

The fight took place in a town outside Fresno, called Lemoore, which looks as though it consists mainly of farmland, then all of a sudden the Palace Indian Gaming Casino pops up out of nowhere. Rachel, Goossen Tutor's PR executive, made sure I was taken care of. Anything I needed I got. No one ever treated us as well as Rachel. Oscar Larios was the favourite going into the fight but that was expected because he was the champion. The fight was televised live on a Fox TV show called the *Best Damn Sports Show Period*.

I met Larios for the first time at the weigh-in and we had respect for one another. He knew I was tough since I'd been in with all the best names in my division, and I respected him because he was the champion, making the sixth defence of his title. Our friends from Los Angeles brought a lot of people to Lemoore for the fight and Cheryl's family had flown over from Belfast. Brian, Craig, Matt and Tommy, another guy I was training, came too. Frank brought his son, Jason. So even though it was a Mexican region, I had loads of fans in the arena.

I was confident going into the fight but my hand was still giving me a little trouble. The injection had helped but it was not pain-free. I was in the dressing-room waiting to go out into the ring with a friend, Kieran. He was more nervous than I was, but Cheryl kept him company and they had a laugh. That's the way I like my dressing-room. I love to have fun and relax before I get into the ring. I don't like it when people are in there looking worried.

Jimmy Lennon Jnr announced the fight – it's always an honour to share the ring with him. As the opening bell rang, I walked straight out and started punching. My plan was to throw long left hooks and right-hands, and to keep my hands up. My right-hand to the head was working well and I was slipping a lot of punches. I was thinking about everything Freddie had taught me and it was working. A big straight left-hand knocked his head back and I was hoping I'd catch him early and it would be over. No chance!

In the first couple of rounds I stayed close and worked his body underneath. He found it hard to keep me off. Larios was only an inch taller than me, but he looked a lot bigger because of our styles. He stands up tall, while I fight small. I was stalking him and I didn't take a backward step. The pace was fast and I was throwing well over a hundred punches a round. Larios was just trying to stay in there with me.

In the third round Larios was trying to land his double jab and uppercut, and he was finding it harder to cope with my non-stop punching. No matter what he did, I had a punch in his face. My body work was fantastic. The left hook to the head was working brilliantly. After the third I told Freddie I'd hurt my hand and even though I kept throwing it, it didn't have the same effect. Macka Foley, a former heavyweight fighter, was working my corner with my doctor Sam Colarusso and my cutman Ray Rodgers, but Freddie was the one doing all the talking – as it should be.

Larios kept hitting me with low blows, but he wasn't being warned for it. I was constantly attacking him with big, long lefts and I stunned him in the fourth. By the fifth round he looked like he was getting tired. He finally got warned for a low blow, but he kept loading up with them. He was throwing lots of right-hands but I blocked most of them. I threw an overhand right in the fifth round and cut him. Sean O'Grady, commentating for Fox TV, said I had 'batteries in [my] gloves'. 'He just keeps going and going,' he said. He had been saying that about me since early in my career.

During the sixth round I could see Larios had faded, so I kept on the pressure. The long left hooks were catching him almost every time. A few times I hit him with body shots and I could hear him groaning. They were hurting him, so I continued to throw them. At the end of the round Larios was really weak. I thought I could come out in round seven and stop him. I felt like I'd taken the fight out of him.

I sat in the corner and Freddie told me: 'You're ahead in the fight; the plan's working. Keep doing what you're doing.' But something came over me. Everything stopped for a second. I was blankly gazing in front of me – I just wanted to get up and walk out of the ring. I can't explain it, even to this day. I don't know what it was. I just felt detached from the fight. I started to feel a little weary. Maybe it was the long layoff, I don't know. Whatever it was, it took over me for a few rounds.

Larios could see I had completely slowed down in the seventh and he stepped up the pace. He landed a good right and a left uppercut to my chin. He hit me two more rights and I dropped my hands as if to say, 'I really don't care.' Larios got his rhythm back, but I was still landing and forcing him back; however, the effect was gone from my punches and my left hand was hurting really badly. At the end of the round, I landed a big overhand right to his chin. That let him know I was still in the fight. Both Sean O'Grady and Barry Tompkins had me ahead after seven rounds. I was up by one point on Barry's card and three points on Sean's.

When I threw a combination in the eighth round, I would start with the body and then come up top and finish with the head. I was trying to confuse him and it seemed to be working. I was forcing the champion to fight. Over the next couple of rounds it was evident that I had nothing in my tank, and, although no one watching the fight on TV would have known it, I felt it. Some of the rounds were close, but I felt I was making the fight – although I knew I was fading because his right-hands were catching me more easily.

My mind was still not really in the fight from round nine through eleven, but I wasn't taking a lot of punishment. Halfway into the ninth round I dropped my hands. I wasn't concerned about being hit, but still he couldn't stop me. I didn't know what was going on. Freddie told me at the end of the ninth round that if I dropped my hands again, he would stop the fight. I knew he meant it.

In the tenth round, Larios was fighting me and I wasn't really punching back. I was doing just enough to stay in the fight and his punches had no effect on me whatsoever. He was a good puncher but nothing like Morales or Hamed, or even Zaragoza.

The doctor came into the ring in between rounds ten and eleven to check on me. 'Get out of the way and let me do my job,' I told him. I knew I had another two rounds in me and there was no way I was going to let him take that away from me. In the 11th round I was blocking shots well and fighting back. I gave him too much room to punch, which was a mistake because then I was fighting his fight. Both of us were tired by this point, but I knew I had to push him in the last round. I knew I had to finish strong to take the Belt from him. Even though I hadn't really fought as well as I could have from the seventh, I felt as if I was well ahead on the cards and I only needed to win the last two rounds.

The crowd was on its feet at the beginning of the 12th round. A lot of people didn't even expect me to be around this long when I came into this fight. People were saying Larios would knock me out. But I had never shown signs of going down in past fights, let alone being stopped, so why should this fight be any different? I started boxing Larios in the last round, sticking my jab in his face. He didn't know what to make of me. He was expecting me to stand toe-to-toe and trade, but I moved around him, picking him off. The crowd was shouting 'McCullough! McCullough!' Barry Tompkins said the fight was so close it would come down to the final round. Larios was trying to box at long range, but it wasn't working for him. I threw a double jab right-hand that rocked his head back. I knew I was winning the last round easily and I really pushed myself in the last minute.

Sean had me one point up going into the last round. He was saying, 'This is what World Championship boxing is all about. There were rumours about McCullough being washed up, but I think that's kinda shot outta the window.'

With 15 seconds to go, I pushed Larios around the ring, landing head shots and body shots. I threw over 190 punches and won the last round without question. I had done enough to take the title, but, if I'm being totally honest, I knew I wasn't going to get the decision. When the scores were read out, I just stood in disbelief. I walked straight over to Larios and shook his hand. I had no hard feelings; he didn't score the fight. I was obviously disappointed, but I wasn't about to complain or make excuses. I had nothing to be ashamed of. Barry Tompkins told the viewing audience that the bout might be the fight of the year.

We went back to the dressing-room and an Irish journalist came in and handed Cheryl the official scorecard. Amusingly, the scores had been tallied up on the wrong side of the page: according to the scorecard, I was the winner. It was obviously a mistake – or was it?

Everyone was telling me that I had won the fight or at least deserved a draw. Rafael Mendoza, Larios's manager, came in and said it was a great fight. He talked about us fighting a rematch. I was thinking, 'If I lost the fight, why would he be offering me a rematch?'

When I arrived back home, our neighbours had decorated our house – inside and out. There were balloons everywhere and a big poster that read 'Our Champ!' Even though I didn't get the Belt, I was still the people's champion.

* * *

The months were ticking past and I was getting frustrated. I was concentrating on my personal training business. Craig and Matt were in the gym three days a week. They had come so far and I was proud of how skilful they were. I had taught them everything I knew – well, not everything.

In April I was helping Arturo Quintero get ready for a fight. We always go toe-to-toe in sparring and on one day in particular this was no different. I threw a right-hand to his body but he brought his elbow down at the same time and my thumb connected with his elbow. I thought I'd broken it. I went to see my doctor to get some medication and was hoping a cortisone injection would take care of the pain. But that wasn't what he had in mind: he put a cast on my hand to prevent me from moving my thumb. He said if he gave me a brace, I'd have taken it off to train. He was right. I had to keep the cast on for two weeks. There were a couple of nights I went to bed tempted to cut it off.

* * *

I continued to put pressure on Cheryl to ask Dan to schedule another fight. By the time May came along, there was nothing on the cards. We attended the Boxing Writers Association of America dinner, where we sat at a table with James Toney and Dan and Debbie Goossen. There were over 20 world champions at the event – more than had ever attended before. Even though I was a world champion myself, I still like to acknowledge others' achievements and am always honoured to have my picture taken with world champions on occasions like this.

I walked up behind Bernard Hopkins and Oscar de la Hoya, who promote Larios. I had met both of them a few years earlier and I was ready to reintroduce myself to Hopkins, a former world champion, when he turned around to me and said, 'Pocket Rocket, you won that last fight against Larios. We promote Larios, but there's no way he won that fight. I want you on my card in July.' De la Hoya was standing beside him, but he didn't say a word. After he had finished talking – and, boy, can he talk – I asked for a photo with him.

I marched straight back to Dan to tell him what Hopkins had said.

Dan looked straight at me with his trusty grin and said, 'That's what I've been working on!'

21

WHY?

Wayne McCullough is the true essence of a great person and an excellent fighter. As a fighter, Wayne demonstrates great skill, passion and heart, with true grit and dignity – a combination rarely found in athletes today.

James 'Smitty' Smith, host of In This Corner

The rematch was set for 16 July 2005 as the chief supporting bout to the Bernard Hopkins v. Jermain Taylor fight. I couldn't believe I was going to be fighting at the MGM Grand Garden Arena. I was so happy. When I moved to Vegas, I dreamed of fighting on a big fight card. Vegas is the boxing capital of the world.

* * *

My thumb was still giving me trouble, and I'd also injured my right knee at a church teen event. I was supposed to be making sure the teens didn't get hurt on the inflatable bouncy castle, but instead I got on for a laugh and twisted my knee. I was given two cortisone injections – one in my knee and one in my thumb – and told I'd need surgery on both, but not immediately.

I met up with Eva Futch the weekend before I left for training camp. Cheryl keeps in touch with her and we arranged to have a coffee before we went to Los Angeles. We chatted for a while about my fights, then about Wynona, and as usual the conversation turned to Eddie. Eva had brought a gift for me: it was a Golden Gloves pin that Eddie had won back in the 1930s. I was flattered. She knows how much Eddie meant to me and I am privileged to have such a piece of history. Before she left, she told me that Eddie called me his 'modern day Joe Frazier'. It was one of the best moments in my life.

* * *

Cheryl had arranged for us to rent an apartment in Los Angeles, which was going to cost us $3,000 for the month. We thought an apartment would be ideal, but it turned out to be anything but. When we walked in, the smell of smoke hit us right in the face. Cheryl organised for us to transfer to another apartment in a much nicer area. It was right across the street from LA's famous Grove Shopping Center – I think Cheryl planned it that way. It was absolutely beautiful. There was a park across the street and I was content.

We'd been in Los Angeles from the Sunday evening, but with the apartment problems I hadn't been to the gym. When Cheryl phoned on the Wednesday to tell Freddie we were coming in, Justin Fortune told her Freddie was in Chicago with another of his fighters and he wouldn't be back until the weekend. So, over the next few days, I worked with Justin instead.

We bumped into Rich Marotta while out for dinner one evening and he invited us over to his house to watch the Kevin McBride v. Mike Tyson fight on TV. That weekend we went to watch the fights with Rich and his wife Helen. I was picking Kevin to win because he was my friend and we go way back. Everyone thought I was nuts. We all had a lot of fun, cheering for Kevin. I was delighted when he beat Tyson.

On the Sunday we went to a friend's house for a BBQ. We sat by the pool. When we were leaving, Cheryl looked at her phone – which had been inside the house – and noticed she had a message. It was from Freddie. He had been called to testify in a lawsuit in New York and would be gone for the next two weeks.

He advised us to go home and train there. I was happy and sad at the same time – I wasn't going to be able to work with Freddie, but I knew what to do.

I had already arranged for Brian Clements and Craig and Matt to come in and spar with me in Vegas. I wanted to work with people I could trust because I didn't need any more injuries before the fight. Brian gave me great-quality work, and Craig and Matt gave me the rounds I needed. I felt it was the best training camp I'd had in my boxing career – amateur and pro. We did about a hundred rounds of sparring, although the best part was we had so much fun. The gym was touching 100 degrees every day, but it didn't stop us from working hard and I was in tiptop shape.

I brought Kenny in two weeks before the fight and when he found out who my sparring partners were he was worried. He said Brian was good but he wasn't sure about Craig and Matt – they had never boxed before, so he didn't know what to expect and he knew they were dancers. But when he saw them spar, the first thing he said was: 'This is the kind of sparring you need, Pocket.' He was impressed when I told him I had taught them how to box. I'd put them in with anybody; I know they can handle themselves.

Freddie arrived into camp a week before the fight. He'd been getting updates and knew everything had gone well. During the last days of camp, he sharpened me up on the pads. Cheryl and I had a hotel room at the MGM Grand from the Tuesday, but I was more comfortable at home, so we moved to the hotel the night before the fight. Rachel had come to Vegas for the week of the fight to take care of my PR. I don't know what I would have done without her that week. I didn't go to the public workout because Golden Boy Promotions had scheduled it at the same time as my usual workout. A few people complained, asking why I wasn't there, but they were told my own workout was more important.

The press conference was on the Wednesday. The only Irish journalist who turned up was Tomas Rohan, who operates his own boxing website, www.Irish-Boxing.com. He and his girlfriend have attended a lot of my fights. Over the years, we have become good friends. He's a great guy. There was no Belfast press represented for what could have been my last fight and, who knows, maybe they've missed a piece of history.

A lot of people thought I had won the first Larios fight, but he was still favourite going into our rematch. Larios was very respectful to me at the press conference, although he did say he wanted to find out who had the bigger *cojones*. I knew I did! He thought he could knock me out and predicted that's how the fight would end. In our first fight Larios made the excuse that he hurt his right bicep but said it had healed. I never made any excuses about my left hand last time, and I knew both of us were injury-free for this fight and there could be no excuses.

Usually I get about ten tickets for a World Championship fight but for this fight I only got four. So we spent over $5,000 on tickets for family and friends, but it was worth every cent. Both of my purses combined for the Larios fights were under $100,000, so I certainly wasn't fighting him for the money; however, I knew if I beat him, I could step up and get a fight with one of the bigger names in the division.

Before the weigh-in we sat down with the HBO commentary team. They were talking to me about retiring. I wondered why I was even there. The only individuals who seemed interested in me were the renowned sports reporter Bob Costas and boxing trainer Emmanuel Steward.

Right before I weighed in I was standing offstage. Cheryl was in the arena to record me weighing in on our camcorder and Freddie was in the arena making sure Larios didn't weigh in before he was supposed to. I was standing between managers and fighters and everything around me started moving in slow motion. The people around me were irrelevant in my life and I thought, 'I'm on my own.' It was surreal. We weighed in and, although I was 2 lb under, I felt really strong. Larios was bang on the weight and he looked skinny as usual.

On fight day, Cheryl, Wynona and I relaxed. We ate lunch with Freddie and met up with Kenny. About two hours before I was due to get into the ring we headed downstairs to the arena. I did the pre-fight drug test in my dressing-room.

I am a regular on the Las Vegas fight scene as a result of my commentating and reporting for *Ring*, so I know all the commissioners and I felt like I was at home. Freddie and I got a good sweat going in the dressing-room and I put on my new Everlast ring outfit. We were ready to go and win the Belt.

I knew I was going to have a lot of support in the arena. I'd had plenty of emails from fans telling me they were coming to the fight or watching on TV. I even got a message from an army sergeant stationed in Iraq who told me he and his battalion were staying awake to watch the fight at 3.30 a.m. I was thrilled.

Craig, Matt and Brian were supposed to walk me to the ring, and they had credentials to do so, but on the way a police officer stopped them and told them they couldn't follow me. He looked at me and said, 'Your music's playing, get moving.'

I turned to him and said, 'Yeah, right.' He had no right to tell me what to do.

The support was fantastic, but everything just felt wrong – from training camp in Los Angeles right through to the fight. The crowd booed Larios as he came into the ring, which surprised me. Freddie, Kenny, Ray and Dr Danny Antonino, who had been working on my hands for a few years, were in my corner. I knew I was in good hands.

My strategy was to begin where I left off in round 12 of our last fight. When the opening bell rang, I started to box Larios on the outside. I'm sure he thought I couldn't do that. Everyone expected me to stand and trade with him. A right-hand over the top cut Larios over his left eye a minute into the fight and I planned to work on the cut and open it up more and cause problems for him. Larios was trying to bomb me out, but I was prepared for that. I had a good first round and when I looked at Cheryl at the end, she agreed. In between rounds, Freddie told me to use my jab and right-hand to the body. In the second round, Larios was throwing low blows, but once again he wasn't getting warned for them. He was still finding it hard to tag me because I was moving and boxing around the ring. In between rounds two and three the word from Larios's corner, as heard on the HBO telecast, was that I was stronger and faster than in the last fight. In the last minute of the third round I had Larios flustered, but he still fired back. He threw an overhand right that landed on my ear. As soon as it connected I heard ringing and knew he had burst my eardrum. I cut him over the right eye in the third and the crowd was roaring with excitement. He was fighting my fight.

Richard Steele, the referee, came to my corner after round three to tell me that the second cut was caused by a head-butt. I protested, but he was adamant. As he walked away, Freddie and I looked at each other and said in unison, 'It was a punch!'

I was moving my head well in the fourth and I kept the pressure on him. I was trying to capitalise on my success in the last round. His face was covered in blood and I thought, and hoped, the referee would step in and stop him. I was punching non-stop and catching him with almost everything I threw. I knew I was hurting him with my body shots. I finished the round with a left-right combination to his head.

I threw a punch-stat record of 170 punches in round four, almost one punch a second. Afterwards, Jim Lampley, of HBO, said, 'And they're alive in Las Vegas. Thank you, Wayne McCullough!'

Over the next couple of rounds Larios was working his left hook to my body but I was throwing punches in bunches right back at him. I didn't want to let him take control. I was landing the better shots. He had to battle to keep up with me. Larios's corner wanted him to land a couple of shots and then move because they thought my shots were counting.

Round seven was definitely his best round in the fight. At this point I thought I was comfortably ahead, but I should have known better. I was going through the motions in this round and decided to take a breather. But I gave him too much room and he was getting his punches off. Larios landed a big overhand right to the side of my head and I stumbled, slightly off balance. He thought he had hurt me, so he stepped in and landed another right-left-right combination flush on my chin. I was angry that I had allowed myself to get hit, but I knew Larios still couldn't stop me. With 30 seconds to go in the round, he hit me three right-hands, but I just banged my gloves off my chin. The fans went crazy – they were probably wondering what I was doing. I came straight back at him and landed a left-right that rocked him to end the round.

I knew I couldn't take another round off and realised I had to get back into the fight. Once again, I'd proved my opponent's predictions wrong: there was no way he was knocking Wayne McCullough out in round seven – or any round, for that matter.

However, at the start of the eighth, I decided to use my face to catch his jabs. With just over a minute to go, I landed a right to his chin and, at the same time, he slipped on some water in his corner and went down. I wanted them to call it a knockdown, but they didn't!

Dr Margaret Goodman came to my corner after the eighth round to check on me, but I told her I was fine and asked her to just let me fight. In round nine Larios hit me two clean low blows that the referee could see. When I dropped my hands to complain about them, he hit me on the chin. I shrugged my shoulders. What did I have to do to be treated fairly? It seemed like everybody was against me.

At the end of the ninth Freddie asked if I was OK. I told him I was fine. 'Better go out there and let your hands go, and not get hit so much or I'm gonna stop the fight. OK, son?' Richard came to my corner and asked me, 'How do you feel, man?' and I said I felt fine. He told me, 'You can't keep taking shots,' to which I responded, 'Richard! I'm fine.' Larios's trainer told him after the ninth round to forget about knocking me out and just box me instead. There were only three rounds to go.

In the tenth round I knew I had to do something or Freddie was pulling me out. Larios hit me with an uppercut and a jab and I put my hands out and shrugged my shoulders again. I came back and landed three left hooks to his head. Not to be outdone, he came back with a good left-right-left uppercut to my chin.

I got back to the corner and Freddie asked again: 'How do you feel? Talk to me, Wayne. I'm gonna stop the fight.'

I protested. 'I'm fine,' I said. Which I was. I knew I was taking fewer shots than I had in previous bouts. I knew I only had two rounds to go. Everyone knows 11 and 12 are always my best rounds. Freddie was fine with that until Richard walked to my corner with Margaret Goodman, the doctor. I knew something was wrong. I knew what she was there for and knew I'd have to plead with her. The conversation went something like this:

'Wayne, I know you're fine.'

'I know where I am and everything.'

'Wayne, I think it's enough.'

'Margaret, please.'

'I know, Wayne.'

'Come on, Margaret. Give me a round.'

'I have so much respect for you. But it's just too much.'

I got up off my stool to protest but her mind was already made up. 'Two rounds to go. Two rounds to go. Margaret, two rounds to go. Please, please.'

'Oh, I'm sorry, Wayne. You know I have so much respect for you.'

'I'm fine.'

'Oh, I know you're fine.'

She walked towards me and it looked as if she was thinking about letting me continue. I knew I was fine. She knew I was fine – she'd shone her light in my eyes and seen nothing to worry about. Everyone knew I was fine. But she advised Richard to stop the fight. And he did. I was absolutely devastated. I cannot even put into words exactly how I felt at that moment.

'I'm sorry, Wayne.'

I broke down in tears. 'Please, don't stop it.' But the decision had been made. My protests fell on deaf ears. The crowd was in uproar. The fans didn't want the fight stopped either. They booed as Larios raised his hands.

I didn't agree with Margaret's decision, but I hugged her anyway and accepted what she had done to me. I later came to terms with the stoppage, but only because the doctor caused it. I can still say I was never stopped by a fighter.

What was the justification in stopping me? My eyes were clear and my legs were strong. Medically, there was nothing wrong with me – a clear CT scan a few days later proved that. I think my age played a part in it. I honestly thought I'd get a fair shake in my home town, but I didn't. I didn't expect to be robbed of six life-changing minutes.

Cheryl could see I was able to fight back and defend myself. I think Margaret made it look as if Cheryl didn't care that I was getting hit, but Cheryl and I have talked about this in private, how if she ever thought I was hurt she would be the first person in the ring and I would not protest. I know I get hit, that's my style, but I don't get hit as much as people think I do. If I did, after 27 years of boxing, I probably wouldn't even be able to speak.

People have said, 'What about ten years down the line?' But in Proverbs 27:1, the Bible says: 'Boast not thyself of tomorrow; for thou knowest not what a day may bring forth.' To me, boxing is the greatest sport in the world, but being nice in this sport has made me a target for people to take advantage of. Nobody loved boxing more than I did. I think I was overprotected in my fight with Larios and that has hurt me more than anything.

* * *

In my dressing-room Freddie asked me to come and work as his assistant in Los Angeles. Dan told me he was going to work me into his company. I know I can do other things outside of boxing, but at that moment in time I couldn't even think straight. Freddie, Matt, Craig, Brian, Kenny, Stuart, Danny, Cheryl and Wynona were all there. While most of them were watching the Bernard Hopkins fight, Cheryl said, 'You can watch these fights, but I can tell you that you will never see another fight as exciting as one my husband has been in.' I got a round of applause and a lot of hugs in the dressing-room that night and I could feel the love. She was right, though. I gave my all to boxing every time I stepped through those ropes.

Boxing has been good to me. I've been places in the world I never thought possible and it has made me a better person. But I feel as if some people involved in my beloved sport let me down.

When the fight was over, I went back to my hotel room. I thought I'd be alone since I'd just lost a World Championship challenge. But my room was filled with family and friends. I was touched. Kieran and Rachel came to the room and, even though we were having as much fun as can be expected at that point, they left in tears. My pastor and his wife, along with their son Matt, our youth pastor, and his wife, came to see me. Pastor Teis prayed for me and that definitely had an emotional impact on how I was feeling.

Michael Flatley called me the day after my fight to tell me how proud he was of me and my performance. He has called me after each and every one of my fights that he hasn't been able to attend since the Hamed fight – win or lose. That shows the character of a true friend.

Even more people have said I should retire, but it hasn't crossed my mind. It is, however, the first time in my career that I haven't gone straight back into the gym. I am disgusted with the people who control boxing, a sport that I have loved for over 27 years. I haven't even gone near my own gym since the fight. On the last day of training I left my black gloves on the side of my ring and four weeks later those gloves are still sitting in the same spot I left them on 15 July 2005.

I have been good for boxing: a role model for children; loyal, honest, clean-living and true. True to myself, true to my wife, true to my family and, as I'm constantly reminded, true to my fans. If I never box again I know I could follow in the footsteps of Eddie Futch and Freddie Roach as a world-class trainer or move into journalism or commentating. I can have a fantastic life outside of the boxing ring.

I believe we're all put on this Earth for a reason. I believe God gave me the talent to box. By the time we are born, God has already chosen the day for us to die.

> Seeing his days are determined, the number of his months are with thee, thou hast appointed his bounds that he cannot pass.
> Job 14:5

If I am meant to die in the ring, then so be it.

> I have fought a good fight. I have finished my course. I have kept the faith.
> II Timothy 4:7

I recently received this letter from the president of the WBC, my dear friend Jose Sulaiman. I cannot begin to express how I feel about being presented with such an honour. I vow to represent the WBC in the same way I have carried myself throughout my life: with dignity, honour and grace.

WBC

Jose Sulaiman Ch.
President

World Boxing Council
Consejo Mundial de Boxeo

August 17, 2005

Wayne McCullough

I am, as President of the World Boxing Council, very proud to have been a boxing commissioner during the era of Wayne McCullough, as he is one of the most courageous and determined boxers that I have seen in my lifetime, while also being a gentleman in his life, as an example for the youth of the world.

Based on those merits it is on behalf of the Board of Governors of the World Boxing Council, I hereby appoint him officially a WBC Boxer's Ambassador of the world.

With my deepest respect and admiration.

Jose Sulaiman
President

Appendix

WAYNE McCULLOUGH'S BOXING RECORD

DATE	OPPONENT	RESULT	
23 February 1993	Alfonsa Zamora	TKO	4
18 March 1993	Sergio Ramirez	KO	3
26 March 1993	Oscar Zamora	PTS	4
16 April 1993	Oscar Lopez	KO	5
4 May 1993	Manuel Ramirez	TKO	5
1 June 1993	Luis Rosario	TKO	5
18 June 1993	Conn McMullen	KO	3
24 September 1993	Boualem Belkif	TKO	5
9 November 1993	Andres Gonzalez	KO	2
30 November 1993	Jerome Coffee	KO	6
18 January 1994	Javier Medina	KO	7
NABF bantamweight title			
19 March 1994	Mark Hargreaves	KO	3
17 June 1994	Victor Rabanales	W	12
NABF bantamweight title			
15 September 1994	Andres Cazares	KO	3
12 November 1994	Fabrice Benichou	W	10
14 March 1995	Geronimo Cardoz	KO	7
30 July 1995	Yasuei Yakushiji	W	12
WBC bantamweight title			
2 December 1995	Johnny Bredahl	TKO	8
WBC bantamweight title			

30 March 1996	Jose Luis Bueno	W	12
	WBC bantamweight title		
13 July 1996	Julio Cesar Cardona	W	12
11 January 1997	Daniel Zaragoza	L	12
	WBC super bantamweight title		
17 April 1998	Antonio Oscar Salas	W	10
19 May 1998	Juan Polo Perez	W	10
31 October 1998	Naseem Hamed	L	12
	WBO featherweight title		
30 August 1999	Len Martinez	W	10
22 October 1999	Erik Morales	L	12
	WBC super bantamweight title		
12 January 2002	Alvin Brown	KO	2
14 September 2002	Johannes Maisa	TKO	4
2 November 2002	Nikolai Eremeev	TKO	4
22 March 2003	Scott Harrison	L	12
	WBO featherweight title		
23 September 2004	Mike Juarez	TKO	2
10 February 2005	Oscar Larios	L	12
	WBC super bantamweight title		
16 July 2005	Oscar Larios	L	12
	WBC super bantamweight title		